"Dr Ryan-Morgan draws on her vast kr
ethical issues involved in this burgeonin
on the empirical literature yet at the sa
relying solely on data in a reductionist wa
forefront and provides an invaluable 'route map' for those working within
this field. As a consequence, this should be an invaluable text for practitioners, expert witnesses and those in the legal profession seeking guidance in
this complex and often challenging area."

– Dr Chris L Hamilton, Cons. Clinical Psychologist

"The case studies in this book are admirably knotty, requiring the precise
level of detailed assessment and consideration demanded of practitioners on
the ground. The author is to be heartily congratulated on undertaking an
important contribution to the field of mental capacity."

– Alex Ruck Keene, Barrister, 39 Essex Chambers

"Clinicians and lawyers alike are certain to welcome this book which weaves
together the complexity of clinical presentation, legal definition and case
law. The assessment of mental capacity is a complex area where the fields of
neuropsychology, mental health and the law overlap. This unique volume
sets out guidance on how to structure complex capacity assessments with real
examples set within the legal framework. An excellent, practical introduction for those new to the field but also of great value to those who regularly
work within medico-legal settings."

**– Dr Sal Connolly, Head of Clinical and
Neuropsychology, Ascot Rehabilitation**

Mental Capacity Casebook

The Mental Capacity Act 2005 (MCA) provides a legal framework for acting on behalf of individuals who lack the capacity to make decisions for themselves. The *Mental Capacity Casebook* showcases numerous real-life case studies in accordance to this Act. Through the exploration of various mental capacity assessments, this book highlights the psychological needs of the individuals who are supported and protected by the MCA (2005).

Dr Tracey Ryan-Morgan, a Consultant Clinical Neuropsychologist, is the first to bridge the gap between the individual's psychological requirements and the legal framework surrounding them. Not only does this book present true, often complex, mental capacity assessments, it does so with legitimate corresponding commentaries. Each case outlines the presented problem along with its background, social context, psychological matters, the overriding opinion and concluding learning points.

This book provides a unique standpoint, offering insight into the complexities of the Act and practical guidance on how to conduct assessments. It serves as essential reading for those looking for guidance whilst making complex capacity decisions, such as clinical neuropsychologists, social workers and legal professionals.

Dr Tracey Ryan-Morgan is an HCPC Registered Consultant Clinical Neuropsychologist, an Associate Fellow and Chartered Member of the British Psychological Society, as well as a Chartered Scientist, a Regional Fellow of the Royal Society of Medicine and is listed on the Specialist Register of Clinical Neuropsychologists. She has worked in the NHS, charity and independent sectors. Tracey has consulting rooms in Wales and London.

Mental Capacity Casebook

Clinical Assessment and Legal Commentary

Dr Tracey Ryan-Morgan

Routledge
Taylor & Francis Group

LONDON AND NEW YORK

First published 2019
by Routledge
2 Park Square, Milton Park, Abingdon, Oxon OX14 4RN

and by Routledge
711 Third Avenue, New York, NY 10017

Routledge is an imprint of the Taylor & Francis Group, an informa business

British Library Cataloguing-in-Publication Data
A catalogue record for this book is available from the British Library

Library of Congress Cataloging-in-Publication Data
A catalog record has been requested for this book

ISBN: 978-1-138-09789-6 (hbk)
ISBN: 978-1-138-09792-6 (pbk)
ISBN: 978-1-315-10466-9 (ebk)

Typeset in Goudy
by Swales & Willis Ltd, Exeter, Devon, UK
Printed by CPI Group (UK) Ltd, Croydon CR0 4YY

To Cian & Ffin. Love always.
To Kerry-Ann. For everything.
To Glyn Edwards. This book is your fault . . .

Contents

Foreword

The law, at least in England and Wales, divides adults[1] into those who have the mental capacity to make relevant decisions and those who do not. This distinction is crucial in many different contexts, above all that of health and social care, not least as it answers the questions: (1) can I rely on this person's consent to an action that I want to carry out; (2) can I override this person's refusal to consent to an action that I want to carry out; or (3) can I proceed even though the person does not appear to be able to give me consent?

In theory, applying the law – in England and Wales the Mental Capacity Act (2005) (MCA) – will always tell us the answers to these questions. However, the Committee on the Rights of Persons with Disabilities has issued a stark challenge to the very foundations of the MCA (2005), not least because they assert:

> Mental capacity is not, as is commonly presented, an objective, scientific and naturally occurring phenomenon. Mental capacity is contingent on social and political contexts, as are the disciplines, professions and practices which play a dominant role in assessing mental capacity.[2]

Does that mean that we should simply abandon the concept of mental capacity? It is undoubtedly under sustained pressure as a valid concept, although it does appear to share many of the characteristics ascribed to democracy by Winston Churchill – i.e., it is the worst approach to these issues except all other forms that have been tried from time to time.[3]

---

1 The position in relation to those aged 16 and 17 is complicated by the fact that both the MCA 2005 and the common law doctrine of parental responsibility apply; the Supreme Court are grappling with precisely how the two interrelate at the time of writing in the appeal from *Re D (A Child)* [2017] EWCA Civ 1695
2 Paragraph 14 of the General Comment No 1 (2014) issued by the Committee on the Rights of Persons with Disabilities ("the Committee") entitled 'Article 12: Equal Recognition before the Law' ("the General Comment"), available at http://tbinternet.ohchr.org/_layouts/treatybodyexternal/Download.aspx?symbolno=CRPD/C/GC/1&Lang=en
3 Winston Churchill; Hansard, HC Deb 11 November 1947 vol 444 cc206. See also, for a discussion of these issues, Ruck Keene, Alex. (2017). Is mental capacity in the eye of the beholder? *Advances in Mental Health and Intellectual Disabilities*, 11(2), 30–39

The challenge from the Committee on the Rights of Persons with Disabilities does, though, place a particular, and acute, focus on the difficulty of applying the legally "neat" concepts of the functional model of mental capacity enshrined in the MCA (2005) across the full complex spectrum of human life. Further, it is undoubtedly the case that there are situations in which determinations of mental capacity are reached which any fair-minded observer would consider to be problematic. Some of these arise because those involved have been either unable or – let us face it – unwilling to take the steps required of the Act itself, not least to comply with its injunction (in section 1(3)) to take all practicable steps to support the person to take their own decision before concluding that they lack capacity. Some of these, however, arise because of the difficulty of translating the apparently simple words of the MCA (2005) into actual practice, and the lack of guidance to assist practitioners to do so that reflects the particular contexts within which are operating.

Much work is being done in different places to try to plug this translation gap.[4] This book adds invaluably to the project by giving detailed real-life case studies from across a range of the most common areas in which capacity comes up (including, for instance, medical treatment, sex, making a will). Each case study outlines the presenting problem/question, background, the assessment process, the opinion and a legal commentary. Reflecting the adage that it is impossible to make up scenarios in this field that outdo reality, the case studies are admirably knotty, requiring precisely the level of detailed assessment and consideration demanded of practitioners on the ground. It is also invaluable that the case studies are followed by legal commentaries: reaching the right decision on capacity is a joint effort between the law in setting the framework and those on the ground charged with applying that framework.

Even if the author makes a strong pitch that clinical neuropsychologists are particularly well-equipped to deal with complex cases, the book is equally useful and applicable to those coming from other disciplines. She, and her contributors, are therefore to be heartily congratulated on undertaking so important a part of the task of bringing mental capacity home.

Alex Ruck Keene
Barrister, 39 Essex Chambers
Wellcome Research Fellow and Visiting Lecturer, King's College London
Honorary Research Lecturer, University of Manchester,
Research Affiliate, Essex Autonomy Project

---

4 See, for instance, the work being done under the auspices of the Wellcome-funded Mental Health and Justice Project (www.mhj.org.uk)

Acknowledgements

I would like to place on record my thanks to Alex Troup, Abigail Bond, Richard Stead and Simon Morgan of St Johns Chambers, Bristol, to Paul Sankey and Andrew Hannam of Enable Law, Bristol, and to Katherine Barnes of 39 Essex Chambers, London, for their considerable contributions to this book, a debt of honour which I can never hope to repay in full.

I am sincerely and inestimably grateful to Richard Dawson (retired District Judge) who inspired me to develop my ideas which gradually took shape in this book. I hope he knows how touched I have been by his kind and thoughtful support, particularly in the early stages of developing the manuscript.

Disclaimer

I am extremely fortunate in that I have been able to avail myself of the monumental cerebral resources of a number of keen clinical and legal minds in the development of this book. I am eternally grateful for the support and encouragement of such esteemed colleagues. However, I feel compelled to offer the disclaimer that any errors of understanding, omission or commission are entirely my own and I respectfully ask the reader to be both patient and forgiving when encountering the same. Mea Culpa.

Part I
Introduction

1 Introduction to the Mental Capacity Act (2005)

Dr Tracey Ryan-Morgan

The purpose of this chapter is to set the scene for the book, to describe the key components of the Mental Capacity Act c. 9 (2005) (MCA) and to explain its relevance to clinical considerations of decision-making.

The MCA (2005) is predicated on the basis that an adult retains capacity to make decisions about money, health, welfare and relationships without interference from others, unless there is robust evidence of an underlying brain injury or impairment to suggest that his/her decision-making abilities are impaired. The presumption is of a presence, rather than an absence, of capacity. In England and Wales, the burden of proving an absence of capacity lies upon the person who raises those concerns and the standard of proof is the Civil Standard on the balance of probabilities.

Comparable legislation

In Scotland, the framework for safeguarding the welfare and/or managing the finances of adults who are deemed to lack capacity because of mental disorder or inability to communicate due to a physical condition is provided by the Adults with Incapacity (Scotland) Act asp 4 (2000). The burden of proof falls on the person who seeks to assert that capacity is lacking and the Civil Standard applies. In 2018, the Scottish Government has been consulting on changes to changes to current guardianship arrangements, emergency placements and restrictions on liberty.

In Northern Ireland, there is the Mental Capacity Act (Northern Ireland) c. 18 (2016). This is a fusion of mental capacity and mental health legislation and it also incorporates criminal justice provisions. It provides a framework for decision-making which includes a statutory presumption of capacity, a requirement to support decision-making, mechanisms to allow individuals to plan for times that they do not have capacity, and safeguards to protect the rights of individuals when compulsory interventions or substitute decisions are required. It removes the potential for a person to be treated for a mental health condition against their wishes if he or she retains the capacity to refuse such treatment, putting it on a par with the rights that individuals currently enjoy to make decisions regarding physical health treatment. As with the comparable legislation in the other devolved nations of the United Kingdom, it falls to the person questioning the individual's capacity to establish the lack of capacity.

This book is exclusively focused on the MCA (2005) because this reflects the geographical area of clinical practice of the author. However, in terms of clinical assessment, there are likely to be significant areas of relevance to practice across all of the devolved nations of the United Kingdom.

The key elements of the Mental Capacity Act (2005)

The main aim of the MCA (2005) (according to the Code of Practice: Department for Constitutional Affairs, 2007) is, "to protect people who lack the capacity to make particular decisions, but also aims to maximise their ability to make decisions, or to participate in decision-making, as far as they are able to do so". The Code of Practice is an excellent source of advice and provides many useful illustrative examples of relevance to clinicians.

The MCA (2005) does not replace Common Law nor can it overpower the provisions of the Mental Health Act (2007). The Mental Health Act provides a statutory framework for treating mental disorder in the absence of consent (which absence could either be due to a lack of capacity or to a valid refusal of treatment). Whereas the MCA (2005), as outlined above, provides a framework for decision-making on behalf of someone who lacks the capacity to do so for themselves.

A particular strength of the MCA (2005) is that it is founded on five robust principles, derived from the European Convention on Human Rights (ECHR), and outlined in section 1 of the Act:

1 A person must be assumed to have capacity unless it is established that he lacks capacity;
2 A person is not to be treated as unable to make a decision unless all practicable steps to help him to do so have been taken without success;
3 A person is not to be treated as unable to make a decision merely because they make an unwise decision;
4 An act done, or decision made, under this Act on behalf of a person who lacks capacity must be done, or made, in their best interests; and,
5 Before the act is done, or the decision is made, regard must be had to whether the purpose for which it is needed can be as effectively achieved in a way that is less restrictive of the person's rights and freedom of action.

Unlike the previous legal framework which predated this Act, an individual cannot be deemed to lack capacity due to a clinical diagnosis (for example, schizophrenia or learning disability) or due to having made what might be deemed an unwise decision (for example, giving away significant resources to a casual acquaintance). Considerations of capacity are not so simplistic as to be binary; in the wording of the legal test of capacity there is a recognition that mental faculties can fluctuate. This consideration gains weight in direct proportion to the magnitude of the decision being made. For instance, the purchase of a pair of shoes is of less concern than the purchase of a house; both require a financial-based decision, but one carries greater potential consequences than the other.

The Act enshrines in law a two-stage test of mental capacity. *Stage One* requires there to be evidence of an impairment in the functioning of mind or brain, whether temporary or permanent, which renders the protected party ("P") unable to make a specific decision at the time it needs to be made.

Once stage one has been satisfied, *Stage Two* asks can the person:

- understand the information relevant to the decision;
- retain that information for sufficient time to make use of it;
- use or weigh up that information in the process of making the material decision; and,
- communicate his/her final decision (by whatever reliable means).

Decision-making on behalf of someone who lacks capacity

The first step is to ensure that all realistic and appropriate efforts to maximise P's capacity to make the decision for himself/herself have been attempted. But, if it is, therefore, reliably established that an individual lacks the requisite capacity to make the relevant decision at the material time, the Act provides a clear framework for decision-making on his/her behalf. Moreover, once it is clearly established that the individual lacks mental capacity to make the decision in question, there is a *presumption of continuance* whereby the incapacity is deemed to continue until the contrary is proved by acceptable evidence as helpfully explained by the recently retired Senior Judge in the Court of Protection, His Honour Denzil Lush (1997, p.3).

- **Lasting Power of Attorney (sections 9 to 14 of the Act):** this must be drawn up and registered by the individual whilst they retain mental capacity so that it can be brought into effect if and when that capacity is no longer assessed to be present. Lasting Powers of Attorney can be for financial matters (property and affairs) as well as for personal welfare (health care and consent to treatment) decisions. In 2016, less than 7 per cent of applications for Lasting Powers of Attorney resulted in the Court making an Order (Family Court Statistics Quarterly, https://data.gov.uk/dataset/a89d2f04-86ad-4f75-a4b1-8204dba8e0ed/family-court-statistics)

  In 2014, MORI undertook a poll of the general public on behalf of the Office of the Public Guardian to garner opinion as to LPAs. The results indicated that:

  o   45 per cent of those aged over 45 knew nothing about LPAs;
  o   61 per cent were not interested in setting one up in the future; and,
  o   40 per cent of those asked were not interested in drawing up and registering an LPA as they did not believe that they would lose capacity, did not care or did not want to "tempt fate".

- **Best Interests (sections 4 and 5 of the Act):** Section 4 relates to the process of considering what might be in an individual's "Best Interests". There are two streams of thought: "what is objectively best for the person" as opposed to, "what would they have done or decided for themselves" if they did not lack the requisite capacity, (sometimes referred to as "substituted judgement"). The decision makers need to identify and then consult with the relevant significant others, they need to ascertain the past views of the individual on whose behalf the decision is being made, they need to encourage and promote involvement of the individual as far as is practicable; and they also need to consider whether or not the decision could be delayed until such time as decision-making capacity may return. Series et al (2017) refer to local authorities using a Personal Welfare application to the Courts as a means of achieving actions which are considered to be in the best interests of the person (p.5).

The Supreme Court offers clarity, in relation to adult care in *N v ACCG & Ors*,[1] "it is axiomatic that the decision-maker can only make a decision which P himself could have made. The decision-maker is in no better position than P." The most eloquent summary is provided in *Re Jones*,[2]

> in the ordinary case, the Mental Capacity Act is not a vehicle for imposing on people views, wishes and feelings that clearly are contrary to those they held before losing capacity, do not hold now and would not hold if they regained capacity, however right those views may be, and however unworthy P's views are according to most people's standard. The onset of mental incapacity is not an opportunity for moral correction.
>
> (paragraph 65)

What happens when "Best Interests" cannot be agreed upon by key parties? For example, consider an elderly gentleman with global brain impairment following multiple strokes. He has a dense right hemiplegia (severe right sided weakness/ paralysis) and severe cognitive impairment, including confusion and disorientation leading to verbal and physical agitation.

Professional rehabilitation clinicians undertook a full assessment of his mobility and potential for improvement. It was decided by the clinical team that he would never be able to reliably or safely stand or walk again. However, mobilising him using the least restrictive piece of equipment called a "Stedy" increased his confusion and disorientation and he would try to stand and become agitated when prevented from trying to walk.

The decision was taken to change equipment for mobilising this gentleman to a hoist. The main difference between the two aids is that the former requires active participation whereas the latter allows complete passivity. It was considered

---

1 [2017] UKSC 22 (paragraph 1)
2 [2014] EWCOP 59

that the latter piece of equipment achieved the outcome of moving him safely without providing him with sensory cues which he interpreted as encouragement to stand and walk. This change of equipment greatly reduced his falls risk and also removed the risk to staff of him trying to (unsafely) mobilise when in the Stedy and staff having to catch him when he lost his balance, which happened with alarming frequency.

However, his family were unaccepting of the professional assessments that his confusion and disorientation led him to attempt to stand and walk when it was not safe to do so. The context was that the gentleman's injury had been admitted as arising from clinical negligence by hospital-based staff so the family came to any discussions with health professionals from a position of distrust and disbelief as they believed that he would walk again and would not accept evidence to the contrary. This led to stalemate and the family threatened the clinical team with legal action if the Stedy was not reinstated. A Best Interests meeting was called with the Local Health Board (this is the Wales equivalent of a Clinical Commissioning Group in England). After consideration of all of the evidence, all involved, except the family, accepted use of the hoist to mobilise the gentleman as being in his best interests.

Next steps would typically be to move to mediation/dispute resolution. However, in an attempt to renegotiate the relationship with this gentleman's family, who were key to moving forward, considerable efforts were made on the part of the professionals involved to help the family to better understand the safety concerns and the increased risks to the gentleman of continuing with active mobilisation through use of the Stedy. The family's wishes were actively listened to and an agreement was reached. The family would accept the hoist, and abandon their insistence on the Stedy, if the clinical team could look at safe ways of supporting him to stand so that he could be at the same eye level as everybody else and could give a standing hug to his wife of more than 65 years who missed their physical contact.

Section 5 of the Act, which relates to what is termed "general defence" for acts, in connection with care or treatment, undertaken in the best interests of an individual who is deemed to be lacking capacity, is of relevance here. There is the caveat that the act undertaken should be something that the person could have consented to had they retained mental capacity. The person carrying out this act must have formed a reasonable belief as to lack of capacity and the best interests of the person. Failure to do so is provided for within the Act in section 44 (Ill-Treatment and Wilful Neglect, see below).

- **Court of Protection Order:** The Court of Protection is described by the Ministry of Justice as "a specialist court created under the Mental Capacity Act 2005. It makes specific decisions and also appoints other people (called Deputies) to make decisions for people who lack the capacity to do this for themselves. These decisions are related to their property, financial affairs, health and personal welfare" (Gov.UK, 2011, p.67). It makes an Order on behalf of the incapacitated person.

The direction from the Judiciary in their interpretation of both of the parameters and spirit of the Act is to manage not to avoid risk in decision-making. Munby, J in Re MM[3] opined that,

> The fact is that all life involves risk. And the young, the elderly and the vulnerable, are exposed to additional risks and to risks they are less well equipped than others to cope with [. . .] physical health and safety can sometimes be bought at too high a price in happiness and emotional welfare [. . .] what good is it making someone safer if it merely makes them miserable.

It is informative to study the data which have been recorded by the Court of Protection since its inception. This helps to gain a measure of the impact of the legislation and how effective a vehicle it is for protecting vulnerable members of society whilst also retaining a proactive stance in relation to their rights and freedoms.

Lucy Series undertook a doctoral research programme (PhD) at Cardiff University Law School focused on the Mental Capacity Act in relation to social care and shared the data she collected on a blog "The Small Places" (http://thesmallplaces.blogspot.co.uk). Table 1.1 is a selection of recent data produced in the Family Court Statistics Quarterly (2016) in order to establish the trends in both applications to the Court of Protection and also in the number and range of Orders made.

Table 1.1 Applications to the Court of Protection

Year	Applications Made under MCA (2005)	Applications for a Property and Affairs Deputy	Applications for a Personal Welfare Deputy	Applications for Lasting Power of Attorney	Deprivation of Liberty
2008	22,583	10,218	404	116	-
2009	19,093	11,336	336	305	0
2010	20,459	12,801	339	254	0
2011	23,538	13,585	302	591	152
2012	24,877	14,808	340	1,205	88
2013	24,923	14,850	333	1,124	109
2014	26,272	15,796	242	1,162	525
2015	26,722	14,967	446	1,519	1,497
2016	29,711	16,088	1,014	1,289	3,143
2017	31,332	15,577	968	837	3995

Source: Family Court Statistics, 2018

3 [2007] EWHC 2003 (Fam)

Table 1.2 Orders made by the Court of Protection

Year	Orders Made under MCA (2005)	Orders Made for Appointment of Property & Affairs Deputy	Orders Made for appointment of Personal Welfare Deputy	Orders Relating to Lasting Power of Attorney	Deprivation of Liberty
2008	16,407	10,439	111	76	-
2009	15,043	11,448	136	242	0
2010	17,798	11,769	133	148	0
2011	22,797	14,541	178	438	24
2012	20,043	13,087	139	876	15
2013	21,895	14,158	218	373	17
2014	23,400	14,762	189	160	22
2015	29,083	16,528	276	578	644
2016	26,494	13,372	327	84	1,366
2017	38,945	15,448	420	85	2,477

Source: Family Court Statistics, 2018

The general trends in relation to applications to the Court of Protection over time appear to be that there is an increase in such activities except in relation to Lasting Powers of Attorney. It is also clear that applications for the appointment of a Deputy for Property and Affairs far outweigh those for a Personal Welfare Deputy. Series and colleagues (2017) note that, "in 2008 the number of welfare related applications received by the CoP was fewer than 1000, in 2016 it is greater than 4000 and expected to continue to rise" (p.3).

Specific consideration of these 2016 data indicates that 83 per cent of applications for a Property and Affairs Deputy were so ordered yet only 32 per cent of applications for a Personal Welfare Deputy resulted in an appointment. Questions have been asked about why so few such Orders have been made. The general consensus appears to be that section 5 of the Act contains sufficient provision for someone to make decisions in connections with another's care and treatment without formal authorisation by the Court of Protection. In addition, a Welfare Deputy could be seen as (unfairly) "trumping" a Best Interests consensus of family, professionals, advocates and other interested parties. Either way, the Court of Protection appears to favour the lighter touch approach, which facilitates greater scrutiny, and, which naturally emerges from having the European Convention on Human Rights (ECHR) as the cornerstone of the Mental Capacity Act (2005).

Early indications from 2017 data (source: Minutes of Court User Group Meeting 26.04.17) indicate a decrease in applications in the six months from September 2016 to March 2017 but that the volume of overall applications was noted to be at its highest since recordings began.

Further consideration of these Court of Protection activity data will be left to greater academic minds but the above cursory perusal affords an interesting insight into the demands placed upon the Court and provides context to the clinical assessments reported in later chapters.

- **Court Appointed Deputy**: Deputies have wide powers under the Act but are accountable to the Court for all and any decisions that they make on behalf of the incapacitated adult within the strictures of the Order.
- **Office of the Public Guardian (sections 57–58 of the Act)**: The Office of the Public Guardian has five main roles. First, they keep a register of Lasting Powers of Attorney. Second, they keep a register of the Orders appointing Deputies. Third, they supervise the Deputies appointed. Fourth, they direct visits by, and request reports from, Court of Protection Visitors. Finally, they deal with complaints against Deputies.
- **Deprivation of Liberty Safeguards (DoLS)**: In the future (probably) to be known as "Liberty Protection Safeguards" (Law Commission, March 2017, Mental Capacity [Amendment] Bill, July 2018). Deprivation of Liberty is the lawful act of detention of an adult for their safety. Whilst there is a difference in terms of legal definitions between "deprivation" and "restriction" of liberty, the effect is essentially the same for the incapacitated individual, "A gilded cage is still a cage" (Lady Hale, Supreme Court).

Under the current arrangements, an application for a DoLS has to be made if, in a care context, an individual is under continuous supervision and control and not free to leave. Authorisations can be on an "Urgent" or "Standard" basis. When this level of control is no longer a necessity, it must be immediately removed. There is an automatic right to challenge DoLS contained within current legislation.

There is also provision for DoLS in domestic settings. In *Cheshire West*,[4] the Court confirmed that a Deprivation of Liberty can occur in domestic settings, if the State is responsible for imposing the arrangements. This would also include a placement in a supported living arrangement in the community. Where there may be a deprivation of liberty in such placements, the rules are that it must be authorised by the Court of Protection. *Cheshire West* was expected to open the floodgates to applications for DoLS and although there has been an increase in these, as well as increased delays in applications being processed, "the Cheshire West Tsunami has not materialised in the CoP" (Series et al, 2017, p.3).

In March 2017, the Law Commission launched a set of recommendations for a draft Bill which would update current DoLS parameters and practice. The most significant changes proposed were:

- removal of the power for care homes and hospitals to issue themselves "urgent" authorisations. However, there is the facility for "emergency" DoLS in those cases which require life-sustaining treatment or to prevent a serious deterioration in a person's medical condition;
- introducing an "administrative authorisation process" as a more effective and efficient way to deal with deprivations of liberty. This came about as a result of the Courts becoming *apparently* overwhelmed by applications following the Cheshire West ruling as it widened the working definition of DoLS. However, Series and colleagues (2017) argue that it has led to an increase in the number of welfare cases being brought by local authorities to the CoP (p.3);
- lowering the age of those to whom the law and DoLS arrangements apply from 18 to 16;
- making the "Responsible Body" more accountable than the "Supervisory Body" is under the present DoLS arrangements. In practice, the Responsible Body would consider requests for authorisations, making sure that the required assessments are in place and also giving the authorisation. Effectively it makes this body accountable for the whole process. However, there is also provision for an independent review of this process that is separately accountable;
- replacing the Best Interests Assessor role with that of the Approved Mental Capacity Professional. Their key role will be whether or not to approve the proposed arrangements;

4 [2014] UKSC 19, [2014] MHLO 16

- a new right to appoint an advocate for the deprived person (unless they are otherwise represented). This could be an Independent Mental Capacity Advocate (IMCA). The main difference is that under the new arrangements, advocacy is an opt-out rather than opt-in facility;
- a strong push to follow the direction of the Mental Capacity (Northern Ireland) Act (2016) which fuses mental health and mental capacity legislation.

However, the Mental Capacity (Amendment) Bill, published in July 2018 and proceeding through the House of Lords at time of writing, has manifestly not (yet) adopted many of the Law Commission proposals. Most notably, there is no statutory definition of "deprivation of liberty" provided and the exclusive focus of the Bill is on the revised DoLS, henceforth (probably) to be known as Liberty Protection Safeguards (LPS). Issues such as whether or not 16–18-year-olds will be covered by the revised Act or whether the current dividing line between the MCA (2005) and the Mental Health Act (2007) is to be maintained are being debated as the Bill makes its way through Parliamentary processes. One sticking point is the use of the term "unsound mind" which has attracted much criticism and is likely to be revised. The new Mental Capacity Act will probably enter into statute in 2020 and many further changes may be wrought before it takes its final form.

The issue of the present arrangement of DoLS is considered in further depth in Chapter 12.

- **Neglect/Wilful Mistreatment (section 44):** There are two criminal offences enshrined within the Act, namely ill-treatment and wilful neglect. These apply to anyone caring for a person deemed to be lacking mental capacity. This includes family and professional carers, solicitors and court-appointed deputies. Ill-treatment and wilful neglect are considered to be separate offences. In order to be found guilty of ill-treatment, the person must have either deliberately ill-treated the person or have been reckless in the way that they were ill-treating the person in question. The law does not take into account whether the behaviour was likely to cause, or did actually cause, damage to the victim's health. The meaning of wilful neglect varies depending upon the circumstances but is typically understood to refer to a failure to carry out an act that falls within the person's duty of care. The following are examples of both ill-treatment and wilful neglect that have resulted in prosecutions and convictions:
- Ill-treatment:
  - grabbing a patient's arm to make him go for a walk when he did not want to go;
  - verbal abuse (swearing and threats of harm);
  - withholding food;
  - punching, slapping, kicking, pinching;
  - spraying deodorant on the faces of frail elderly residents suffering from dementia and sitting on their legs;

- o standing on the feet of a young woman with severe learning disability with the aim of making her scream for the amusement of staff;
- o forcing fingers into the mouth of a vulnerable adult causing it to bleed;
- o shutting a vulnerable adult outside in the rain in his socks as a punishment for being loud and agitated;
- o putting hands forcefully around a vulnerable man's neck in order to silence him;
- o pulling a man from a car when he became agitated.

- **Wilful neglect:**

  - o failing to perform CPR on a person in the absence of a Do Not Resuscitate (DNR) order;
  - o leaving a vulnerable adult with dementia on a locked bus overnight without food or water;
  - o failing to ensure that prescribed medication was taken and then disposing of the same in the bin, thereby falsifying medication records (MAR charts);
  - o leaving an elderly man on the floor for over an hour after a fall and then pulling him up by the scruff of his neck and shoving him onto a wheelchair;
  - o disabling the bedside warning alarms of a number of vulnerable care home residents in order to sleep whilst on a waking night shift;
  - o stealing money from a vulnerable person when in a position of trust (close relative);
  - o leaving a number of vulnerable elderly residents in their own waste for several hours in protest as being passed over for promotion;
  - o leaving an elderly dementia patient unsupervised in a bath, against the written care plan, resulting in her slipping out of her lap belt and sliding underwater. She sustained anoxic brain damage having been found cyanose (blue) by a colleague who raised the alarm.

- **Participating in research (sections 30–34):** There are two considerations in relation to research involving incapacitated adults: first, those who commence their participation whilst retaining mental capacity but who lose this during the course of the research; and, second, those who lack capacity at the outset but who would be considered to benefit from participation.

The Medical Research Council (2007) puts forward the view that blanket exclusion of adults who lack capacity from participation in research could be considered discriminatory. Ethical principles have been developed and written clearly as a guide to those considering such research in order to protect the vulnerable:

- o the interests of the individual must always outweigh those of science and society;
- o the research must relate to a condition or impairment that affects the individual or the treatment of this condition;

   o   it must not be possible to conduct equally effective research with adults who have the capacity to consent;

   o   the potential benefits of the project should outweigh the risks: the level of acceptable risk depends partly on the possible benefit to the individual;

   o   views of those close to the participant should always be sought, unless this is not possible due to particular circumstances; and,

   o   a participant who lacks capacity should only be included in a study when there are no indications that he or she objects to this.

- **Making Advanced Decisions (sections 24–26):** The MCA (2005) provides for "Living Wills" in that it makes (limited) provision for advance decisions to refuse treatment. Section 25 makes specific provision for the conditions and formalities for refusing life-sustaining treatment (defined as necessary to sustain life). The Code of Practice helpfully distinguishes between the types of treatment and the circumstances in which it may be prescribed in consideration of whether it is life-sustaining or not. An advance decision may not allow a person to refuse basic or essential care, such as warmth, shelter or personal hygiene but can allow refusal of artificial hydration and/or nutrition.

Despite the Law Commission Proposals of March 2017 gaining general acceptance, there was no corresponding proposal in the Queen's Speech to Parliament of June 2017. Alex Ruck Keene of 37 Essex Street Chambers offered his view on the next ten years for the MCA (2005) on 29 June 29 2017 (Ruck Keene, 2017). Essentially, he proposed a review of the best interest decision-making process as needing to start from the person and "work upwards and outwards". Second, he suggests scrutinising the "authority" for those who reasonably believe the person they are caring for to be lacking in capacity rather than a "general defence" for actions undertaken under the auspices of that belief. Although the Mental Capacity Act (2005) does refer to general defence, Alex Ruck Keene considers that, in practice, it is treated as *de facto* "authority" and that a more delicate balance is needed to ensure less restrictive ways of keeping individuals safe. One of the key messages of Mr Ruck Keene's address is for there to be close scrutiny of those determinations which deem that an individual lacks capacity, ensuring that they are fully defensible and, "to place P's wishes and feelings about any proposed orders at the heart of any application" (Series et al, 2017, p.7).

The NICE Collaborating Centre for Social Care consulted on "Guidance on decision-making and mental capacity" between December 2017 and February 2018 and published definitive guidance in October 2018 (NICE, 2018). The document covers issues such as the training of staff on issues relating to decision-making capacity, to provide guidelines for staff who are tasked with assessing capacity and the issue of Best Interests. It also covers advanced care planning and supported decision-making. However, it also serves to highlight the discrepancies between it and the Code of Practice which warrants an urgent overhaul.

Experienced clinicians are frequently asked to conduct an objective, and defensible, assessment of the decision-making capacity of an individual towards whom they have a duty of care and the NICE guidance will be helpful in that regard. However, it remains that the assessment of capacity is essentially a legal, and not a clinical, one. Clinicians and colleagues in local authorities can conduct assessments, as directed by the Code of Practice that accompanies the Act, but can only ever be in an advisory role to the Court of Protection. Mr Justice Neville, in the case of *Richmond v. Richmond* (1914) offered the view that,

> it is obvious that an idea obtained that this was a question for the doctors to decide . . . in my opinion this is not so; it is for the court to decide, although the court must have the evidence of experts in the medical profession who can indicate the meaning of symptoms and give some kind of idea of the mental deterioration which takes place in cases of this kind.
>
> (reported by Denzil Lush, Master of the Court of Protection, 1997)

References

Court of Protection User Group. (2017). Minutes of Court User Group meeting 26.04.17. Retrieved from http://mentalhealthlaw.co.uk/Court_of_Protection_User_Group

Department for Constitutional Affairs. (2007). Mental Capacity Act 2005: Code of Practice. Retrieved from www.gov.uk/government/publications/mental-capacity-act-code-of-practice

Gov.UK. (2011). Judicial and court statistics (annual) 2011. Retrieved from www.gov.uk/government/statistics/judicial-and-court-statistics-annual

Law Commission. (2017, March). Mental capacity and deprivation of liberty. Retrieved from http://lawcom.gov.uk/app/uploads/2017/03/lc372_mental_capacity.pdf

Lush, D. (1997). Conference slides. Issues in deciding capacity. The British Psychological Society Special Group in Clinical Neuropsychology: Capacity & Neuropsychology, London.

Medical Research Council (2007). MRC ethics guide 2007: Medical research involving adults who cannot consent. Retrieved from https://mrc.ukri.org/documents/pdf/medical-research-involving-adults-who-cannot-consent/

NICE. (2018). Guideline NG 108: Decision-making and mental capacity. Retrieved from www.nice.org.uk/guidance/ng108

Ruck Keene, A. (2017). The MCA – big issues for the next 10 years. Retrieved from www.mentalcapacitylawandpolicy.org.uk/the-mca-big-issues-for-the-next-10-years/

Series, L., Fennel, P., Doughty, J., & Mercer, A. (2017). *Welfare cases in the Court of Protection: A statistical overview.* Cardiff University & Nuffield Foundation. Retrieved from http://sites.cardiff.ac.uk/wccop/files/2017/09/Series-Fennell-Doughty-2017-Statistical-overview-of-CoP-Key-findings.pdf

2 The role of the psychologist in assessments of mental capacity

Dr Tracey Ryan-Morgan

> Capacity is a construct with clinical, ethical and legal referents, and in this regard, it may be unique among clinical constructs.
>
> (Moye & Marson, 2007, p.9)

The need for a mental capacity assessment usually arises in response to an urgent or unforeseen situation and often has to be completed quickly.

In hospitals, there may be sudden pressure for discharge with parallel actions undertaken in terms of locating a suitable discharge destination, preparing a clear assessment and statement of both retained skills and support needs, conferring with appropriate interested parties (usually relatives) as well as exploring funding options for the available placements. Whilst all this is underway, a member of the clinical team will typically be tasked with undertaking an assessment of the individual's ability to make an informed decision in terms of where they wish to live when discharged. This task is typically undertaken by the psychologist.

Another scenario might be that an adult with known and diagnosed learning disability may be attending a day centre where staff have observed that their vulnerabilities may be being exploited, typically by staff but more usually by a fellow service user. Where this occurs, the issues typically relate to alleged sexual, physical, financial or emotional abuse. The psychologist will be tasked with assessing mental capacity urgently whilst alerting the local safeguarding team and ensuring that other remedial actions are taken to protect the vulnerable adult.

It is, similarly, not uncommon for an urgent mental capacity assessment to be requested by a solicitor in a medicolegal setting where an adult with a moderate to severe head injury, living in the community with a significant package of care, is placing themselves at risk perhaps by drinking too much alcohol or by taking recreational drugs when accessing the community and placing themselves at physical risk (of aggression towards or from others).

A further example is provided in the case of an adult who is already deemed to lack capacity coming under significant pressure from close family members to hand over money or to make significant purchases for them, with this expectation being expressed solely on the basis of the nature of the relationship rather than in the best interests of the vulnerable adult. It is not unusual to hear comments such as, "but he's my brother and he knows I would buy this for him if our situations were reversed" or "I've looked after her all of her life and gone without things that I wanted so now she owes me this much." A situation like this can be further complicated when the Court Appointed Deputy is a family member. Although in such circumstances they would be held to account for any financial expenditure, by the Office of the Public Guardian, having an interested party as a deputy seems to remove a layer of protection for the incapacitated adult.

These kinds of situation can lead to significant conflict around the protected party, who may also lack insight into their vulnerabilities. An assessment of the specific decisions being taken by the vulnerable adult has to proceed carefully and sensitively so as to strike the right balance between conducting a robust assessment, and yet protecting the trusted relationships around the individual that are in place to keep them safe. Newberry and Patchet (2008) argue that, "it is clear that sensitivity and skill are required in assessing decision-making capacity, in order to minimise any possible distress to the adult and to arrive at the best possible determination that fully supports the adult's rights" (p.439).

The question of *how to* assess capacity is one which many clinicians find tortuous, mainly because few senior, experienced clinical practitioners will have received specific training in the "how to" of capacity assessments but are more likely to have learned about the "why" it is necessary in the context of the MCA (2005) (the Act). Undertaking assessments of mental capacity intimidates many clinicians. This is presumably because the outcome of such assessments can have far-reaching consequences for the individual in question. A more cynical view might be that there are complex reasons for the reluctance, which stem from professional self-preservation. For example: the removal of immunity from prosecution for "experts" involved in litigation in the *Jones v Kaney* judgment; there may be an over-enthusiastic IMCA who may encourage the individual to mount a legal challenge to the results of an assessment of mental capacity that they do not agree with (the lack of agreement may be due to lack of insight into their own vulnerabilities); and a general avoidance of actions which may give rise to career-changing complaints has given rise to a reluctance to "stick one's professional neck out". Moye and Marson (2007, p.9) offered the view that, "clinical judgements of capacity can often be inaccurate, unreliable and even invalid", and they call for capacity assessment training to become a formal element in the clinical training programme of relevant professionals. NICE issued detailed guidance for staff tasked with assessing decision-making in May 2018 and covered this specific issue in the consultation document (NICE, 2017).

Newby, Anderson and Todd (2011, p.18) advocate for senior colleagues to share their experiences of conducting mental capacity assessments via the teaching and training of others. There is published, general advice about how to conduct such assessments, but these "template" approaches rarely fit the particular circumstance of what is often a complex clinical situation. One only has to look at the hypothetical scenarios described above to appreciate that most assessments of mental capacity that are placed before the clinician are complex and multi-faceted with significant potential consequences for the parties involved, whether capacity is deemed to be retained or absent.

The Code of Practice which accompanies the Act is helpful in that it offers a prescriptive and transparent approach to assessments of capacity, naming psychologists as recognised assessors of capacity in complex cases (paragraph 4.42, Department for Constitutional Affairs, 2007, p.54). However, a note of caution is sounded by Denzil Lush who, when Master of the Court of Protection, offered advice that, "although psychometric testing is a valuable tool for assessing the individual's ability to reason and his or her cognitive skills generally, you must not allow any other test to usurp the actual legal test" (1997, p.8). Clinical and neuropsychologists should always do more than just administer psychometric tests when undertaking any assessment and not rely on a single source of evidence. Moye and Marson (2007, pp.4–5) discuss the notion of standardised assessment instruments being, "meant to supplement not supplant clinical judgement about capacity. Because of the interactive and contextual nature of capacity, a test score alone cannot substitute for a professional clinical judgement" (citing Kapp & Mossman's 1996 paper in support of this view).

The question is how to protect the unique set of skills that is brought to capacity assessments by clinical neuropsychologists who are able to draw together objective neuropsychometric evidence and consider the same through the subjective filter of "clinical judgement". In February 2013, the Division of Neuropsychology (British Psychological Society) issued clarification regarding the use of titles for applied psychologists in the field of Clinical Neuropsychology when working with the public. It was made clear that Full Membership of the Division of Neuropsychology is a grade of membership and not a statement of competency to provide clinical neuropsychology services. In order to use the title "Clinical Neuropsychologist", the practitioner must be entered onto the Specialist Register of Clinical Neuropsychologists held by the Division of Neuropsychology. The only means of being entered on this register is to successfully complete the post-doctoral Qualification in Clinical Neuropsychology, having first been registered as a Practitioner Psychologist with the Health & Care Professions Council (British Psychological Society, n.d.). These checks and balances exist because the title is not protected by statutory regulation yet.

Clinical neuropsychologists are, therefore, uniquely placed in terms of capacity assessments, to understand both the workings of the brain and the, often, idiosyncratic patterns of behaviour which can follow changes to the brain. There are essentially two different approaches that are equally useful, which the profession adopts when undertaking assessments of competence. Can the person perform a function: yes or no/pass or fail? The alternative approach to this is to ask that if they can, how well can they do it? It is the combination of these approaches that underpins the assessment.

A comprehensive neuropsychological assessment comprises numerous elements that have equal and mutually validating influence in considerations of mental capacity:

- subjectively reported symptoms at interview;
- information from collateral informants such as care staff, family and close friends. Wood and Bigler (2017) comment that, "it is unwise, even negligent, to form opinions on how test performance is likely to influence everyday behaviour without carefully interviewing those with direct experience of the person's real-world behaviour over a period of time" (p.93). This is particularly critical in cases of brain injury involving the prefrontal cortex where "frontal lobe paradox" is evident (George & Gilbert, 2018);
- full clinical history via interview and review of clinical records;
- current medications;
- clinical observations such as how alert the person is, looking at how they approach the assessment, can they concentrate on what is being said, can they follow the conversation element of the assessment, are they able to communicate effectively, are all important considerations. Essentially, has the person had sufficient information for their attempts at decision-making to be fully informed?
- neuropsychometric testing (filtering results through base rate data and including objective assessments of performance and symptom validity).

The clinical neuropsychologist then considers all of the information that results from a comprehensive neuropsychological assessment against known (researched and published) models of brain function. However, there is additional information to be obtained, which is critical to a *comprehensive* assessment of mental capacity:

- assessing if the person is aware of the reason(s) for the assessment;
- establishing information about current living and support arrangements already in place, including their effectiveness and any gaps in provision that give cause for concern;
- assessing the potential risks presented by and to the person by virtue of their brain dysfunction; and,
- identifying any cultural or religious factors that may have a bearing on the assessment or the presenting circumstance.

What is vitally important is how the information obtained from such an objective and structured assessment can be applied to the established two-stage legal test enshrined in the MCA (2005). For Stage One (which is, essentially a diagnostic test) to be satisfied there would need to be clinical evidence of brain injury or dysfunction and, ideally, this evidence would be derived from more than one source. For example, a diagnosis of vascular dementia would need to be made clinically via interview *and* neuroradiological scanning for it to have sufficient weight.

For Stage Two to be satisfied (which is a functional approach to capacity), it is useful to consider the neurocognitive functions associated with each of the four limbs and to devise standardised means to assess these. This approach was developed by Newby and Ryan-Morgan (2013), see, for example, Table 2.1.

Table 2.1 An example of the neurocognitive functions associated with each of the four limbs of stage two of the Mental Capacity Act (2005)

Understanding the information relevant to the decision	• Comprehension of orally and visually presented materials • Visual perception
Retaining the information for sufficient time to use it in the decision-making process	• Autobiographical memory • Semantic memory • Auditory and visual attention • Working memory • Immediate and delayed verbal and visual memory
Using or weighing up the information in the decision-making process	• Deductive reasoning • Cognitive flexibility • Consequential reasoning • Impulse inhibition • Social perspective taking • Judgement • Integrating feedback from experience
Communicating the decision by any reliable means	• Verbal expression • Motor control (drawing, writing, pointing) • Eye gaze/movement

When the assessment has been carried out, there are still checks and balances that need to be considered. For example, are there factors present which may be amenable to treatment? If so, is it possible to delay the outcome of the assessment or to suggest a repeat assessment after an appropriate interval in order to compare the results if improvement is expected? Are there environmental factors that are contributing to a fluctuation in capacity which could be better controlled? One of the most important factors for this author is that relating to reasonableness, that is, has the benchmark for the assessment been set too high? Is too much being expected of the vulnerable individual which might not be expected of a peer?

Baker[1] suggested that, "it is not necessary for a person to demonstrate a capacity to understand and weigh up every detail of the respective opinions, but merely the salient factors" (paragraph 69). There is an earlier case[2] where the Judge had made this exact point, "the person under review must comprehend and review the salient details relevant to the decision to be made. To hold otherwise would place greater demands on (x) . . . than others of her chronological age/commensurate maturity and unchallenged capacity" (paragraph 58).

1 *CC v KK and STCC* [2012] EWHC 2136 COP
2 *LBL v RYJ and VJ* [2010] EWHC 2655 COP

In a now somewhat dated, yet still influential, paper, Sullivan (2004) asks the question, "what level of impairment constitutes incapacity remain(s) largely unresolved" (p.131). This represents the underpinning view, that the Act attempts to engender, that, "decision-making capacity is an attribute that people possess in varying degrees" (p.132). This moves away from the binary consideration of "can the person decide or not?" to "under what circumstances might the person be most effectively supported to decide?". This latter hypothetical question encapsulates the ECHR thread running through the Act, which seeks to not only maintain and uphold but also to promote the decision-making rights of individuals. This is also referred to by Moye and Marson (2007) as a, "fundamental tension between two core ethical principles: autonomy (self-determination) and protection" (p.3).

Ruck Keene (2014, paragraph 37) provides an extremely useful outline of a "good" capacity assessment, summarised below:

1   Be clear about the capacity decision that is the subject of the assessment;
2   Be clear that you and the person being assessed are in possession of the concrete information relating to the choices available;
3   Be clear about the salient details that the person needs to understand in order to inform their decision-making;
4   Be clear about the efforts undertaken in order to maximise the person's potential for decision-making;
5   Be clear about the nature of the impairment, once identified, and its impact on the decision-making process;
6   Be clear about why this is an incapacitated rather than unwise decision.

There are both general and specific tests which can be administered to assist in the assessment of mental capacity. Sullivan (2004) refers to "general ability tests" which measure cognitive or independent living skills and "purpose-built capacity assessment tools" which would include vignette-based assessments of mental capacity (p.135). Inclusion of the cognitive tests is on the basis that there is an underlying neurological substrate to decision-making which can be quantified and, therefore, also measured. Sullivan (2004) poses an argument in support of this approach, that "general cognitive abilities such as memory are (also) thought to underlie decision-making capacity and have a common neurological basis" (p.140).

The inclusion of tests of everyday living is to ensure that there is a degree of ecological validity to the assessment. It is not unusual, for example, for an individual with executive dysfunction arising from frontal lobe injury, to be able to "pass" clinic-based tests of executive function but to be observed to actively struggle with everyday life tasks in their usual environment. This is known as the "frontal lobe paradox" (Wood & Bigler, 2017, p.92 citing Walsh, 1985; George & Gilbert, 2018) or "a failure to apply intelligence adaptively" (Wood, 2015) and emphasises the crucial importance of focusing on the functional elements of mental capacity rather than a diagnostic approach alone. Prior to the MCA (2005) considerations of mental capacity focused on diagnostic or outcome (or after-the-fact)-based information. Thus, a diagnosis of, say, schizophrenia or a spending-spree resulting in an inability to make a rent payment might each have led to an automatic presumption of mental incapacity.

There is a recognition that, "clinicians from different disciplinary backgrounds may vary in their capacity assessment approach and outcomes" (Moye & Marson, 2007, p.8). Church and Watts (2007, p.304) emphasise that, "good practice in assessing capacity . . . depends upon the exercise of clinical judgement within a valid and contestable process", and put forward a flow chart of such a process to illustrate their argument. This supports the view expounded by Lush (1997, p.8) that the assessor should always make a, "comprehensive record of your examination and findings," as a "record which fails to explain the reasons why the assessor arrived at his or her decision is likely to be of little value as evidence" (p.2).

The British Psychological Society (2010) provides an Audit Tool designed for use by applied psychologists and other professional colleagues allied to medicine. The guidance highlights four key standards which are required to be in place to ensure a robust capacity assessment. The purpose of the guidance is to ensure that everything that should be done is done. If these standards are not being met, as confirmed through review of practice against the template, then clear areas for improvement will be highlighted. The Audit Tool emerged from a collective professional anxiety as to what constitutes a "good enough" assessment of mental capacity by:

- clarifying standards within capacity assessments;
- identifying the sources of advice and expertise;
- assisting in ways of addressing complexity; and
- drawing this together in a user-friendly way (p.4).

The Audit Tool also comments upon the necessary skills and competencies required by the assessor and how to address any identified deficits.

It is true to say, therefore, that sufficient guidance exists to ensure that the process of assessment of mental capacity is transparent, based on sound clinical and psychometric evidence, by those with the appropriate qualifications, experience, training and competencies and also includes sufficient information from key sources as well as being defendable.

The next chapter will consider the various extraneous, often unmeasurable, factors which will need to be considered to ensure that the individual who is subject to assessment is protected appropriately.

References

British Psychological Society. (2010). *Audit Tool for Mental Capacity Assessments.* Leicester: British Psychological Society, Social Care Institute for Excellence.

British Psychological Society. (n.d.). Specialist register in Clinical Neuropsychology. Retrieved from www.bps.org.uk/lists/SRCN

Church, M. & Watts, S. (2007). Assessment of mental capacity: A flow chart guide. *Psychiatric Bulletin, 31,* 304–307.

Department for Constitutional Affairs. (2007). Mental Capacity Act 2005: Code of practice. Retrieved from www.gov.uk/government/publications/mental-capacity-act-code-of-practice

George, M. & Gilbert, S. (2018). Mental Capacity Act (2005) assessments: Why everyone needs to know about the frontal lobe paradox. *The Neuropsychologist, 5,* 59–66.

Kapp, M. B. & Mossman, D. (1996). Measuring decisional capacity: Cautions on the construction of a "capacimeter". *Psychology, Public Policy, and Law, 2*(10), 73–95.

Lush, D. (1997). Conference slides. Issues in deciding capacity. The British Psychological Society Special Group in Clinical Neuropsychology: Capacity & Neuropsychology, London.

Moye, J. & Marson, D. C. (2007). Assessment of decision-making capacity in older adults: an emerging area of practice and research. *Journal of Gerontology, 62B*(1), 3–11.

Newberry, A. M. & Patchet, A. K. (2008). An innovative framework for psychological assessment in complex mental capacity evaluations. *Psychology, Health & Medicine, 13*(4), 438–449.

Newby, G., Anderson, C. & Todd, D. (2011). It takes time, practice and thought: Reflections of a neuropsychologist's experience in implementing the Mental Capacity Act 2005. *Clinical Psychology Forum, 218,* 16–20.

Newby, H. & Ryan-Morgan, T. (2013). Assessment of mental capacity. In Newby, G., Coetzer, R., Daisley, A. & Weatherhead, S. (Eds.), *The Handbook of Real Neuropsychological Rehabilitation in Acquired Brain Injury* (pp. 179–207). London: Karnac.

NICE. (2017). Decision-making and mental capacity: Consultation draft. Retrieved from www.nice.org.uk/guidance/ng108/documents/draft-guideline

Ruck Keene, A., Butler-Cole, V., Allen, N., Bicarregui, A. & Kohn, N. (2014). A brief guide to carrying out capacity assessments. Retrieved from www.39essex.com/docs/newsletters/capacityassessmentsguide31mar14.pdf

Sullivan, K. (2004). Neuropsychological assessment of mental capacity. *Neuropsychology Review, 14*(3), 131–142.

Walsh, K. (1985). *Understanding brain damage: A primer of neuropsychological evaluation.* London: Churchill Livingstone.

Wood, R. Ll. (2015). Disorders of behavioural self-regulation after Traumatic Brain Injury. Retrieved from http://neurorehabilitering.dk/wp-content/uploads/2015/09/Disorders-of-Behaviour-Self-Regulation-Final.pdf

Wood, I. I. & Bigler, E. (2017). Problems assessing executive function in neurobehavioural disability. In T.M. McMillan & R. Ll. Wood (Eds.), *Neurobehavioural disability and social handicap following traumatic brain injury* (pp. 88–100). Oxford: Routledge.

3 Guiding principles and common pitfalls

Dr Tracey Ryan-Morgan

With Simon Morgan

Whilst legal professionals and clinicians hold each other, generally speaking, in high positive, mutual regard, there can be fundamental misunderstandings of the strengths and powers associated with their respective roles and functions. Both need to acknowledge the underlying truth, that certainty of professional opinion rarely exists. Mason (1993) explores this concept of "uncertainty" eloquently and in a way which can be meaningful to assessments of mental capacity. The narrative is, that we seek certainty in order to reach a robust position of "knowing". Indeed, the clinician is appointed as the expert for the purposes of the assessment and for the explicit purpose of assisting the Court to "know" and, therefore, to act accordingly. However, psychologists (in particular) are familiar with the concept of "premature certainty" (Stewart et al, 1991 – cited in Mason, 1993, p.191) where knowing too soon can actually prejudice an assessment and lead to opinions founded on insecure, incomplete or inaccurate information.

Kapp and Mossman (1996) continue this move against absolute (or unsafe) certainty in our professional opinions and place their exhortations to caution in the context of the measurement of capacity, "although there is a clear consensus that it is essential to assess decision-making capacity . . . there is also agreement as to the lack of generally accepted, reliable, valid and simple assessment techniques" (p.75).

A measurement of capacity issue requiring consideration is that relating to whether it is a normative or threshold/criterion-related concept. In other words, "will individual performances be compared with those of a representative sample of presumably competent individuals or with a pre-established performance criterion?" (Edelstein, 2000, p.430). The problem with the former approach is that the normative sample will have to be matched for age, gender, educational attainment, socio-economic status, health, medications and numerous other variables. In practice, this would require a vast norm population so that all relevant variables could be controlled for, but that each stratification sample of the pool of comparator adults would still contain sufficient numbers to be representative. The difficulty with the latter (threshold-based) approach is that a person could pass or fail the test (according to established criteria) but that this does not provide direct evidence of an ability to satisfactorily accomplish the task at hand. A "pass" score could still yield an unsatisfactory performance. Therefore, "the importance of a multimethod comprehensive assessment cannot be over emphasised" (Edelstein,

2000, p.431). An additional caveat to adopting an actuarial approach to assessing capacity is that the numerical values or scores that are produced in such objective assessments of function cannot reflect contextual factors such as the complexity of the decision. Edelstein confirms this view, "the amount and complexity of information can potentially influence performance as a function of the individual's ability to comprehend and retain the information needed to make an informed and rational decision" (2000, p.426).

Section 3(4) of the MCA (2005) confirms that there should be an understanding about the reasonably foreseeable consequences or deciding one way or another, or of failing to make a decision. Edelstein (2000) supports this view that the individual needs to understand the concepts of risk and benefit associated with decisions which fall under the remit of the Act. As Newby and colleagues (2011) point out, "each situation or decision can be treated on its own uncertain merits and may have unusual and unique solutions" (p.17).

There is, therefore, a tension between ensuring that the individual is in possession of sufficient information to assist, support and maximise autonomous decision-making, with the person facilitating the decision-making process in maintaining an objective role and a position which does not result in influence. Mason (1993) explores the notion of the "observer" being unable to adopt an objective position by nature of the fact that we effect change through observing and measuring. It is crucial to be aware of, and control for, potential sources of bias during an assessment. McMillan (1996) discusses these in depth. For example, the assessor could misinterpret a response, the test environment could influence the individual by being too busy or distracting, the person could be acutely unwell, tired or unmotivated to fully participate. In addition, the format of the assessment is critical, particularly if there is a relatively brief window during which the person may be able to reliably take part. Finally, the nature of the responses required from the individual can bias the outcome of the assessment, for example, if the preferred mode of response is by eye movement or gesture, such as finger pointing, but the assessor expects or requires a verbal response.

However, away from such unintentional, probably unconscious, effects lies the notion of deliberate exertion of influence which often rears its ugly head in complex decisions of capacity. Individuals with impairments of mind or brain are often in receipt of support (whether physical or psychological) or attention that introduces a power imbalance, through dependency, into such relationships. This, in turn, can lead the individual with the impairment to make decisions that are driven by the need to seek the approbation of those upon whom they are dependent, such that this factor may achieve equal or ascendant merit in their minds on the decision-making balance sheet.

Skowron (2018) has explored the interaction between autonomy and capacity. There is an important distinction to be made between retaining capacity and being sufficiently free from coercion or influence as to retain autonomy also.

Influence has been referred to as *actual* or *presumed*, but this dichotomy has come in for criticism by the Judiciary, "a division in to cases of actual and

presumed undue influence is illogical. It appears to confuse definition and proof."
(Lord Clyde, *Royal Bank of Scotland v. Etridge*,[1] paragraph 92). It is established
that the legal burden of proving undue influence always rests on the party making
the allegation. However, a complicating factor is the acceptance that, in certain
relationships, a presumption of influence exists. For example, a parent can influence
a child under the age of 18, a husband may influence a wife, a doctor may
influence a patient, a lawyer may influence a client, and a religious advisor may
also bring influence to bear by nature of their position and role. Professor David
Archard (Lancaster University) asks if any decision is actually "free". In reality,
many of the decisions which are considered within the remit of the MCA (2005)
occur under conditions of considerable personal stress and with time pressure
being brought to bear.

A clinical understanding of undue influence is provided by Moye and Marson
(2007), "it generally relates to some form of coercion of a vulnerable adult to
do something that will benefit the coercer" (p.8). This leads the authors into
an exhortation to understand the contribution played by the dynamics of social
decision-making in clinical judgements of capacity. In their December 2017
Newsletter, 39 Essex Street Chambers Report Team comment that,

> One of the (possibly unanticipated) consequences of the decision in
> Cheshire West is that there is no place within the exercise of determining
> whether a person is deprived of their liberty to ask whether there is any ele-
> ment of compulsion or coercion being exercised, either by State agents or
> private individuals.
>
> (Essex Street, 2017, p.1)

Prospect Theory is not a new concept in psychological research. It was first
proposed by Kahneman and Tversky (1979) and predicts that individual preferences (decisions) will depend on how a problem (or question) is framed, which
in turn, influences how an individual perceives risk and outcomes. The authors
argue that, "it is often possible to frame a given decision-problem in more than
one way" (Tversky & Kahneman, 1981, p.453). Buchanan (2004) argues that,
"whether or not a treatment decision is to be respected depends on the terms
in which the question is couched," (p.417). This topic is returned to, in more
depth, in Chapter 9.

It is the principles of this approach that underpin the neuropsychometric
assessment commonly referred to as the Iowa Gambling Task (IGT) (Bechara
et al, 1994). The IGT was designed to assess risk preferences by simulat-
ing real-life decision-making using uncertainty, rewards and penalties. It was
originally used to compare individuals with prefrontal lesions of the brain with
healthy individuals so that their decision-making processes could be explored.
In the game, players are given four decks of cards and a fund of virtual money

1   (No. 2) [2001] UKHL 44

(e.g., $2000). Players are instructed to select cards one at a time with the aim of trying to lose the least amount of money and, by default, to win the most.

Turning a card results in a reward ($100 in decks A and B and $50 in decks C and D) or a penalty (large in decks A and B and small in decks C and D). Playing from decks A and B leads to an overall loss, while playing C and D leads to an overall gain. Players do not know how many cards will be in the decks. After encountering a few losses, healthy participants begin to avoid the decks with large losses. Patients with bilateral damage to the ventromedial prefrontal cortices do not.

To see Prospect Theory in action, consider an adult male, aged 60, with severe and extensive brain damage following a car accident. He is considered to lack capacity to manage his financial and property affairs and has a Court Appointed Deputy. He is currently resident in a Registered Care Home for people with brain injury and is detained under a Deprivation of Liberty Safeguards (DoLS) with a 24-hour support package in place. He is challenging the DoLS on the grounds that he does not need any help or support. He has identified a property that he has asked his deputy to purchase for him and plans to live there with minimal or no support as he displays a complete lack of insight into his cognitive deficits, his established pattern of behavioural risk-taking, and his need for support for reasons of his own personal safety. Without realising it, he has conflated the location of his residence with his need for support. Prospect Theory could inadvertently be employed to frame the questions posed to him in the capacity assessment where his ability to make a decision about his future residence and care needs was under scrutiny. For example, if the individual posing the question to the gentleman seeks the preferred outcome of the assessment being for him to remain where he presently lives, and also therefore remains safe, the following two options could be presented to frame the choice in such a way as to influence his decision-making process:

> *Option 1*: move to a place of your own in the community but the 24-hour care and support package would remain in place and would probably comprise many, if not all, of the current staff who are employed for that purpose. The DoLS would continue.

> *Option 2*: stay in your current flat in the Registered Home as this is familiar. However, the clinical team will work with you and the Best Interest Assessors (DoLS) will put a plan in place where you are able to learn to do more and more for yourself so that we can reduce the level of support and increase your independence. We can also look at supporting you to find some new interests and activities in the local community. This will be easier to put in place from where you live now as you won't have to get used to a new environment or routines first.

The framing of the decision depends upon which is the more powerful motivator for this gentleman – living in his own home or not being on DoLS and, by implication, having more personal freedom.

However, this approach would be unethical on two counts, at least. First, it would conflate the two decisions of where to live and what level of support is needed. Second, and of greater concern, it would conflate the assessment of decision-making capacity with what would be in his best interests, the "protection imperative" referred to by Lush (2015, p.10), and is to be avoided at all costs. The point of this illustration is to demonstrate how relatively easily one can inadvertently (or deliberately) influence the decision-making of a vulnerable adult, thus highlighting, "the dangers of being drawn towards an outcome that is more protective of the adult and thus fail to carry out an assessment that is detached and objective" (*A Local Authority v TZ*, by his Litigation Friend the Official Solicitor).[2]

Where this approach can be seen to work positively in neurorehabilitation following brain injury is reported succinctly in "Making the Abstract Real" (Acquired Brain Injury and Mental Capacity Act Interest Group, 2014, pp.11–13). The case reported relates to a Mr Jones who, as a result of a brain injury, lacked insight, displayed aggression towards others and was manifestly unable to feed himself, keep himself clean and healthy or engage with support. He had been assessed repeatedly over many years by non-brain injury specialists who had uniformly deemed his refusal to be an inviolable human right. Eventually, he was assessed by professionals qualified and experienced in brain injury who, rightly, established that he lacked capacity with decisions relating to his health and welfare. He was placed in a rehabilitation community where the clinical team worked to consistently reduce his choices by providing structure whilst protecting his sense of needing to be in control. The example provided in "Making the Abstract Real" describes the techniques considered, rejected and, finally, selected to ensure that Mr Jones took a regular shower. If told or asked to have a shower, he would refuse or delay and then refuse later. If provided with written or electronic prompts to shower, he would be overwhelmed and would not follow the instruction which followed. However, if provided with the choice between two different coloured shower gels, with staff holding the two gel bottles and physically offering these to him, Mr Jones would select a product and proceed to shower. "Supporting Mr. Jones in this very highly structured way creates a sense of capacity, it supports Mr. Jones to look, act and feel more capable than is accurate . . . Mr. Jones is not capacitous, it is a highly structured and managed environment that sustains this" (p.13).

Suggestibility is the quality of being inclined to accept and act on the suggestions of others, without considering the possible motives or consequences (Gudjonsson, 1984). It is a term often coined in the circumstances of questioning of a key individual such as a witness, suspect or vulnerable adult; this is referred to specifically as *interrogative suggestibility*. This is an essential consideration in the context of an individual expressing, or appearing to express, uncertainty. Having started this chapter from the perspective of professional uncertainty in mental capacity assessments, it is now critical to consider any uncertainty expressed on the part of the individual being assessed.

2 (No. 2) [2014] EWHC 973 (COP)

Uncertainty might be implied by apparent confusion, by a change of mind or by a reluctance to engage. In *LBL v RYJ and VJ*,[3] paragraphs 33, 49 and 50 refer to the fact that,

> inadequate regard had been paid to the young woman's potential to teenage ennui, manipulation and fickleness, which were not traits confined to those lacking capacity ... if an initial expression of views was effectively challenged by continual repetitive questioning ... any person, even one without impairment, might begin to doubt his or her initial response.

The warning to clinicians and other professionals instructed to undertake assessments under the MCA (2005) is clear, "it is therefore crucial that we understand how clinical judgements of decisional capacity relate to the social dynamics of decision-making" (Moye & Marson, 2008, p.8). Knowing that an individual can be subject to intentional influence, to fickleness, to capriciousness or simply the desire to change their mind, whether for good or ill, means that the assessor of capacity must be vigilant to avoid the pitfall of assuming incapacity, or *knowing too soon*.

In *PC v City of York Council*,[4] paragraph 54, it is argued that,

> there is a space between an unwise decision and one which an individual does not have the mental capacity to take and he powerfully argues that it is important to respect that space, and to ensure that it is preserved, for it is within that space that an individual's autonomy operates ["he" refers to Mr. Paul Bowen, QC].

Here are some key aspects of good practice which may assist the objectivity of planned capacity assessments:

- Ask the key questions more than once, framed differently each time, but avoid repetitive or leading questions which may influence the decision-maker to acquiesce;
- Do not ask questions that require just a binary response (unless the individual has communication difficulties);
- Look for consistency of decision or, where there is inconsistency or confusion, make all efforts to mitigate this;
- Assess the person alone, away from the real or perceived influence of significant others (family, friends, care staff including those who might purport to give factual support of the position); and
- Look for the individual's ability to apply knowledge in an adaptive way to ensure that there is congruence between knowing and doing.

---

3 [2010] EWHC 2665 (COP)
4 [2013] EWCA Civ 478

If the opinion is that the individual lacks capacity, form a view as to whether or not this may be a permanent position or one which may change. Give advice as to when it might be reasonable to reassess capacity. The presumption of continuance (Lush, 1997, p.3) is that, "once incapacity has been established, it is presumed to continue until the contrary is proved by acceptable evidence." However, this principle was established prior to the MCA (2005) and it is unclear if this still holds.

However, what is the position when it becomes clear that an individual may retain capacity for some decisions but not all? *PC v City of York Council*,[5] paragraphs 51 and 61, "where a person has capacity to make other, related decisions, there is a need to delineate why and how her mental impairment is sufficient to be the cause of her asserted inability to make the decision at issue." The advice is that, where an apparently vulnerable adult wishes to make what may be considered to be an unwise decision, care needs to be exercised to ensure that the autonomy of the individual is not eroded by the Court.

This chapter has focused on how not to undertake assessments of capacity, in that it has clearly framed the pitfalls to avoid along the way. These include influence (whether intended or inadvertent), suggestibility, coercion, conflating capacity with Best Interests, allowing for capricious decision-making and the changing of minds at a level permitted to those whose capacity is not in question. Indecisiveness is not an indication of lack of decision-making capacity. The rights of the individual are not to be removed lightly or without full and due consideration. As Mr Ruck Keene argued in his address on the 10th anniversary of the MCA (2005) (Ruck Keene, 2017) the person's wishes, beliefs and decision-making powers should be the starting point from which everything else moves outwards and upwards.

References

Acquired Brain Injury and Mental Capacity Act Interest Group. (2014). Making the abstract real. Acquired Brain Injury and mental capacity: Recommendations for action following the House of Lords Select Committee Post-Legislative Scrutiny Report into the Mental Capacity Act. Retrieved from www.biswg.co.uk/files/2214/1285/3006/DoH_MCA_ABI_17_09_14.pdf

Bechara, A., Damasio, A. R., Damasio, H. & Anderson, S.W. (1994). Insensitivity to future consequences following damage to human prefrontal cortex. *Cognition*, 50(1–3), 7–15.

Buchanan, A. (2004). Mental capacity, legal competence and consent to treatment. *Journal of the Royal Society of Medicine*, 97(9), 415–420.

Edelstein, B. (2000). Challenges in the assessment of decision-making capacity. *Journal of Aging Studies*, 14(4), 423–437.

Essex Street. (2017). December newsletter. Retrieved from https://1f2ca7mxjow 42e65q49871m1-wpengine.netdna-ssl.com/wp-content/uploads/2017/12/Valid-Consent-Discussion-Paper-December-2017.docx.pdf

5 [2013] EWCA Civ 478

Gudjonsson, G. H. (1984). A new scale of interrogative suggestibility. *Personality and Individual Differences, 5*(3), 303–314.

Kahneman, D. & Tversky, A. (1979). Prospect Theory: An analysis of decision under risk. *Econometrica, 47*(2), 263–292.

Kapp, M. B. & Mossman, D. (1996). Measuring decisional capacity: Cautions on the construction of a "capacimeter". *Psychology, Public Policy, and Law, 2*(10), 73–95.

Lush, D. (1997). Conference slides. Issues in deciding capacity. The British Psychological Society Special Group in Clinical Neuropsychology: Capacity & Neuropsychology, London.

Lush, D. (2015). What the Court expects. British Psychological Society: Neuropsychiatry and Mental Capacity: an update.

Mason, B. (1993). Towards positions of safe uncertainty. *Human Systems: The Journal of Systemic Consultation & Management, 4*, 189–200.

McMillan, T. (1996). Neuropsychological assessment after extremely severe head injury in a case of life or death. *Brain Injury, 11*(7), 483–490.

Moye, J. & Marson, D. C. (2007). Assessment of decision-making capacity in older adults: An emerging area of practice and research. *Journal of Gerontology, 62B*(1), 3–11.

Newby, G., Anderson, C. & Todd, D. (2011). It takes time, practice and thought: Reflections of a neuropsychologist's experience in implementing the Mental Capacity Act 2005. *Clinical Psychology Forum, 218*, 16–20.

Ruck Keene, A. (2017). The MCA – big issues for the next 10 years. Retrieved from www. mentalcapacitylawandpolicy.org.uk/the-mca-big-issues-for-the-next-10-years/

Skowron, P. (2018). The relationship between autonomy and adult mental capacity in the law of England and Wales. *Medical Law Review.* doi:10.1093/medlaw/fwy016

Stewart, K., Valentine, L. & Amundsen, J. (1991). The battle for definition: the problem with (the problem). *Journal of Strategic and Systemic Therapies, 10*, 21–31.

Tversky, A. & Kahneman, D. (1981). The framing of decisions and the psychology of choice. *Science (New Series), 211*(4481), 453–458.

Part II

Case presentations and commentaries

4 Capacity to make decisions about own finances

Dr Tracey Ryan-Morgan

With Alex Troup

> Financial capacity comprises a broad range of conceptual, pragmatic, and judgment abilities that are critical to the independent functioning of adults in our society . . . Financial abilities range from basic skills of counting coins or currency to conducting cash transactions, managing a checkbook and bank statement.
>
> (Moye & Marson, 2007, p.7)

Newby and Ryan-Morgan (2013) exhort the assessor of an individual's mental capacity to manage finances to steer away from considering the matter in binary terms but rather to see a continuum of complexity in decision-making regarding finances and property. For example, being able to make day-to-day decisions about essential goods to purchase such as bread and milk is more straightforward than deciding between two competing investment opportunities with different degrees of risk attached. It is not unusual for a person to have a court-appointed deputy for property and financial affairs to manage their overall finances and assets but for them to receive several small deposits each week, on pre-arranged days, in order to manage their own grocery shopping or other modest, regular, expenses. The principle is one of managing financial risks whilst promoting independence in decision-making in a safe way which seeks to empower the individual wherever possible.

Moye and Marson (2007) helpfully consider three separate elements to financial decision-making which can be adopted as an assessment framework for the clinician. The first tier of decision-making requires what is referred to as *declarative* knowledge. This refers to facts and concepts such as loans, interest rates and personal financial information such as the type of bank account or investment. The second level can be described as *procedural* knowledge, or the awareness of routine and repetitive actions that are related to money management such as withdrawing from a cashpoint machine, paying money in to an account, paying bills and writing cheques. The final element is the ability to form judgements so as to solve financial "problems". For example, how to pay for a holiday through budgeting, saving regularly and setting limits to expenditure, or considering the implications of withdrawing money from a savings account to make a large-scale purchase with the associated need to realise that the money can only be used once and may not be easily or quickly replenished.

As outlined in Chapter 2, one of the assessment tools available to the clinician is a structured interview. The following is a list of areas which would ideally be included in such an assessment of financial awareness and capacity for making financial decisions, having first established the current level and extent of financial decision-making that takes place, with or without support (Suto, Clare & Holland, 2007, provide a useful resource to support this approach):

- Identify the source(s) of income currently available to the person;
- Name the number and type of bank/building society accounts that the person currently has access to;
- Establish what the person currently knows and understands about money (this may be as basic as identifying coins or notes of currency to being able to work out change from a purchase);
- Identify how the person currently withdraws or accesses their money;
- Establish what kind of support (if any) the person currently receives in relation to their money and from whom;
- Establish the person's typical financial needs/demands each week/month;
- Ask how the person would deal with unexpected/unplanned financial events/ occurrences such as a boiler breaking down or an unexpected bill;
- Establish the person's understanding of a typical range of bills that need to be considered including rent/mortgage; utilities; groceries; clothes; petrol/ transport fares and similar;
- Establish the person's understanding of how to access different sources of money such as credit agreements, loans, mortgages, equity from assets;
- Find out whether the person has encountered financial difficulties in the past and, if so, how these came about and were resolved; and,
- Ask if the person believes that they need help with their finances.
- It can also be instructive to pose the question, "what would you do if somebody gave you thousands of pounds tomorrow?"

Empowerment Matters (2014) provide a detailed, well-structured, step-by-step guide to assessing financial decision-making which is useful to clinicians carrying out such assessments.

Legal context

The question whether a person ("P") has capacity to manage his property and financial affairs will be determined by reference to the principles set out in s.1 of the MCA (2005), and the two-stage test set out in sections 2 and 3 thereof. Stage One involves asking whether the person has an impairment of, or a disturbance in the functioning of, their mind or brain. If so, Stage Two is to ask whether the impairment or disturbance means that the person is unable to make the specific decision when they need to. Any such capacity assessment should not be carried out in the abstract but rather by reference to the specific decisions which it is likely that P will have to make in the foreseeable future, taking into account the value and complexity of P's property and financial affairs and the extent to which P can be supported in making decisions. The assessor should also take into account all aspects of P's behaviour and personality, including vulnerability to exploitation, although vulnerability does not of itself mean that P lacks capacity.[1]

The degree of capacity required will differ as between (for example) managing day-to-day affairs, managing the complexities of a personal injury claim and managing a large financial settlement, such as that awarded as damages. Even if P is assessed as lacking capacity to conduct certain financial decisions, the assessment should also consider what decisions P *can* make so as to promote his independence and autonomy. This approach is in line with the common law position: see *Masterman-Lister v. Brutton & Co*[2] where the Court of Appeal held that the test of mental capacity was issue-specific and depended on the nature and complexity of the transaction in respect of which the decision as to capacity fell to be made.

The following are drawn from historic cases that illustrate some of the difficulties involved in assessing capacity to make decisions regarding finances and property. All names and identifying factors have been changed to protect confidentiality.

Case 1: AA

Presenting question/problem

This is a case of a young lady who had just turned 18 years old. She suffered a serious brain injury in a car accident whilst a young infant. She had identifiable brain changes, attributed reliably to the accident, and attended specialist schools for all of her educational life and is attending further education college with support. She receives 24-hour care and support from family and is unable to manage day-to-day life without this input. Her solicitor asked for an assessment about her capacity to manage her finances in the context of an impending financial settlement for her personal injury claim for damages incurred in the car accident.

Background to the case

Clinical issues

At the age of 3 months, AA was a passenger in a car which was involved in a road traffic collision. She was resuscitated by a passer-by and was breathing spontaneously when she arrived at Accident and Emergency. GCS (Glasgow Coma Scale) had been 5–6.

---

1 *Lindsay v. Wood* [2006] EWHC 2895 (QB)
2 [2003] 1 WLR 1511

Neuroradiology confirmed diffuse subarachnoid blood and a basal skull fracture. (This matured into left fronto-temporal and right superior frontal lobe cerebral damage, with a small hippocampus and a thinning of the corpus callosum noted on subsequent scanning.) Over the next 24 hours she experienced several seizures, for which she was medicated, and an EEG confirmed sub-clinical sharp waves over the left hemisphere.

In addition, AA was diagnosed with cardiac difficulties which required surgical interventions in the form of pulmonary artery banding and cardiac catheterisation. Professional opinion was that the cardiac condition was independent of the accident.

Over the coming months and years, AA appeared to experience developmental delay, which had not been present prior to the accident. AA is left-handed.

Family/social context

AA lives with her mother and younger sister who provide 24-hour support in the form of prompting to personal hygiene and care, including helping her to choose clothes to wear which are appropriate to the weather and circumstance. AA is unable to shop, cook, manage day-to-day money or undertake other important activities of daily living that subserve independence. AA is engaged to be married to a young man she met in college who has moderate learning difficulties. The support that she receives is competence-promoting and generally empowering.

Psychological/neuropsychological matters

AA was noted to experience symptoms of anxiety throughout her childhood. She found it difficult to be around others and required significant support. Cognitively, she was regularly formally assessed using standardised psychometric tests. The results confirmed the developmental delay and noted specific difficulties in terms of attention, concentration and memory, sequencing motor movements, fine manual dexterity and co-ordination. Cerebral palsy was excluded as a diagnosis. This picture continued throughout her childhood and into early adulthood and was consistent with the early brain injury as a result of the accident.

Assessment and rationale

Neuropsychometric testing in the context of mental capacity included a brief assessment of neuropsychological functioning, two short tests of executive functioning (problem-solving, judgement and evaluation, sequencing and sustained attention) as well as a brief measure of general cognitive function. In addition, AA's adaptive skills were assessed in the context of developmental delay. AA, her mother and sister were all interviewed. The assessment took place over three appointments on different days and at different times of day to mitigate possible fatigue.

The results of the neuropsychometric tests indicated that AA is functioning in the bottom 5th centile of the population for her age in terms of overall cognitive function with her Full-Scale IQ lying between 72 and 82. (The average IQ of the general population lies between 90 and 109.) This is classified as borderline learning disabilities. Evidence from neuropsychological testing also pointed to specific problems with attention, immediate memory, visuospatial-constructional skills and language (fluency and comprehension).

Structured interviews, with individually tailored visual aid resources, were used to assess AA's understanding of basic financial concepts such as number ordering, number familiarity, number value and money familiarity as well as the concept of income and savings. The results suggested that she was functioning at a rudimentary level in terms of these skill areas. The resources used included laminated cards with roman numerals and also a set with groups of different amounts of dots clearly visible. Actual coins and paper currency were used as well as pictures of a piggy bank and bank cards, all of which were designed and prepared specifically for the assessment. In relation to the concepts of income and savings, AA struggled to manage her benefits without the support of instructive and directive financial planning from her mother. She was able to adhere to a routine that had been established, such as saving a set amount each week because she had been told to.

AA follows the process of withdrawing money from her bank account into which her benefits are directed from her mother's account, with support to remember her PIN number, and placing this in a dedicated jar which has been labelled "savings". Evidence from mother indicated that AA becomes easily confused when working out what she needs her savings for and how to spend it in a managed way, such as trips to the cinema or a brief holiday. She is presently unable to successfully budget independently such as for clothes or leisure purchases (e.g. DVDs or music CDs). If not closely supported, AA would spend her savings on items which catch her eye without being able to consider the consequences in terms of delaying the desired financial goal for which she is saving. There appears to be a disconnect in her mind between the money she physically spends and where it comes from. For example, she would take £10 out of her savings jar and spend it on a desired object or activity but then appear confused when she returned to the savings jar to find that the £10 has gone.

It was possible to establish that in her daily life, AA currently makes very few choices without support. Her clothes are selected for her on the basis that she will choose clothes which are inappropriate for either the weather or for her environment if not supported. Her meals are planned and prepared by others, she is prompted to all aspects of her personal hygiene and her established daily routines run smoothly with little change or flexibility. This would suggest that there is scope to extend her decision-making skills generally with a view to potentially involving her in a level of financial decision-making at some point should she so wish. At present, AA has indicated that she does not seek further financial independence as she feels overwhelmed by both the skills and knowledge needed and the responsibilities associated with this.

Opinion/outcome

There is sufficient neuroradiological and neuropsychometric evidence to indicate that Stage One has been satisfied in that there is unequivocal and permanent damage to AA's brain.

Stage Two requires consideration of AA's ability to understand, retain, weigh up and communicate her decisions regarding money in the context of managing a potentially large financial settlement.

The results of the formal testing and structured interviews indicated that AA has some grasp of the most basic financial concepts but is unable to extrapolate and generalise from these in order to weigh up information considering consequences and implications in order to arrive at financial decisions, such as how much to save and for what purpose or how long she may have to save for in relation to the target item. For example, she knows that she has been advised to put money aside each week for "shopping" but was unable to explain what this shopping might entail or how much she might need.

There is potential to augment AA's capacity to manage small amounts of money, which could be developed through skills-based learning such as teaching her functional budgeting and day-to-day money management skills on a task-by-task basis. The aim should be to achieve a weekly budget with clear lines of expenditure planned in advance and learned by AA so that although she will have achieved a degree of financial independence, this will be done safely, within safe parameters that would not increase the risks to her, for example, of being exploited by others or of spending in excess of income and having to go without basic supplies.

There is also merit in considering the development of a Financial Passport (Suto et al, 2007) with AA. However, it is unlikely that she would reach sufficient level of ability and skill in the matter of financial management in order to achieve capacity to manage her own financial affairs, particularly in the context of a potentially large award for damages.

Legal commentary

The above assessment rightly and helpfully distinguishes between what AA cannot do (i.e. manage her impending personal injury award) and what she might be able to do with appropriate support (e.g. manage small amounts of money).

The fact that AA lacks capacity to manage her impending personal injury award means that the Court of Protection will have jurisdiction either to appoint a deputy to manage the award on her behalf, or alternatively to direct the creation of a trust of AA's assets under s.18(1)(h) of the MCA (2005).

The differences between these two options, and their respective advantages and disadvantages, were explored in detail in the two cases of *Re HM*[3] and *Watt v. ABC*.[4] In the latter case the court accepted that where (as in the

---

3 [2012] WTLR 281
4 [2016] EWCOP 2532

present case) P may have capacity with appropriate support to make certain decisions, one advantage of a deputyship is that it may promote autonomy and flexibility. This is because unlike a trustee, a deputy is only permitted to take a decision if P lacks capacity to do so (s.20(1) MCA (2005)) and must apply s.1(5) MCA (2005) (Best Interests) and s.4(4) MCA (2005) (participation by P). Thus, in the present case a deputy would be required, so far as reasonably practicable, to permit and encourage AA to manage small amounts of money, or to improve her ability to do so.

Discussion/learning points

One particularly powerful learning point in this case is that when it becomes apparent that a vulnerable person is being supported intensively, consideration needs to be given as to how best to manage the potential for safe decision-making in order to maximise potential for capacity that fully supports the individual's rights (Newberry & Patchet, 2008).

There is always a balance to be struck between providing an individual with sufficient support to protect their vulnerabilities without this being paternalistic and, inadvertently, denying rights and freedoms in the process. For example, a weekly allowance may not allow for sufficient freedoms for leisure or social activities once essentials are purchased. A monthly allowance may give too much room for overspend well before the next deposit is available. The amount and frequency of allowance needs to be titrated to suit the needs of the individual simultaneously meeting the need for greater independence whilst managing the risks of restricting financial freedoms and potential for exploitation.

Case 2: AB

Presenting question/problem

This is a 92-year-old gentleman with a longstanding diagnosis of mixed dementia with a registered Enduring Power of Attorney in place since 2007 which requires his two daughters to act jointly on his behalf. However, the daughters are estranged and mistrustful of each other's actions and intentions. His solicitor was seeking to establish whether or not he retained capacity to manage his day-to-day finances.

Background to the case

Clinical issues

AB has a diagnosis of mixed dementia which refers to a combination of clinical features of both vascular and Alzheimer's dementias. Full medical records were available for the purposes of the assessment. He was under the care of a local consultant psychiatrist at the time of the assessment.

Family/social context

AB has two daughters who are named jointly in the registered Enduring Power of Attorney but who are estranged. Both daughters are in contact with AB but take care never to meet face-to-face due to being antagonistic towards each other. Each believes the other to have malign intentions towards their father's financial assets.

Psychological/neuropsychological matters

An established diagnosis of mixed dementia gives a clear framework within which to conduct the assessment of capacity to manage financial affairs. Typically, vascular dementia proceeds in stepwise deterioration with periods of stability in-between. Cognitive effects are more widespread due to general ischaemic damage. Alzheimer's dementia has a more progressive deterioration with key features of cognitive change at each stage of the disease. It is important to establish if there is retained insight into cognitive decline as this can render the views of the individual more reliable and informative, if awareness is present.

Assessment and rationale

AB was interviewed alone. He was unable to recall how much money he has and masked his lack of knowledge by repeating "not a lot" as the questions were repeated and reframed. He considered that he only needs money to buy newspapers but that each cost no more than 20 pence. He was firmly of the view that he is responsible for his own money and that he or Daughter 1 collect it from the Post Office. However, Daughter 2 has been designated as his "Appointee" by the Department of Work and Pensions in order to have authorisation for AB's state pension and pension credit. Daughter 2 collects his pension from the local Post Office on his behalf. AB did not appear to be aware of this arrangement during the assessment. It is possible that he was previously aware of the arrangement and has forgotten.

When asked if he had access to any other monies AB replied, "no ... can't remember ... don't know". When asked what he would do if he had more money each week or received a large cheque in the post unexpectedly, he replied, "don't know". He was clear that he does not consider that he needs help from anybody to look after his money. He was unable to state how much money he had, from where it comes or where it is kept.

An assessment was made of the level of choices that AB currently makes, and he confirmed that he chooses which clothes to wear each morning, although he may elect to wear clothes which perhaps should be washed before being worn again. There are personal hygiene concerns.

He believed that he chooses his breakfast, lunch and dinner. However, it became apparent that most meals were being prepared for him by his daughters. The assessment results indicated that he generally makes choices from a limited range of options frequently needing only to give yes/no answers. He lives alone but receives significant support from his daughters each day.

Whilst AB was able to correctly recite his name, date of birth and address he firmly believed that the day of the assessment was Monday when in fact it was a Friday and that it was January 1990 (actual date was January 2009) and that Margaret Thatcher was the current Prime Minister, which was not the case. He was able to correctly identify the town where the assessment was conducted but unable to name the offices or road where the assessment took place, despite this taking place in the offices of his solicitor which he had been attending for many years in a town where he had lived all of his life. His answer to the question of "where are we now?" was that he was, "not in jail anyway". He thought his mother's forename was Angela but was rather unsure of this. (Records indicated that this was incorrect. This had been his late wife's name.) The results of this element of the assessment suggested that AB was only partially orientated, a finding which corresponds to those reported in his medical notes where it was stated, a year earlier, that his "Dementia has progressed to moderate stage".

It had been planned to undertake a wider range of psychometric tests at the outset, including Digit Span and List Learning subtests of the Wechsler Memory Scales and the Matrices Subtest from the Wechsler Abbreviated Scale of Intelligence. However, it was noted in medical records that AB becomes markedly anxious when subjected to formal psychometric testing and is severely hard of hearing. With that in mind it was decided to administer the MEAMS (Middlesex Elderly Assessment of Mental State). The MEAMS is a widely used, relatively brief, screening test used to detect gross impairment of specific cognitive skills in the elderly. The subtests of the MEAMS are sensitive to the functioning of the different areas of the brain. This was administered to AB and the results indicated that he failed 9 of the 11 subtests confirming wide-ranging cognitive impairment across a number of key neuropsychological domains.

AB was assessed through the medium of English although his native language was Welsh. This decision was taken on the basis that there are no formal measures of cognitive function available in the Welsh language. He was sufficiently fluent in English and content to be assessed through that medium. At various points during the interview, his answers in English were confirmed through the medium of Welsh to ensure reliability of response.

Opinion/outcome

AB is a 92-year-old gentleman with a diagnosis of mixed dementia, at a moderately advanced stage, currently under the care of Dr PP, Consultant Psychiatrist at a local hospital. There is no question but that AB's condition is a deteriorating one such that his "impairment of mind or brain" (Stage One of the MCA (2005) test) is permanent.

In terms of the Stage Two test of capacity, it is noted that AB had limited comprehension skills in general but, specifically, also displayed a compromised understanding of his present financial affairs. His memory dysfunction was marked in terms of autobiographical detail (such as the names of his grandchildren or the name of the daughter who collects his pension) and was also impaired for acquiring new information (learning) such as would be critical to managing his affairs. In terms of executive functions (which directly mediate decision-making skills), it was clear that verbal fluency, naming and mental flexibility skills were compromised to a significant degree. He was unable to make choices in a range of contexts in daily life. With reference to communication skills, AB retained the ability to make his views known whether such views are reliably held or otherwise. His compromised orientation was also a critical factor to consider in the context of mental capacity.

On the basis of the above assessment, and within the terms of the MCA (2005), AB lacked the capacity to manage his financial affairs. The court could have been directed to note that two years previously, he had been deemed, by his treating physician, to lack the capacity to consent to an invasive medical procedure (which was a matter of record in his medical notes).

Legal commentary

The fact that AB lacks capacity to manage his financial affairs means that the daughters will continue to manage his affairs on his behalf under the registered Enduring Power of Attorney. There must be some concern that the daughters' estrangement may in practice make it difficult for them to act jointly as attorneys. If so, then an application may need to be made either to cancel the registration of the Enduring Power of Attorney on the basis that one or both of the daughters are unsuitable to act as attorneys,[5] or to appoint a deputy to manage AB's property and affairs instead of the daughters.[6]

Discussion/learning points

The key learning point when assessing an individual who has a longstanding diagnosis of degenerative cognitive impairment and where reliable collateral information may not be available from family members, is that full medical records are critically important in order to check recollections of key clinical facts and features of presentation. In this case, AB had an appointed social worker, so much of the autobiographical information and details of financial benefits were available as a matter of record. Where such records are not available, it is essential to speak to professionals involved to check facts and share impressions from the assessment in order to ensure accuracy and reliability of opinion. For example, it could be the case that the individual's abilities may be known to fluctuate. It could be that recollections which seem implausible may be accurate, or *vice versa* and erroneous assumptions could be made by the assessing clinician.

---

5 Under MCA (2005), Sch.4, para. 16(4)(g)
6 Upon the appointment of a deputy the court should direct the revocation of the EPA: MCA (2005), Sch.4, para. 2(9)

Case 3: AC

Presenting question/problem

This is the case of a 56-year-old lady, AC, who was born prematurely, experienced developmental delay and has had seizures throughout her life as a result of the underlying perinatal brain injury. Her fits had been poorly-controlled and she has also experienced several episodes of profound depression which have resulted in hospital admission under the Mental Health Act (1983) primarily as a result of parasuicides. The referral question was in relation to her capacity to manage her day-to-day finances in the context of one of her family members (who provides care for her) having been charged with criminally defrauding AC of substantial amounts of money.

Background to the case

Clinical issues

AC had a lifelong history of learning disability, right sided hemiplegia from birth, poorly controlled epileptic seizures (occurring, at best, with frequency of one tonic-clonic seizure per week and, at worse, with several such seizures per day resulting in regular admission to hospital on an emergency basis), reactive depression and parasuicides. All her suicide attempts had been by means of overdosing prescribed medication and one had resulted in a cardiac arrest requiring external cardiac massage in order to preserve life. She also experienced several falls which were presumed to be seizure-based but neuroradiological investigation, via CT, reported an old infarct in the right lentiform nucleus. (The role of this brain structure is to maintain muscular control of the body and to assist in controlling movement.)

Family/social context

AC is married and her husband also has learning disability. She receives significant support from a sister and a sister-in-law (her husband's sister). Concerns were raised, primarily by her GP but also, latterly, by other professionals, that she was financially vulnerable. She had a mobility car which her sister kept outside her own house and made full use of. AC had been looked after at home by her mother and brother until her mother's passing some years before. Her sister had got AC to sign papers re-mortgaging her house, ostensibly without AC's understanding, knowledge and consent, and had retained the proceeds for herself.

Psychological/neuropsychological matters

Records indicated that AC had never had to live without 24-hour support, which she had received from her mother and brother for many years then received from her husband and husband's sisters. She was known to Social Services and had voluminous hospital notes from psychiatric and health services. Notes indicated that, "she was more comfortable in hospital than at home", which indicated that she struggled without intensive support, at least for certain periods during her life. There were significant entries over many years indicating a consistent diagnosis of "reactive depression" which supported the view that she is easily overwhelmed.

Assessment and rationale

AC's knowledge was assessed by means of unstructured and structured interview as well as by means of psychometric testing to establish the nature of her learning disability in terms of cognitive strengths and weaknesses. Her mood was also formally assessed. She was accompanied by sister-in-law, X, who remained present throughout.

During the initial part of the interview, AC was engaged in indirect discussions about relations with various family members in order to ascertain her support network within her wider family group. She talked frequently about her sisters-in-law X and Y (presumably because she sees these more often and they are reported to provide the majority of the care and support to AC alongside her husband). She reported not seeing her brother (A) very often and informed that she currently has no contact with her sister, Z (who is the subject of the criminal investigation).

It was explained to AC that the purpose of the assessment was to find out what she understood about money and how to make decisions about money and she appeared to understand and consent to this.

A series of colour laminated sheets were shown to AC with pictorial representations of different coins and notes within the sterling currency as well as a picture of a bank and a piggy bank and debit and credit cards. These were used to form the basis of an assessment of AC's knowledge as to currency and the various means of having savings and spending the same. It was clear that she was able to identify coins and notes, although she was only able to identify the "savings" role of a bank. She recognised credit and debit cards although was unable to differentiate these and confirmed that she had neither as she did not know how to use them although she knew that "people cashed their money in" using the cards.

AC was asked how much money she has personally, in her purse or elsewhere and she was unable to say. She appeared to guess that she had £50.00 in her purse at that time although X queried this. AC did confirm that her husband looks after their money (it is understood that he only does so with assistance) and that he does tell her how much they have but she cannot remember and that she is not sure whether her husband (B) actually knows how much money they have.

At this stage in the assessment, several vignettes from Suto and colleagues (2007) were administered to AC. She incorrectly added together two 20 pence pieces and a 10 pence piece as totalling 60 pence and could not see the error when pointed out to her. AC was unable to identify the issues required in each of the vignettes in order to make a financial decision.

AC was then asked if she knew what a mortgage was. She replied, "it's for money". When then asked if she had a mortgage, she replied, "think so". AC was then asked how much her mortgage is for. She replied, "a lot". She was asked where she gets her money from and she responded with, "the bank". She was then asked who gives her money when she needs it. AC replied, "one of my sister-in-laws". At this stage, X confirmed that B is taken to do the shopping and he does all of the cooking. AC does not have a mobile telephone as she does not know how to use one and confirmed that whilst she is able to answer her landline telephone, she struggles to use it and cannot make outgoing calls independently.

An attempt was made to ascertain the level of decision-making that AC currently enjoys. It appears that apart from choosing her own clothes each day, AC makes few if any other independent decisions. X confirmed that as far as meals are concerned, B does not offer choices to AC but is aware of her likes and dislikes and accommodates these. If required to make a choice from two or three items, X confirmed that AC would be able to make a reasonable choice.

AC responded to the question "who helps you to decide things?" with "B, X and Y." AC and B were married before her mother passed away.

AC confirmed that she does not see her brother (A) often but that Y and her partner come to stay once or twice a week to help with cooking, offer company and bring their dog (which is loved by AC). They sleep at the house when visiting. X supervises AC's medication.

X confirmed that AC used to have more regular contact with social workers but last saw one approximately six months ago. Neither AC nor X were able to clarify the purpose of Social Work involvement.

It appears that AC used to attend a day centre (details unknown) and enjoyed this but stopped going because she was pestered by another service user. She would like to attend a day centre again and it is felt by X that it would be good for AC to get out of the house and to be more occupied, as although she greatly enjoys drawing this is a largely solitary endeavour.

Psychometric assessment of general cognitive function resulted in a Full-Scale IQ of 51–59. This indicates that AC is functioning in the lowest 0.1 per cent of the population in terms of cognitive function. In other words, 99.9 per cent of her age peers are functioning at a higher cognitive level. Her results place her in the "severe impairment of intellectual functioning" category (British Psychological Society, 2000). The profile of scores is "flat" and is concordant with a lifelong developmental disability, as indicated in AC's medical records.

The average IQ for the general population lies between 90 and 109. Standard units of measurement away from this average are expressed in the form of a "standard deviation". It is accepted, when discussing general cognitive function, that a standard deviation is equivalent to 15 and that two or more standard deviations away from the average (i.e. 100) is considered to be "abnormal". Therefore, the maximum IQ that a person can have and still be eligible for the diagnosis of learning disability is 70. An IQ of 70 is equivalent to functioning in the bottom 2 per cent of the general population. It is standard practice for clinical psychologists to report IQ figures in ranges to allow for measurement error.

The Clock Drawing Test is a widely accepted means of assessing broad neurocognitive function as it taps into a wide range of skills and abilities including:

- visual attention;
- working memory;
- planning, co-ordinating, sequencing;
- visuospatial skills;
- rule-following; and
- concrete knowledge.

It was first established that AC could read a clock face and was able to tell the time. At this point, the Clock Drawing Test was administered to AC who registered a score of 6 out of a possible maximum 13. She dropped marks for the following errors:

- adding in numbers in excess of the 12 required;
- misplacing the number sequence by going from top left round to top right (i.e. counter-clockwise);
- placing the hands in the wrong positions; and
- confusing the numbers 3 and 5 when writing.

Her low score on this test is consistent with an individual with severe intellectual impairment.

The Comprehension subtest (from the Weschler Adult Intelligence Scales IV) is designed to assess an individual's understanding of general principles and social situations. It was administered to AC who registered a raw score of 6, which converts to a scaled score of 2. (The population average for a scaled score is 10, with a standard deviation of 3. Scores below two standard deviations from the average are considered to be "abnormal".) This reflects AC's difficulties in understanding and her performance is consistent with an individual with severe intellectual impairment.

The Picture Naming subtest (from the Cognitive Linguistic Quick Test) is a brief test of confrontation naming which measures an individual's ability to name everyday objects presented in line drawings. It was chosen on the basis that the drawings are clear and simple. AC scored 9 out of a possible 10. Although dysarthric, she does not appear to have any difficulties with finding the correct words for objects, thus indicating that her speech difficulties are more likely to be mechanical (speech musculature) rather than cerebral.

The Gudjonsson Suggestibility Scales are a well-established measure of interrogative suggestibility, that is, the tendency of individuals to accept suggestive information in the context of being interviewed. It is based on a theoretical model of suggestibility which contends that this characteristic is mediated by an individual's cognitive abilities, mental state and personality characteristics.

This test was administered to AC who was unable to freely recall any of the read-out story under immediate or delayed recall conditions. It was, therefore, decided to administer the questions which follow free recall in an attempt to ascertain if any of the information contained within the story had been retained by her. The results indicated that AC's free recall is severely impaired, and that she is somewhat amenable to suggestion under conditions of interrogative suggestibility.

The Social and Moral Awareness Test is a relatively new test (2010) which assesses social-moral knowledge and reasoning in individuals with a learning disability. It was administered to AC who demonstrated a reasonable knowledge of socio-moral imperatives (24 out of 30) but an impoverished ability to use this knowledge to reason (9 out of 30) as she frequently made inappropriate or irrelevant answers to reasoning items on this test. This test is a useful means of illustrating the dissociation between holding concrete knowledge and being able to apply this knowledge in an adaptive way, sometimes referred to as a dissociation between "knowing" and "doing".

Opinion/outcome

Stage One of the MCA (2005) test would be satisfied in that there is considerable, reliable evidence of impairment to AC's mind and brain, which is permanent.

Stage Two of the MCA (2005) test requires evidence of AC's ability to understand, remember, weigh up and communicate information regarding financial decisions. The current assessment has indicated that she had only the most basic understanding of money and how finances work (including a failure to understand a mortgage), was unable to recall key financial information with respect to her own assets, was unable to weigh up financial information in order to inform decision-making but was able to communicate her wishes, even when based on incomplete or erroneous knowledge. It was of concern that she was vulnerable to influence through suggestion and, therefore, unable to protect herself from financial exploitation. AC clearly does not retain capacity to manage her day-to-day finances. There is scope for augmenting her ability to handle small sums of money, should she so wish, without overwhelming her. A first step would be the development of a Financial Passport (Suto et al, 2007). Financial skills training might aim to support her to take responsibility for making specific purchases during each week in order to contribute to the running of the family household, such as buying all the milk or bread that is required.

Legal commentary

In view of the conclusion that AC lacks capacity to manage her day to day finances and is vulnerable to exploitation, this seems an appropriate case for the appointment of a deputy to manage her property and affairs.[7] The Court of Protection will select the deputy based upon P's Best Interests, but it applies a *prima facie* order of preference which favours a spouse, family members or close friends over professionals or local authority departments.[8] In the present case the Court of Protection would plainly not countenance appointing the sister Z to act as deputy, given Z's apparent financial abuse of AC and the criminal proceedings against her. AC's husband's

---

7 Under s.16(2)(b) MCA (2005)
8 *Re AS* [2013] COPLR 29

learning disability may make him an inappropriate candidate, depending upon the extent of his disability and its effect upon his own capacity to manage financial affairs. It appears that AC's sisters-in-law, X or Y, may be appropriate choices.

If a deputy is appointed, then he or she will not automatically be authorised to pursue litigation on behalf of AB against the sister Z. Instead the deputy will need to consider whether it is in AB's best interests to pursue such litigation, taking into account all the circumstances of the case and the relevant factors set out in s.4 of the MCA (2005). The relevant circumstances will include, among other things, the merits and quantum of the claim against Z (and for that purpose it may be necessary for the deputy to obtain an opinion from counsel), the size of AB's estate and the affordability of the proposed litigation, and the enforceability of any judgment obtained against Z.

Discussion/learning points

Individuals with a learning disability are able to learn and to live lives with differing degrees of independence. The key is to ensure that support is competence-promoting and empowering by focussing on skill acquisition rather than "doing for" the person who requires support and assistance. AC is more likely to benefit from a supportive intervention if she can understand its relevance to her daily life which the new skills would be designed to augment. The focus would need to be facilitative rather than paternalistic and should, by definition, only provide the skills that AC herself wishes to acquire.

Case 4: AD

Presenting question/problem

AD experienced a severe head injury at the age of 22 when struck by a car at a ski resort. AD was walking through the main road which ran through the town when he was struck by a vehicle which was travelling in the same direction as that in which he was walking. Following the accident AD was initially treated in Switzerland before being evacuated to the UK where he received inpatient rehabilitation at a specialist centre.

He was pursuing a legal claim for damages and his solicitor was concerned as to whether or not he retained the mental capacity to manage his finances in the context of a potentially substantial settlement. At the time of the assessment, his recovery of cognitive function was still underway.

Background to the case

Clinical issues

AD experienced retrograde amnesia of several hours and post-traumatic (anterograde) amnesia in excess of four weeks' duration. His GCS at scene had been 12.

It is well-established that the most important prognostic GCS score is that obtained on arrival at A&E (Lesko et al, 2013) but this information was not available. He spent over three weeks being medically managed and stabilised before being able to be repatriated, as an inpatient, to a regional neurorehabilitation centre in the UK where he spent several more weeks.

Family/social context

At the time of the accident, AD was in the final year of a four-year degree studying law. Following the accident, he was able to return home to live with his parents in order to continue his neurorehabilitation. His father, in particular, was supportive of AD in terms of assisting him with practical arrangements by liaising with insurers and the university to establish a supported return to study at the appropriate time. AD also entrusted his father with his overall money management until he felt able to resume the responsibility. AD had a large circle of supportive friends both at home and at university.

Psychological/neuropsychological matters

AD had previously been very physically active, engaging in a range of outdoor pursuits and sports, and was finding it difficult to adjust to enforced inactivity. He did respond well to encouragement and was motivated to fully engage in his neurorehabilitation. He retained full insight into his injuries and was aware of the level of support that he required at each stage of his recovery. His expectation was of a full recovery.

Assessment and rationale

Records provided included results of psychometric testing undertaken within the first few weeks of being repatriated. These data were useful for comparison for the purpose of tracking neurocognitive recovery.

AD's general cognitive function was re-assessed and the data from early (3 months post-accident) and current (12 months post-accident) administrations demonstrated consistent improvement in all areas. Specifically, his Verbal IQ had increased from 99 to 111; his Performance IQ had improved from 85 to 99; and his Full-Scale IQ had changed from 93 to 107. It should be pointed out that the Performance IQ index score is derived from tests which are largely timed. This places the individual under pressure to address a speed-v-accuracy trade-off which is often compromised by brain injury. A significantly lower PIQ than VIQ is typical after head injury as it is primarily reflective of a slowed processing speed that accompanies traumatic brain injury. However, overall, the picture of AD's cognitive function was one of continuing improvement.

When AD's memory was tested, a similar picture of improvement emerged although his 1-year post-injury scores were still below normal, highlighting residual difficulties with acquiring new information into memory (learning) for both verbal and visual material. The position was fairly typical of post-brain injury function in that AD needed more repetition and rehearsal of information than pre-injury in order to ensure it was registered into memory storage but that it also decayed sooner than would have been expected but for the brain injury. In other words, it took him longer to learn new things and he forgot things more quickly than previously. However, it must be remembered that this was still an improving picture.

With respect to executive function, which captures the skills of applying judgement, problem-solving, weighing up information from different perspectives and evaluating potential consequences as well as measuring cognitive flexibility, testing revealed that his abilities were continuing to improve but that there was still evidence of impairment, particularly with mental flexibility, visual attention and working memory which were all below where they would have been before the injury.

Observation during assessment highlighted a mild speech impairment with word-finding difficulties as well as a degree of impulsive responding on occasion but not throughout. Performance-validity testing had produced results indicative of adequate effort on the part of AD.

Opinion/outcome

Stage One of the MCA (2005) test was met in that there was evidence of impairment to AD's brain, which was permanent, at the time when material decision-making in connection with financial affairs needed to be made.

Stage Two indicated that he had no impairment of understanding, with mild but improving difficulties with recalling key information but a retained ability to seek the missing information and answers when needed. In terms of being able to weigh up information relevant to financial decision-making, AD had ensured his father's assistance and was able to evaluate information with this reliable support. He did not experience any significant communication difficulties which would impede his capacity.

Final opinion was that there was insufficient evidence to rebut the presumption of capacity to manage property and financial affairs. AD had experienced a significant (moderate) brain injury but was 1 year into recovery and with targeted neurorehabilitation in conjunction with natural and spontaneous recovery processes was continuing to improve. He retained insight into his difficulties and, particularly with respect to finances, had put structures in place (with his father) to ensure safe management and expenditure of his finances and was fully engaged in his programme of neurorehabilitation. His prognosis was robust for continued recovery.

Legal commentary

What underpins this positive capacity assessment is firstly the presumption of capacity in section1(2) of the MCA (2005), and second the principle in section 1(3) that a person is not to be treated as unable to make a decision unless all practicable steps to help him to do so have been taken without success. The assessment has, therefore, rightly taken into account the substantial assistance given to AD by his father in the management of his finances. The fact that AD has capacity to manage his finances, including a substantial damages award, means that the Court of Protection will have no jurisdiction in this case.

Discussion/learning points

A key learning point is that when assessing capacity, consideration must always to be given to the possibility that capacity may fluctuate, particularly in the context of a prolonged period of recovery, as is the case with brain injury. For example, if the decision in question does not need to be made at the present time and the person is in a period of recovery, the Act would exhort one to wait until the person being assessed is at their best and has received robust support to maximise their potential for capacitous decision-making (Department for Constitutional Affairs, 2007, Chapter 3).

References

British Psychological Society. (2000). *Learning disability: Definitions and contexts*. Leicester: BPS.

Department for Constitutional Affairs. (2007). Mental Capacity Act 2005: Code of Practice. Retrieved from www.gov.uk/government/publications/mental-capacity-act-code-of-practice

Empowerment Matters. (2014). Making financial decisions: Guidance for assessing, supporting and empowering specific decision making. Retrieved from https://empowermentmattersweb.files.wordpress.com/2014/09/assessing-capacity-financial-decisions-guidance-final.pdf

Lesko, M. M., Jenks, T., O'Brien, S. J., Childs, C., Bouamra, O., Woodford, M. & Lecky, F. (2013). Comparing model performance for survival prediction using Total Glasgow Coma Scale and its components in Traumatic Brain Injury. *Journal of Neurotrauma, 30*, 17–22.

Moye, J. & Marson, D. C. (2007). Assessment of decision-making capacity in older adults: An emerging area of practice and research. *Journal of Gerontology, 62B*(1), 3–11.

Newberry, A. M. & Patchet, A. K. (2008). An innovative framework for psychological assessment in complex mental capacity evaluations. *Psychology, Health & Medicine, 13*(4), 438–449.

Newby, H. & Ryan-Morgan, T. (2013). Assessment of mental capacity. In Newby, G., Coetzer, R., Daisley, A. & Weatherhead, S. (Eds.), *The Handbook of Real Neuropsychological Rehabilitation in Acquired Brain Injury* (pp. 179–207). London: Karnac.

Suto, I., Clare, I. C. H. & Holland, T. (2007). Financial decision making: Guidance for supporting financial decision-making by people with learning disabilities. BILD Publications.

5 Capacity to make welfare decisions

Dr Tracey Ryan-Morgan

With Abigail Bond

Series and colleagues (2017) note that,

> the most common cases heard under the CoP's welfare jurisdiction today concern: where a person should live; how they should be cared for; and questions about relationships such as whether contact with particular individuals should be restricted, and whether a person has the mental capacity to consent to sex or marriage.
>
> (p.2; the latter issue is dealt with in
> Chapter 7 of this book)

The court can only embark on making decisions as to "welfare matters" if it has acquired jurisdiction to do so under the MCA (2005). Since that jurisdiction arises only where a person lacks "capacity" to make the decision with which the court is asked to concern itself, this question of "capacity" needs to be determined as a preliminary issue.

The principles to be applied when addressing questions of capacity are set out in sections 1–3 MCA (2005) (see Chapter 1). There are, in addition, two principles which can be said to be of particular significance for clinicians undertaking assessments about a person's capacity to make decisions about living or care arrangements, or with whom they should have contact.

The first is that whilst it is recognised that the opinion of the treating clinician (or healthcare professional with experience of working with P) will in many cases be as valuable and, in some cases, more valuable than the opinion of a jointly instructed independent expert, there is a risk that the close relationship that the clinical/professional has with P might drive them towards the most protective outcome and obstruct the need to undertake a detached, objective assessment. Highlighting this hypothetical risk in relation to vulnerable adults, in *PH v A Local Authority v Z & R*[1] at para. 16 (xiii), Baker J drew an analogy with what has been referred to in proceedings brought under Part IV of the Children Act 1989 as the "child protection imperative" or "the need to protect a vulnerable child".

1 [2011] EWHC 1704 (Fam)

Further, in repeating this point in *CC v KK & STT*,[2] Baker J reminded himself that the court too, in assessing whether a person has the capacity to decide where to live and what their care needs are, must be careful to avoid being influenced by sympathy for a person's "perfectly understandable" wish to return home.

The need for the assessment to be thorough and objective cannot be overstated. For example, a social worker's assessment which concluded that P's "lack of insight" and "inflexibility of thought" meant that "on the balance of probabilities [P] lacked the mental capacity to make the decision as to where he should live" did not contain sufficient forensic rigour or provide reasons adequate to justify its conclusion. Nor was it rescued by the addition in oral evidence that P was "unable to sift and weigh the issues": Hayden J in *London Borough of Wandsworth v AMcC, AJ, CJ and JJ*.[3]

The second principle is that, whilst the court will consider the opinion of the jointly instructed expert as part of its duty to consider all the relevant evidence on the issue, it is important to remember that the roles of the court and the expert are distinct and that the determination of capacity is ultimately a decision for the Judge and not for the expert. In most cases, the opinion of the expert will be confirmed by the other evidence, but there will be cases where the court reaches a different conclusion. In some cases, where it is not practicable for the court to make a single declaration or decision of incapacity, and where it is likely that future or ongoing decisions need to be made for someone whose condition makes it likely that they will lack capacity to make further decisions in the future, the court can appoint a deputy to act for and make decisions for that person. The power to appoint a deputy is set out in section 16 of the MCA (2005):

(1) This section applies if a person (P) lacks capacity in relation to a matter or matters concerning, (a) P's personal welfare, or (b) P's property and affairs.

(2) The court may, (a) by making an order, make the decision or decisions on P's behalf in relation to the matter or matters, or (b) appoint a person (a deputy) to make decisions on P's behalf in relation to the matter or matters.

(3) The powers of the court under this section are subject to the provisions of the Act and, in particular, to section 1 (the principles of P's best interests).

(4) When deciding whether it is in P's best interests to appoint a deputy, the court must have regard, in addition to the matters mentioned in section 4, to the principles that, (a) a decision by the court is to be preferred to the appointment of a deputy to make a decision, and (b) the powers conferred on a deputy should be as limited in scope and duration as is reasonably practicable in the circumstances.

(5) The court may make such further orders or give such further directions and confer on a deputy such powers or impose on him such duties as it thinks

2 [2012] EWHC 2136 (COP)
3 [2017] EWHC 2435 (Fam)

necessary or expedient for giving effect to or otherwise in connection with an order or appointment made by it under subsection (2).

(6) Without prejudice to s.4, the court may make the order, give the directions or make the appointment on such terms as it considers are in P's best interests, even though no application is before the court for an order, directions or an appointment on those terms.

(7) An order of the court may be varied or discharged by a subsequent order.

(8) The court may, in particular, revoke the appointment of a deputy or vary the powers conferred on him if it is satisfied that the deputy, (a) has behaved or is behaving in a way that contravenes the authority conferred on him by the court or is not in P's best interests, or (b) proposes to behave in a way that would contravene his authority or would not be in P's best interests.

Guidance as to the appointment of personal welfare deputies is found at paragraphs 8.38 and 8.39 of the Code of Practice:

> 8.38 Deputies who have personal welfare decisions will only be required in the most difficult cases where important and necessary actions cannot be carried out without the court's authority or there is no other way of settling the matter in the best interests of the person who lacks capacity to make particular welfare decisions.
>
> 8.39 Examples include when someone needs to make a series of linked welfare decisions over time and it would not be beneficial or appropriate to require all of the decisions to be made by the court. For example, someone such as a family carer who is close to a person with profound and multiple learning disabilities might apply to be appointed as a deputy with authority to make such decisions. The most appropriate way to act in the person's best interests is to have a deputy who will consult relevant people but have the final authority to make decisions; if there is a history of serious family disputes that could have a detrimental effect on the person's future care unless the deputy is appointed to make decisions; the person who lacks capacity is felt to be at risk of serious harm if left in the care of family members. In these rare cases, welfare decisions may need to be made by someone independent of the family, such as a local authority officer. There may even be a need for an additional court order prohibiting those family members having contact with that person.

As for the identity of the deputy, paragraph 8.33 of the Code provides:

> In the majority of cases, the deputy is likely to be a family member or someone who knows the person well, but in some cases the court may decide to appoint a deputy who is independent of the family; for example, where the person's affairs or care needs are particularly complicated. This could be a professional deputy.

However, whilst recognising that the fact that the family is the cornerstone of society and that a person who lacks capacity should, wherever possible, be cared for by members of his natural family, in G *v* E (*Deputyship and Litigation Friend*),[4] Baker J warned at paragraph 61 that that did not justify "the appointment of family members as deputies simply because they are able and willing to serve in that capacity. The words of section 16(4) are clear. They do not permit the court to appoint a deputy simply because

> it feels confident it can but only when satisfied that the circumstances and the decisions which will fall to be taken will be more appropriately taken by a deputy or deputies rather than by a court, bearing in mind the principle that decisions by courts are to be preferred to decisions by deputies. Even then, the appointment must be as limited in scope and duration as is reasonably practicable in the circumstances. It would be a misreading of the structure and the policy of the statute and a misunderstanding of the concept and role of deputies to think it necessary to appoint family members to that position in order to enable them better to perform their role as carers for P.

Case 1: BA

Presenting question/problem

BA is a 70-year-old gentleman with lifelong learning disability as well as long-standing symptoms of anxiety and depression who was accommodated, on an emergency basis, when his living arrangements broke down. He had been cared for by a relative whose motives and behaviours were being brought into question by the Local Authority. Advice was sought, within the terms of the MCA (2005), as to whether BA retained the ability to choose where to live, who to live with and with whom to have (unsupervised) contact.

Background to the case

Clinical issues

BA had recently been given a diagnosis of vascular dementia against a context of learning disability and mood disorder, comprising symptoms of anxiety and depression. Of concern, he had recently been found to have a number of unexplained bruises on his body in areas that could suggest that he was being grabbed, forcefully, by the arm. Bruising had been noted in his groin area and inner thigh and also on his trunk. These had occurred in recent weeks. It was noted that BA is on anti-coagulant medication and he reported, when questioned, that he bruises easily. This may or may not explain the *pattern* or *cause* of bruising.

4 [2010] EWHC 2512 (COP), Fam [2010]

Family/social context

BA had lived with a nephew who received a financial allowance for providing him with 24-hour care prior to admission, on an emergency basis, to a local nursing home. His nephew had been observed by domiciliary care staff to be shouting at BA and being verbally abusive on several occasions. BA, when questioned, alleged that his nephew shoved him whilst verbally abusing him. This alleged assault had occurred after BA was incontinent of urine in the chair whilst watching television. BA reported being frightened of his nephew. In this incident, he may have left it too late to go to the toilet, was too frightened to go/move earlier, or an unwitnessed incident, which caused him to be afraid and to lose bladder control, occurred just prior to the accident.

The nephew was subsequently the subject of an immediate safeguarding investigation, of which he was unaware at the time of the emergency removal of BA to the nursing home. The nephew had also had his access to BA's finances blocked.

BA had grown up in care and held deep distrust of care institutions. He had been married in his early twenties and had two daughters. His marriage broke down and he has been estranged from his daughters for many years. He had moved to the area to live closer to a brother who, sadly, passed away within a short time.

Psychological/neuropsychological matters

BA had expressed on several occasions that he was frightened of his nephew and no longer wanted him to live at his house.

He had been given a diagnosis of vascular dementia some four years prior to the present circumstance and was also being treated for depression and symptoms of anxiety. He had not been assessed by a clinical neuropsychologist as part of the NHS service provision but a psychogeriatrician had reported a Mini Mental State Examination (MMSE) score of 13/30 indicating moderately advanced dementia. Co-morbidities included essential hypertension, atrial fibrillation, asthma, type 2 diabetes mellitus and emphysema. CT and MRI investigations of his brain had reported general atrophic (shrinkage) changes with little change over a 4-year period, calling into question the earlier diagnosis of vascular dementia.

Assessment and rationale

Since his emergency admission BA had become much less anxious and more settled. He had eaten well and gained an appropriate amount of weight.

Staff at the nursing home confirmed that BA required a significant amount of care in the form of monitoring and prompting. For example, he needed prompting to wear slippers. He needed assistance with bathing and personal care and some direction with food. He did not appear to mobilise independently around the nursing home. Staff did not agree that BA could live independently without significant care and confirmed that he had confided to staff that he wished to remain living at the nursing home and not to return to his own home.

However, it is not known if he expressed this view based on the belief that his, allegedly, abusive nephew might still be living there.

The assessment interview focused on the kind of choices that BA might currently be making whilst at the nursing home. He was found to be able to make what are termed "forced choices" such as whether or not he wants a drink or food rather than to decide at what time he might want a cup of tea or whether he might prefer a different beverage or even where he might like to drink it.

BA was presented with a genogram of his family but frequently confused the names of family members. The assessment took place over several assessment visits so that a view could be formed as to his ability to recall information between appointments.

BA's behaviours in the nursing home were highly routinised. He had meals and activities at set times every day, getting up and going to bed also conformed to routine. He reported that he found it difficult to socialise spontaneously as he was concerned what the other residents might be saying or thinking about him.

BA was disorientated to place (gave the wrong address as his home), could not recall how long he had been living at the nursing home, got the ages of his daughters wrong and did not know the day or date at the time of assessment.

In terms of formal psychometric assessment, the Adaptive Behaviour Assessment System was administered. This is an assessment measure of an individual's ability to adapt their functioning and is completed by caregivers to the person in question. The results indicated that in all aspects of daily functioning, BA's abilities would be classified as "extremely low". This confirms the subjective impression that BA would be unable to live independently without significant care support to ensure his health, well-being and safety.

The Montreal Cognitive Assessment (version 7.1) was also administered. This is a widely available, brief, screening instrument designed to detect the presence of cognitive impairment across a wide range of neuropsychological domains. It is considered to have excellent sensitivity (identifying those with cognitive impairment) and excellent specificity (ruling out those who do not). BA's total score on the MOCA was 4/29. This represents significant and gross cognitive impairment and illustrates widespread neuropsychological dysfunction. It is possible that the low scores on testing were consistent with lifelong learning disabilities or were attributable to the clinical presentation of the neuropathological processes underpinning his dementia. Whatever the origin of his difficulties, his level of functioning clearly indicated a range of disabilities that compromise the possibility of capacitous decision-making.

It was also decided to administer selected subtests of the CamCog-R. This is a well-established means of assessing cognitive function in elderly adults where there is suspected cognitive dysfunction. A selection of brief sub-tests was administered to BA. He experienced marked difficulty with visual problem-solving skills, indicating that he struggled with both the understanding and execution of the task.

Finally, the Glasgow Depression Scale for People with a Learning Disability was administered to BA. This is a valid and reliable self-report measure of depressive symptoms for adults with learning disability. The cut-off score is 13 (yielding

96 per cent sensitivity and 90 per cent specificity). It was administered to BA who registered a score of 14 indicating the presence of depressive symptoms. It appears from records that BA has experienced symptoms of mood disorder across his adult life but more specifically since the loss of his brother.

Opinion/outcome

BA was co-operative throughout the assessment and complied with all that was asked of him. It was noted that BA responded well to positive reinforcement and his evident anxiety at the outset of the assessment was able to be reduced considerably through the appropriate use of reassurance and encouragement, as well as by keeping sessions brief.

The results of the assessment indicated that BA lacked the capacity to make considered decisions about with whom he should have contact as he appeared unable to retain information regarding his current lack of contact with certain family members, which then would become confused in his mind. He was unable to apply abstract reasoning skills in order to formulate an opinion and was also unable to calculate implications or consequences of contact with various family members. The two issues of returning home and of living with his nephew were conflated in his mind, despite efforts to assist him to separate the two. BA expressed, unprompted, the view that he no longer wished his nephew to live at his home. He expressed the view that the nephew had provided only minimal care and support and that he no longer wished to live with him anywhere. However, this view appeared to be predicated on the basis on somewhat confused recollection as to whether BA was no longer allowed to see his nephew or whether the nephew was no longer allowed to see BA (he had not been officially told that his nephew had been prevented access to the nursing home).

BA had expressed contentment about his current placement at the nursing home and also about his professional carer, who regularly took him out on a Sunday afternoon. He was able to express whether or not he was happy with such care but lacked the mental capacity to formulate considered responses to detailed questions about his care needs, which are relatively complex due to his cognitive difficulties, impaired insight, mood disorder and significant health problems.

Whilst it is recognised that capacity can fluctuate, it was clear from the available medical records that BA was experiencing a degenerative cognitive condition, which overlaid his lifelong learning disability. This was further complicated by the presence of symptoms of depression and anxiety which appeared to be longstanding. Whilst there may have been minimal day-to-day fluctuations in mood there was unlikely to be any significant fluctuation in underlying cognitive ability or functional capacity. It was considered unlikely that, in the future, BA could regain capacity in respect of the issues under assessment. The opinion was expressed that he lacked the requisite capacity to choose where to live and with whom to have contact. However, he was able to express wishes which were taken into account in a Best Interests process which followed the assessment.

Legal commentary

There are three elements to the test for capacity, ie:

(1) "The functional test." Is the person unable to make a decision? If so:
(2) "The diagnostic test." Is there an impairment or disturbance in the functioning of the person's mind or brain? If so:
(3) "The causative nexus." Is the person's inability to make the decision because of the identified impairment or disturbance?

The strict adherence to this ordering (as set out in section 2(1) of the MCA (2005) and in contrast to the Code of Practice which puts the diagnostic test first) avoids a discriminatory and simplistic approach. In this case it avoids the risk of falling into the trap of moving from the finding that BA has moderately advanced dementia to concluding that he lacks the capacity to make the decisions about where to live or who to see. Importantly, when it comes to the application of the "functional test", the court needs to consider the capacity for decision-making not in general terms but in relation to each specific area of decision-making under consideration, which means that the results of the MoCA do not of themselves determine the issue.

Each case of course depends on its own facts, but helpful guidance as to what needs to be taken into consideration in determining whether a person has the capacity to make specific welfare decisions is provided by Hedley J in *A Local Authority v FG, AG and HG*.[5] In relation to the question of capacity to decide where a person should live, which is so often a choice between family and local authority provision, Hedley J considered that this was "a relatively sophisticated process" which "involves an ability to understand what the issues are that determine family or local authority provision, what the consequences of any such decision are, and how they are likely to impact on a person's emotional, physical and educational welfare." An ability to say yes or no to a specific offer, or to make a choice of one between two, does not go far enough where there is evidence that a person would be overwhelmed by the requirement to digest information relating to the nuances of these choices. What will be important in this context is ensuring that the court has up-to-date information about BA's understanding of the choices available to him, especially in the light of his reduction in anxiety and the report that he has become more settled since his emergency admission.

Hedley J also gave guidance in relation to the capacity to make judgments about whether or not a person should see their relatives or the context in which they should do so, which he described as requiring 'an understanding of quite complex emotional issues.' Cobb J in *WBC v Z, X & Y*[6] expressed in similar terms what was involved in decision-making about contact:

5 [2011] EWHC 3932
6 [2016] EWCOP 4

An informed choice about contact with others would include an understanding of the positives and negatives of having contact, or a relationship, with another individual, and an ability to assess the risks posed by another individual or situations from which to extricate herself if she were vulnerable to exploitation.

Importantly, a person's capacity to make judgements about whether or not he or she should see their family members, or third parties, needs to be distinguished from their capacity to decide on any individual occasion whether to take up the offer of contact that has been made (per Hedley J in *A Local Authority v FG, AG and HG*[7] at paragraph 19). It follows that if it were found that BA did not have capacity to make judgements about whether or not he should see his family members, his wishes and feelings in response to a decision to allow a visit by, for example, his daughters, should be respected.

Discussion/learning points

In terms of what could be added to the present assessment, it would have been informative to take BA to visit his home and show him that his nephew no longer lived there in order to reassure him and also to inform his view as to future residence. Unfortunately, his physical health precluded this coupled with the assessment having taken place in the depth of winter in a mountainous area with frequent snow and heavy ice fall. Trips out would have increased his already considerable falls risk. As an alternative, photographs could have been taken of his former home, both outside and internally, for these to be used to guide and prompt discussions. However, the concern in this instance would have been how to avoid undue influence in someone who was already suggestible in presentation. Showing him such photographs may have been interpreted by BA as a wish on the part of the assessor for him to return there whether he wished to or not due to his limited understanding and impaired insight.

Case 2: BB

Presenting question/problem

This case relates to a 45-year-old lady with learning disability who had always been cared for by her mother. Upon the death of her mother she was subsequently supported by a family member, but evidence came to light that within the wider family, BB was being physically abused and that monies of hers were going missing. A further complicating factor emerged when one of the accused family members subsequently made a counter-claim that the professional carers in the residential home, where BB had been placed for her protection, were financially exploiting her. The assessment specifically requested an assessment of BB's capacity to manage her own finances, make day-to-day financial decisions, decide where she lives and who she can have contact with.

Background to the case

Clinical issues

There were no particular clinical issues at play in this assessment. BB had a life-long learning disability which was well-established and documented. She had accessed specialist support services for many years. There were no significant health issues.

Family/social context

For many years, BB had lived at home with her mother and her brother. She had a sister who lived next door, but this sister was estranged from the mother and brother and for many years there was no contact between the parties. This changed suddenly when the sister reported to the police that the brother had assaulted BB and her mother. The police arrested the brother, investigated the allegations, but found no case to answer. A consequence of this event was that the brother moved away and no longer provided support to BB or her mother. The estranged sister stepped into the breach.

Within a few months, the mother resumed contact with the brother, as a result, the sister removed BB from respite care and refused to disclose her whereabouts to the Local Authority on the grounds that she did not trust anyone to protect her vulnerable sister. When BB's social worker was able to contact and meet with BB, she disclosed that she was afraid of the sister who had removed her, and a safeguarding procedure was initiated. BB was removed to a placement within supported accommodation and her sister was prevented from having access whilst the investigation was underway. Once completed, contact was resumed and within a short period of time, the sister was appointed deputy for financial affairs for BB.

There followed a complaint by BB that her sister had struck her, and a further safeguarding investigation resulted in the sister, once again, being prevented from accessing BB. The sister then sought legal representation and made a formal complaint against the provider of the supported accommodation where BB resided, expressing dissatisfaction with the care provided and making allegations of financial exploitation of BB by staff. Members of the wider family then also expressed concerns that they were being prevented from visiting BB due to false allegations of undue influence. In view of the breakdown in relationships between BB, her sister, the wider family and the accommodation provider, the Local Authority sought to remove the sister as financial deputy. The care provider made a statement to the effect that oversight of the care and support provided to BB was occurring through regulatory and governance procedures and could be safely and accountably managed outwith the remit of the Court of Protection in a way which would empower BB.

Psychological/neuropsychological matters

BB was assessed by an experienced speech and language therapist who reported the opinion that BB was "a competent, confident communicator within the environments she accesses . . . by using methods to supplement verbal language BB is able to make her needs known and communicate effectively with her peers and carers." It was considered important to establish this at the outset.

GP records indicated that her general practitioner, who had been treating BB for many years and was familiar with her needs, was of a similar view with regards to BB's ability to make her needs and wishes known.

Historical records evidenced a general cognitive assessment in adulthood which confirmed an IQ in the range of 60. (The average IQ of the general population lies between 90 and 109.) BB had attended a range of specialist day services and centres for most of her adult life. There was no evidence of psychological difficulty other than at periods of acute distress in connection with documented family schisms.

Assessment and rationale

The assessment was planned to include formal interview of BB with her independent advocate present, interview with the social worker, interview with the care home provider, interview with her sister and formal, structured assessment of BB's adaptive behaviour skills in the context of daily living. The sister refused the invitation to interview.

BB was interviewed with her advocate present. The early stages of the assessment focused on BB's capacity to manage her property and financial affairs. It became clear that many day-to-day choices are taken away from BB by the current financial arrangements (with her sister as deputy). Money or items had to be requested, and the need demonstrated to the satisfaction of the current deputy, in order for money to be forthcoming. For example, BB could not choose which clothes to buy or which toiletries to purchase for personal use. However, on a day-to-day basis she was able to choose which clothes to wear, which meals to eat and make decisions on a (limited range) of leisure activities, dependent on available resources. BB was also able to elect to go to the toilet when necessary.

BB made it clear that she would like a hairdresser to visit the house and to have her hair cut and coloured. It became clear at the outset of this interview that BB was not aware of the full extent of her financial resources. She did not know how much money was kept on her behalf or whether the resources extended to more than just financial income. For example, BB was unaware if she is part-owner of a property or any other assets. When asked what she would do if she received more money or a cheque in the post, BB became excited and said she would have more money and be able to "do more things". The current financial arrangements appeared to be unnecessarily complicated. BB had made it clear that she wanted to make more choices and have more involvement in decisions about her money. BB also made it clear that she trusted the current Home Manager to assist with managing her money on a day-to-day basis.

The second part of the structured assessment involved decision-making about residence. BB was able to confirm that before she lived at her present address, she lived with her brother but was vague about details. At this point BB became very quiet and her body language was withdrawn. It was confirmed that she had not been allowed to tell of her whereabouts when living with her brother and she still found it very difficult to talk about this. She had not understood why she was being asked to "tell lies" and knew it was wrong but could not make sense of it. She confirmed that she had been able to be involved in the decision to move to her present address and also confirmed that she is happy where she is. Initially, she had not felt happy there because her sister had been calling all the time. At this point BB started pulling her hair and gestured using her finger tips the path tears would take down her face. BB had asked staff to keep her bedroom curtains, and the curtains downstairs, closed so that she could not see her sister arriving. It was reported that BB used to hide from her sister, and she called the Home Manager and asked her to stop her sister from coming but her sister did not abide by this request.

When asked what she did and did not like about where she presently lived BB was unable to offer any information about anything she did not like but confirmed that she enjoyed sewing, knitting, watching television and putting on nail varnish. She expressed that she was happy with the residents that she shares the house with and considers one of them to be her best friend. BB also confirmed that she had been involved in choosing the colour scheme for her bedroom as well as her bedding and curtains.

The subsequent part of the structured interview related to decisions about shopping, buying and spending. It was confirmed that BB attended a day centre every weekday between 9.00am and 3.30pm. She attended different centres on different days. She was involved in playing bowls, cooking, yoga and having physiotherapy and spending time in activities with her best friend who she lives with. BB made it clear that there were staff that she has bonded well with at the day centres and she enjoyed going with them for meals, shopping and to the cinema. BB expressed a desire to attend college as several of her friends do.

In relation to shopping BB confirmed that she did go shopping with her best friend and staff and was encouraged to select those items for which she has money. BB became very animated when discussing shopping suggesting that this is an activity she enjoys significantly. When asked about the last thing BB had bought when she went shopping, she initially had difficulty recalling as there had been several weeks of snow and she had been unable to get out regularly. However, when prompted about Christmas shopping BB was able to recall that she had bought herself a bag and was very pleased with the purchase.

It was confirmed that BB only has help to choose what to buy when she asks for that help. When asked about going on holiday it was confirmed that her sister used to decide when and where to go on holiday and takes BB. BB made it very clear at this stage that she did not wish to go on holiday with her sister again as she had not enjoyed the last holiday. She was able to communicate through gesture and verbal sounds that her sister had made her sad and made her cry when they were on holiday last. BB was aware that several of her friends were able to go on overnight stays and for weekends away as holidays and BB was clear that she would also like to engage in such activities if she was to be able to make more financial decisions.

The subsequent stage of the interview related to BB's family. BB was asked who was in her family and she informed that her family consists of the sister she does not wish to have contact with, a brother whom she would not talk about and a second sister. Further prompting and encouragement enabled BB to refer to this brother (who had previously been accused of assaulting her) but she gave the impression that she was not permitted to talk about him and felt uncomfortable doing so such that this was not pursued further.

When asked who she had contact with in her family and what different activities she undertook with people in her family BB confirmed that she did not like to see her family members and she did not undertake any activities with them. BB was then asked why she did not like seeing family members and she reported that she did not like seeing any of them because they might make her see the sister who she did not like and that she specifically did not wish to have any contact with this sister.

It came to light during the interview that BB did not receive any post at her home as this had been redirected by the sister who was her deputy to her own house, without BB's consent. It appeared that the mail was not then forwarded to BB and that she had recently got into difficulties as she had no written documentation to prove where she lived and did not have access to her passport or other such documents.

At this stage of the interview BB was very clear that she did not want a copy of the present report to go to her sister and therefore wished to ensure that her solicitor would send her a copy via her Independent Advocate.

In relation to BB's contact with her advocate this often took place on an unplanned basis by telephone and face-to-face and always proceeded well. BB was aware that she could pick up the telephone and contact her advocate although it appeared that contact was usually initiated by the advocate. BB confirmed that she liked all of the staff in her present house, was very happy there and that advocacy worked very well for her.

At this stage, the staff who worked with BB on a daily basis were asked to complete the Adaptive Behaviour Assessment Scales. The results indicated that that there were particular areas of strength in terms of independent living skills demonstrated by BB which included leisure, social skills and self-care. These skills specifically related to the basic care of her home including cleaning, food preparation and performing chores. It also related to skills needed for engaging and planning recreational activities, including playing with others, engaging in recreation at home and following rules in a game. BB had strong skills in the area of personal care including eating, dressing, bathing, toileting, grooming and hygiene and also the skills needed to interact socially and get along with other people including having friends, showing and recognising emotions, assisting others and using manners.

At interview, the social work team leader expressed her view that BB did not require a deputy as she was able to make supported decisions and that there were sufficient checks and balances in place with current regulatory and governance arrangements to ensure that BB's needs and rights were protected. However, she also expressed the view that BB is suggestible, and that specific care would have to be taken to mitigate against the risk of undue influence.

An interview with the director of the housing provider indicated that she had grave concerns about BB's sister continuing in the role of deputy for financial affairs. She recounted several examples of how the sister was being obstructive in terms of preventing BB access to money for reasonable purchases. For example, BB had a hairdryer which broke. When the sister was approached for money to purchase a replacement, she would not give any money until the broken hairdryer had been given to her to inspect. She was also approached for a specific, and modest, purchase but refused the request on spurious grounds. The director had subsequently written to the Court of Protection requesting an audit of BB's finances and expressing misgivings about the present deputy appointment.

Opinion/outcome

BB was able to make day-to-day decisions about small items of expenditure, within a supported environment, although the current arrangements for managing her finances largely prevented this. It was argued that BB would benefit from the appointment of a deputy who would assist with decision-making in her best interests and with her clearly expressed wishes in mind. The extant arrangements were such that the deputy typically made financial decisions on BB's behalf which disempowered her and denied her access to resources that she wished to have in order to maximise her independence. The present deputy was unwanted by BB and could be replaced with a deputy, appointed by the court, who was not a member of her family.

However, although the assessment highlighted that although BB was able to express views, she lacked the capacity to weigh up options regarding finances. She may be able to decide that she wished to buy a new DVD player but was unaware of the extent of her finances or the competing demands on these such that if she did make the purchases she wished to, she would be unaware of whether this would leave her enough to purchase essentials such as food or bus tickets for that week. She had limited understanding of the value of money and no knowledge of her available resources including the source, extent and frequency of her income.

BB was specifically asked about her family members as part of the structured interview. BB made it clear that she did not wish to have contact with her family members and she did not wish her family members to be involved in making decisions about her life which included decisions about money and decisions about residence, what resources she accesses and how she lives her life.

BB had sufficient communication skills and was able to make herself understood and was able to express clear views about where she wished to live and whether or not she was happy in her residence. However, there were no other options available, or presented, to BB against which she could consider her choices. BB had lived in other places but had never independently chosen where she lived. She had been removed both by family members and by Statutory Authorities from previous residences. She had no sense of permanence and was anxious about whether or not she would be moved out of her present residence and possibly made to return to live with family. However, with respect to her place of residence and choice of contact with others, the assessment clarified that she retained capacity for such decisions. She was able to understand the issues, recall the basis of her decision-making, weigh up the immediate consequences of her choices and communicate these to a level which made her wishes understood. She had also been consistent throughout the period of assessment as to her wishes regarding contact with family and choice of residence.

Legal commentary

This case raises an important point in connection with the "diagnostic test", namely, the extent to which BB, with an IQ in the region of 60 and no other psychological or health difficulties, could be said to be suffering from an "impairment of, or a disturbance in the functioning of, the mind or brain". In *WBC v Z*[8] Cobb J doubted the conclusion of the consultant developmental psychiatrist that a "borderline intellectual disability" would pass the diagnostic test, noting for example that paragraph 4.12 of the Code of Practice contemplates as an example of an impairment or disturbance in the functioning of the mind or brain a "significant" learning disability. Since BB's learning disability falls between "borderline" and "significant" and is likely to be classed as "mild", particular care in the exploration and analysis of her difficulties would need to be exercised here.

Even if the court were to conclude that BB suffered from an impairment of or a disturbance in the functioning of the mind or brain, and agreed with the clinician's conclusion that she was unable to make a decision for herself in respect of budgeting and finances, it would still need to be satisfied that the "causal nexus" between the two had been established. Crucially, the question for the court is not whether BB's ability to make these sorts of decisions is impaired by the impairment of, or disturbance in the functioning of, the mind or brain but rather whether she is "rendered unable" to make the decision by reason thereof (see *Re SB* (A Patient: Capacity to Consent to Termination) above at [38]). What is more, an inability to make a decision by reason of impairment/disturbance must be carefully distinguished, if possible, from an inability to make a decision due to the influence of an over-bearing third party. In this case, BB's ability to engage in financial decision-making has been subject to the invasive control and restrictions exercised by her sister as her deputy: is there room for the argument that BB may well be able to weigh up options regarding finances if, free from her sister's over-protection, she were given more information about the extent of her finances and the opportunity to learn how to budget? Or is there – aside from the issue of third-party influence – additional evidence that she has difficulty retaining information (as to finances) and formulating decisions?

Finally, if the concerns expressed by the director of the housing provider as to the conduct of BB's sister as deputy for her financial affairs are well-placed, the court does have the power to replace an appointed deputy: see section 16(8) of the MCA (2005) which provides that

> The court may, in particular, revoke the appointment of a deputy or vary the powers conferred on him if it is satisfied that the deputy (a) has behaved or is behaving in a way that contravenes the authority conferred on him by the court or is not in P's best interests, or (b) proposes to behave in a way that would contravene his authority or would not be in P's best interests.

The court would need to hear argument on who should replace BB's sister if her deputyship is revoked. Even if there is no suggestion that a proposed deputy would fail to act in P's best interests, the court should only appoint someone in whom all family members having continuing involvement with P have full confidence and trust. In *A Local Authority v M, E and A*[9] the court stressed the need for the appointed deputy to be given the best opportunity to forge a good relationship with everyone in the case and therefore appointed an independent experienced solicitor specialising in Court of Protection work in preference to a social worker employed by the same local authority that had brought and prosecuted the proceedings in the first place.

Discussion/learning points

The Code of Practice (Department for Constitutional Affairs, 2007) states clearly that, "Anyone supporting a person who may lack capacity should not use excessive persuasion or undue pressure" (paragraph 2.8, p.23). Evidence would suggest that the sister has manifestly failed to observe this imperative and that she had made unjustified assumptions about what might be in BB's best interests without consulting her and other family members properly.

Case 3: BC

Presenting question/problem

BC is a 30-year-old with a history of a severe brain injury in adulthood. The nature of his brain injury meant that he had impaired insight into his difficulties

---

and was noted to frequently have followed a course of action that has placed him at risk of harm. His court-appointed deputy requested a capacity assessment in respect of BC's ability to make reasoned judgements around his use of alcohol, his choice and situation of residence and his continued contact with family members with whom he has a tempestuous and, occasionally, violent relationship. The issue of residence was current as he was private tenant in a rented property, but the landlord had received complaints from neighbours about the noisy and aggressive behaviour associated with his drinking of alcohol and his tenancy was at risk.

Background to the case

Clinical issues

BC had sustained his severe brain injury in a fall from a roof. Several experienced clinicians in the field of brain injury had previously assessed BC and concluded as follows:

- His brain injury renders him "suggestible" and "at risk of acting out on misperceptions in ways that could potentially cause distress to himself and others";
- His brain injury has resulted in "poor social cognition (poor insight and judgement) and inability to self-regulate his behavior."

BC had already had two case managers who had attempted to manage the risks posed by his lack of insight into his vulnerabilities. He had asked his deputy to sack both in turn, refusing to work with them or engage with the packages of support that were put in place around him.

There were numerous examples of ill-advised decision-making which had required the involvement of others to avert considerable problems for BC. He had used Facebook to disclose the details of his financial settlement and his address. He had also used Facebook to express abusive opinions about, and towards, people known to him, including his estranged wife, despite strong advice regarding potential consequences to himself. BC had discharged himself from a specialist neuropsychiatry inpatient service against medical advice. This provided further evidence that he had been unable (on occasion) to use the information that had been given to him to weigh up the most appropriate course of action for himself and where he had made decisions that place him at risk of harm or of exploitation by others.

A pressing concern was that BC would drink large amounts of alcohol each day, against clinical advice, which was having the effect of further compromising his judgement as well as substantially increasing his fatigue. This had the knock-on effect of exacerbating his underlying neurocognitive difficulties such that his speech was more slurred than usual, and his balance and mobility were also affected, increasing his falls risk. In fact, he had several falls whilst under the influence of alcohol within the home, two of which had resulted in broken bones.

Family/social context

BC was the oldest of three sons. Two of them were estranged from one another. His father was also on the scene (his mother having died several years previously). There was substantial, corroborated, evidence that his father and one brother, who lived together, both over-used alcohol and brought alcohol to BC's home against strong medical advice not to do so. They also took him to local pubs where the three of them drank heavily during the day and frequently engaged in physical fighting with each other as well as members of the public. There was also evidence that the father and brother were taking BC to visit local prostitutes and paying for their services on his behalf.

BC's estranged brother had refused to have contact with the father and third brother and felt strongly that neither were acting in BC's best interests. He wished to support BC but could not access him without the other family members turning up unannounced and causing conflict around BC.

BC's father had made a number of suggestions regarding the purchase of property (with BC's significant financial settlement) for the three of them to live together and for BC to set up a gardening business for the three of them to work in, and benefit from financially.

There were safeguarding concerns raised by the local authority in respect of the physical violence and potential undue influence of his brother and father. BC would regularly approach his financial deputy for money to give his family (at their request) and would become hostile, aggressive and abusive when such requests were reasonably denied, making threats against his deputy.

BC had three young sons of primary school age and below, with whom he had contact several times per week. Contact was supervised by a local authority registered childminder, at the request of the boys' mother. The arrangement was a voluntary one, but BC frequently bombarded his ex-partner with abusive text messages and phone-calls based on unfounded suspicions as to her behaviour and she was considering taking the matter to the Family Court to request a formal order as he had refused all requests to curtail his inappropriate behaviours.

Concerns were being raised about BC's lack of self-regulation as well as a lack of behavioural boundaries for the children when he had conduct of them. The local authority was working closely with the children's mother to ensure continued contact but there was a significant risk that she would revert to the courts if matters were not able to be managed better for the safety of the children.

It had been difficult to recruit staff to the support package that was in place as BC (and his behaviours since his brain injury) had become somewhat notorious in the local community. There was a high turnover of support staff, many of whom left because of threatening behaviour towards them by BC, which made it difficult to ensure consistency of approach in terms of the nature and level of support provided. This meant that the support package was frequently at risk of breaking down. Alternative care packages were tried which varied from directly employing and training staff to recruiting a care provider to put in their own teams of staff.

Psychological/neuropsychological matters

BC had a traumatic brain injury several years previously following a fall from a roof. He was unconscious at scene with a GCS of 3/15. There was evidence of increased cranial pressure which was surgically addressed through frontal craniotomy and lobectomy. The surgical summary at the time was that BC had experienced a severe traumatic brain injury with right frontal atrophy and a left internal capsule infarct with left cerebellar atrophy. Neuroradiology confirmed extensive cortical and subcortical damage with generalised cerebral atrophy and persisting evidence of a left internal capsule infarct.

There was neurocognitive evidence of impaired reasoning as to consequences, difficulty with focusing on a task, slowed processing of information and responses and marked problems with memory. BC also had dysarthria, manifest as slurred speech, which worsened with fatigue or when under the influence of alcohol, making communication challenging and frustrating for him. His mobility and balance were also affected by the brain injury, fatigue and alcohol such that he struggled to negotiate his ground floor home safely.

Assessment and rationale

In light of the above information, it was considered prudent to administer a formal measure of BC's potential suggestibility to undue influence. The Gudjonsson Suggestibility Scales provided clear and objective evidence of his susceptibility to influence and negative feedback, the latter of which would make him change his mind from a previously held opinion or recollection with only subtle suggestion.

BC was assessed by means of a pre-prepared structured interview, designed to focus on aspects of understanding and reasoning in relation to drinking alcohol, having contact with his father and brother, and consistent thoughts about future residence. Details as to BC's neurocognitive deficits had already been established by court appointed experts in the medicolegal claim which had settled.

When asked about alcohol intake, BC grossly under-estimated his daily intake, a fact which was open to challenge by his support staff who had knowledge of the amount of alcohol stored in the house and whose responsibility it was to dispose of the empty bottles and cans each morning. He also played down the impact of the alcohol on his brain injury despite several attempts to educate him, in a supportive rather than didactic way, about the known effects of alcohol on brain injury. He frequently became agitated during the interviews, which took place over several sessions and the assessment had to be terminated abruptly due to verbal aggression and threats of violence by BC.

An interview took place individually with BC's father, then brother, who lived together, in an attempt to educate them about the effects of alcohol on BC and also to seek their support in limiting his access to alcohol. BC was unable to independently access the community and his alcohol supply was provided by his father and brother. Both father and brother would give the impression of understanding the risk to BC and also agree to reduce the amount of alcohol they provided to him but, in practice, they did not adhere to these verbal commitments.

Conversations were also held, separately, with BC, his father and brother, about the potential consequences of his aggressive behaviour and their physical fighting together. BC lacked any insight into the possibility that his behaviours may compromise his much-valued contact with his children or that potential serious injury could ensue to any of the parties. Given the severity of his brain injury, attempts were made to educate BC to the possibility that further blows to his head could result in catastrophic injury, all to little avail.

In terms of residence, BC was from the local area and had clear ideas about the type of property he wished to settle in. This would require a purchase as few suitable properties were on the local rental market. However, in these considerations, BC's father and brother exerted considerable influence over his decision-making as they made a case for living with him and supporting him in the future, despite a clear lack of evidence of their ability to do so in the present. There was no recognition on the part of any of BC or his father and brother as to the need to adapt any property to meet his mobility needs. Several patently unsuitable properties were suggested by the father and brother which were then subsequently supported by BC.

Opinion/outcome

The results of the assessment clearly indicated that BC lacked the capacity to use any knowledge of his brain injury and its consequences in his decision-making about alcohol, contact with his brother and father, risks to himself, his children or future residence. There was also overwhelming evidence of impaired insight and risky decision-making on a daily basis which supported this view. In addition, there was significant objective and anecdotal, observational evidence as to his susceptibility to influence which rendered him vulnerable.

However, protracted discussions with the deputy for financial affairs indicated that even were a welfare order to be requested of the Court of Protection, particularly in respect of his unsafe alcohol intake, and, even if that request were to be granted (which was considered unlikely), the crux of the problem remained as to how to implement such protective measures in the least restrictive way possible and ensure continued safety unless BC were living in a controlled, residential environment. He had indicated vehemently that he would never agree to living in a formal residential home placement, and psychiatric opinion was that he would not satisfy the criteria which would enable him to be moved subject to a section of the Mental Health Act (2007).

The approach taken was to initiate safeguarding procedures in respect of his father and brother to seek to ensure BC's continued safety and to illustrate to them, in the clearest terms, the risks that their behaviours presented or magnified in BC's life.

The case manager and deputy managed to preserve their working relationships with BC, with considerable effort, and to maintain the consent and co-operation of the children's mother for continued, supervised, access. The staff team were replaced by an experienced local care provider who was recruited to work with BC to put in place a new support team, a strict routine and a contract-of-agreement with BC with respect to alcohol and respectful behaviour. In return, BC was to be supported to access the local community to source an appropriate property, to drink safely and within agreed limits, and, to engage in enjoyable activities each day to improve his quality of life. He also agreed to attend Local Authority parenting classes, with support, and to engage with his children in safe and age appropriate activities. Progress was slow, with several difficult periods where BC would challenge the support provided but some successes were achieved.

The outcome was that BC eventually moved into a suitable property which was purchased and adapted for him and his children. The care team provided 24-hour, competence-promoting support. Contact with BC's father and brother was supported but managed. BC re-engaged with the neuropsychiatrist, on a community basis and, gradually he settled into less challenging patterns of behaviour. His former partner worked closely with the deputy, case manager and care provider to ensure continued contact between BC and his sons as this was a key motivator for him and was valued by the children.

Legal commentary

It is noted that the deputy for BC's property and affairs did not consider that the court would grant a "welfare order" in this case, i.e. an order stipulating where BC should live, restricting his alcohol intake and restricting his contact to his father and brother in particular. Before making any such order the court would of course need to be satisfied that BC lacked capacity in relation to these sorts of decisions, by applying the principles set out in sections 1–3 of the MCA (2005) above. In this case section 3(2) would play a significant role. This provides that

> a person is not to be regarded as unable to understand the information relevant to a decision if he is able to understand an explanation of it given to him in a way that is appropriate to his circumstances (using simple language, visual aids, or any other means).

Likewise, paragraph 4.16 of the Code of Practice states that "It is important not to assess someone's understanding before they have been given relevant information about a decision. Every effort must be made to provide information in a way that is most appropriate to help the person understand." Whilst the clinical assessment of BC had concluded that he lacked the capacity to make decisions about the relevant welfare matters, the success of the supportive work that was subsequently carried out to provide information to him and to get him to engage with a "contract of expectations" suggests that a finding of a lack of capacity may not have been justified. Furthermore, the case illustrates the importance of section 1(4), ie that a person is not to be treated as unable to make a decision merely because he makes an unwise decision (here, his persistence in drinking alcohol).

In any event, even if the court were to find that BC lacked capacity, section 1(6) of the MCA (2005) requires that before any decision is made on behalf of an incapacitated person, regard must be had to whether the purpose for which it is needed can be as effectively achieved in way that is less restrictive of the person's rights and freedoms. In other words, as pointed out by Peter Jackson J in *Wye Valley NHS Trust v B*,[10] a finding of lack of capacity "does not operate as on off switch for [his] rights and freedoms." The painstaking, collaborative, multi-professional approach taken with BC described above led ultimately to an outcome similar to that which would have been achieved by the making of a welfare order under the Act yet in a manner which was far less invasive of his rights and liberty. Nonetheless, if this approach is adopted, great care should be taken in attempting to draw up a "contract" (here in the form of a behavioural contract) with someone who is thought to lack capacity so as to ensure that it is not coercion by another name. See, in a different context, the stark warning against assuming the consent of a parent to the accommodation of their child under section 20 of the Children Act 1989 and the steps needing to be taken by a social worker to satisfy themselves of capacity: *Re CA (A Baby)*.[11]

Discussion/learning points

There is merit in considering a positive risk-management approach in cases of this nature rather than in seeking a restrictive welfare order from the court. In *DM v Y City Council*[12] Bodey J heard an application on behalf of DM by way of challenge to a Standard Authorisation which had authorised his deprivation of liberty at a care home. DM, an abstinent alcoholic with a form of alcohol-related dementia, had lived in a home for people with alcohol-related difficulties for the past five years. He sought to leave the home and to live independently or to live somewhere where alcohol was available. There was clear evidence that he had sustained cognitive deterioration from chronic abuse of alcohol and that he had no insight or comprehension as regards his alcohol problem or his proven inability to care for himself, and a clear finding by the consultant psychiatrist of a lack of capacity to litigate, or to make decisions regarding his care and residence, and his consumption of alcohol. The judgment deals in the main with the Best Interests decision, namely as to whether DM should be required to remain in the home (with his current life expectancy of six or so years) or to be moved to a different residential unit where he could drink (with his life expectancy reduced to as little as two years). Bodey J reminded himself of the dangers of being too paternalistic in such cases and that the purpose of the "Best Interests" test was to look at matters from the incapacitated person's point of view. He also reminded himself of what Munby J, as he then was, had said in *Local Authority X v MM & another*[13] at paragraph 120:

10 [2015] EWCOP 60
11 [2012] EWHC 2190
12 [2017] EWCOP 17
13 [2007] EWHC 2003

physical health and safety can sometimes be bought at too high a price in happiness and emotional welfare. The emphasis must be on sensible risk appraisal, not striving to avoid all risk whatever the price, but instead seeking a proper balance and being willing to tolerate manageable or acceptable risks as the price appropriately to be paid in order to achieve some other good . . . what good is making someone safer if it merely makes them miserable?

Bodey J concluded after considering the pros and cons of each outcome that remaining where he was would be the least restrictive option consistent with his best interests and that, although by moving DM he would be fulfilling his stated wish, DM would be losing much else of real value to his quality of life (loss of meaningful friendship with another resident, deterioration in his physical and mental health, likely further moves if, when drinking, his behaviour became so challenging that the new home declined to keep him). It was, however, a finely balanced decision. In BC's case, the recognition that – even if the court agreed that he lacked capacity – an application for a welfare order would have uncertain prospects of success, led to a more constructive approach being undertaken. What required consideration in this instance was the nature of the relationships within the family prior to the injury, the views and practices regarding alcohol intake prior to the injury and BC's style of parenting prior to the injury. With the right guidance, structure and trained support staff in place, it was possible to manage some of the risks posed by BC's behaviours and judgements.

Case 4: BD

Presenting question/problem

BD is a 30-year-old woman with a lifelong history of learning disability, Cerebral Palsy, Epilepsy and sensory difficulties. The capacity assessment requested a professional opinion as to her ability to decide where she should live and what (if any) contact she should have with family and others. At the time of the assessment, she had been placed in a local authority residential home and her whereabouts were not divulged to her family as there were ongoing proceedings relating to their alleged physical, emotional and financial abuse of her. BD, however, was asking for contact with her mother and was distressed by her absence.

Background to the case

Clinical issues

BD was a young woman with a range of physical disabilities including Sjogren's Syndrome (an auto-immune disorder), motor and sensory peripheral neuropathy, walking and mobility problems and bilateral hearing loss. BD also has epilepsy and has only achieved partial seizure control with medication. A comprehensive speech and language assessment highlighted that BD can process verbal and visual information but achieves incomplete understanding and has slowed processing resulting in unreliable and incomplete communication skills.

Family/social context

BD was sexually abused as a child, within the family. All previous allegations made by BD regarding sexual and physical abuse had been substantiated following investigation. She also witnessed significant domestic violence by her father towards her mother and siblings. Her father physically injured BD on a number of occasions through his rough handling of her. There were significant disputes within the extended family to which BD had been exposed. The local Social Services Department had longstanding involvement in terms of monitoring BD's safety and well-being and providing regular respite for her away from the family home. A Protection of Vulnerable Adults (POVA) process had been followed on numerous occasions but BD expressed high levels of distress when separated from her family, particularly her mother. Social Services staff strongly believed that BD was susceptible to influence and had reason to believe that BD was pressurised to remain in the family home for the financial benefits that this entailed for the family.

Psychological/neuropsychological matters

Records indicated that BD would display non-compliant behaviours when distressed, such as intentional incontinence. At such points, the language used towards her by her family was highly inappropriate and derogatory in that they would call her "an animal". She would also self-harm and express suicidal ideation. A psychiatric review indicated probable post traumatic stress disorder (PTSD) and depression. She expressed low self-esteem.

Matters came to a head when one day, after attending the local day service as part of her routine, BD refused to go home at the end of the session. She was expressing high levels of distress and disclosed that several family members had threatened to kill her if she moved out or moved away. The local authority responded by removing her immediately to an out-of-area emergency placement. The concern was that the family may attempt to locate and remove her from this placement if it was in their local area.

An MRI of her brain revealed no abnormal areas of high signal or masses, indicating that there was no acute neuropathology. Records indicated that BD's clinical presentation was as a result of global, developmental delay.

Assessment and rationale

There were several key areas of neuropsychological and psychological function which required formal assessment.

A comprehensive assessment of IQ was undertaken, using the Wechsler scales, which indicated that BD's level of function was in the range of 55, which is representative of the bottom 0.1 per cent of the general population. Her profile of scores was relatively flat with little in terms of relative strengths and weaknesses. This is a typical pattern for an individual with a history of developmental delay.

An assessment of BD's ability to adapt her behaviour in a range of life contexts was administered. The Adaptive Behaviour Scales indicated that BD experienced difficulties in all aspects of her daily life, including cognition, communication, accessing the local community, carrying out domestic tasks, self-care and self-direction (without prompting) and keeping herself safe. There were no particular strengths identified. Essentially, the results indicate that BD is at a disadvantage (from peers) by not being able to learn sufficiently from experience to adapt her behaviours accordingly.

Given the diagnosis of depression from psychiatric review, it was considered useful to undertake a formal assessment of BD's mood using the Glasgow Depression Scale for Learning Disability. It is a useful tool in that it involves the individual in dialogue about their needs. BD completed a version, as did a professional carer who knew BD well. The results indicated, not unexpectedly, that BD was reporting symptoms which were well-above the threshold established by the test authors for confirmation of depression. Subjective appraisal of the individual items on the measure which were endorsed by BD indicated that she was largely sad and anxious, has low self-esteem and is significantly concerned about making a mistake or disappointing others.

At this stage, it was considered essential to obtain a formal measurement of BD's reasoning abilities. The Social and Moral Awareness Test (SMAT) taps into an individual's ability to reason and connect consequences to actions. The SMAT was administered to BD and the results indicated that she had a rudimentary grasp, in concrete terms, of right and wrong, but was manifestly unable to reason in anything other than immediate, self-focused consequences. She was unable to view situations from the perspectives of others or to generalise a range of possible behaviours or actions.

Finally, an assessment was made of BD's suggestibility, given the local authority concerns that she was susceptible to influence. The Gudjonsson Suggestibility Scales were administered to BD and the results indicated that she was highly influenced by negative feedback and questions designed to make her shift her opinion. Her responses to items were largely acquiescent and she was consistently eager to please.

When interviewed about choices that BD is able to make day-to-day, it emerged that she will occasionally choose her own clothes but that these may not be situation or weather appropriate. She does not choose her meals or mealtimes. She does not choose who visits her or when. She plays no role in her weekly timetable. It was also established that she had no bank account, but the manager of her current residential placement was looking into how to establish an arrangement which would give BD access to small sums of money for daily items such as toiletries or refreshments.

BD was asked for her views as to her placement. She could not remember how long she had lived there but spontaneously volunteered the information that her mother had told her, "you are not my daughter" which caused her to become upset. She then disclosed that she missed her mum and that this made her "cry a lot". When asked about how she felt about returning to live with her mother, BD was unable to give any consistent responses. She did not know where her family lived as she was under the impression that they had moved home since she left. She was unable to state whether or not she might have her own room or be supported to attend Day Services and maintain her social friendships. Throughout the interview, she was unable to give voice to any positives about returning to live with her mother (and siblings).

At this stage, it was considered essential to obtain an understanding of BD's ability to grasp the concept of time as this underpins the permanency of some decision-making. It has already been established that some adults with learning disabilities struggle with this concept (Owen & Wilson, 2006). BD was unable to tell the time using a conventional clock face or digital information. She was unable to grasp the concept of distance or journey times, could not keep track of the days of the week and was unable to work out how long she had lived in the current placement.

Opinion/outcome

In order to decide about where to live, BD needs to be fully aware and understanding of, as well as able to recollect, the details of the options available to her. She also needs to be able to weigh these up, and to give consideration to the different possibilities in order to arrive at a capacitous decision. The present assessment has demonstrated that BD is not aware of the details of the family home (such as where it is, what type of house it is) and whether or not she would have her own room. She appears unable to recollect the reasons or incidents which have led to previous breakdowns in home living arrangements. BD has been noted to be acquiescent in her responses in terms of what she thinks the listener wishes her to say and also overly reliant on set phrases in conversations that she may not follow. To that end, her communication skills are shown to be compromised. It is also clear that she is unable to consider potential consequences and weigh these up for herself. Clinical opinion, based upon the present assessment, is that BD lacks the capacity to decide where she should live.

BD has feelings for her mother and values their contact although it is also the case that the episodes also upset her, "can't help crying". At present, BD does not make choices as to who visits her or when contact takes place and, as such, lacks decision-making experience in this key area of her life. She appears unable to make connections between previously difficult episodes in family relations, with her at the centre, and her present wish to see her mother. Her lack of adaptive skills means that this will probably continue to be the case as she is unable to make the connection between upsetting episodes and contact in general. Clinical opinion, based upon the present assessment, is that BD lacks the capacity to decide what contact she has with family members and others.

The cognitive challenges facing BD are permanent, that is, she has limited abilities to understand and recall information as well as marked difficulties with extrapolating learning from experiences that she has. BD is also extremely limited in being able to weigh up information and consider potential consequences. Of significant concern is her acquiescence and susceptibility to influence which renders her decision-making potentially invalid. It is possible to maximise choices for BD but any choices she is offered should be managed and provided from a limited array that does not challenge her abilities and also does not place her in a position of vulnerability to the influences of others. The limited array should minimise the potential for negative consequences whilst encouraging BD to make more choices in her day-to-day life.

BD is significantly susceptible to influence and is largely acquiescent in her responses, demonstrating a malleability that renders her extremely vulnerable. Any choices that are offered to BD need to be limited to situations where whatever choice she makes cannot place her at risk and can only be considered to be in the wider context of her best interests. This can be achieved by limiting the choices available at the outset. For example, when selecting clothes on a cold day, instead of asking her whether or not she wishes to wear warm clothes, BD would be offered a choice between two or more items of warm clothing. This would ensure that she would be appropriately dressed yet still empower her to choose safely.

In terms of her wish to return home, it would be helpful to consider whether BD is not asked whether she wishes to return home to live but whether she wishes to visit home, accompanied and supported by professional staff, for a limited time period or at an agreed frequency of visit in order for this to be monitored. This would enable her to satisfy her curiosity about the new home and also reduce her feelings of being left out of her mother's consideration by not being at home without her feeling pressure to return to live there.

BD is able to express wishes and views in relation to contact and residence but the concern is that she is doing so in the absence of an ability to draw upon past (negative) experiences, to weigh up potential (adverse) consequences of such a decision and is, most significantly, noted to be highly susceptible to influence which renders her acquiescent to the (perceived) wishes of others.

Her expressed views should be considered within a Best Interests framework which should take account of the views expressed by BD but must also take into account the concerns and views of professionals who are bound by a duty of care towards BD as well as those views of family members.

Legal commentary

This is an example of a case where the presumption of capacity may well not have been rebutted. As far as the functional test is concerned it has been flagged up that there appear to be additional practical ways in which BD can be provided with information about the decision (i.e. of where to live) which have not yet been undertaken with her, such as taking her to visit there. Further, although her global developmental delay and IQ of around 55 would seem likely to satisfy the diagnostic test, the court would need to be satisfied that any inability to make decisions on where to live/with whom to have contact is due to the identified impairment or disturbance rather than being due to her being manipulated or overborne by a third party

It should also be noted that whilst the making of declarations and the exercise of decision-making under the MCA (2005) requires a declaration of incapacity there is nonetheless available the use of the inherent jurisdiction in respect of adults whose capacity is vitiated by constraint, coercion, undue influence, or for some other reason preventing them from forming or expressing a genuine and real consent, i.e. where their capacity to make decisions for themselves has been compromised by something other than the matters covered by the MCA (2005) (see *Re L (Vulnerable Adults: Court's Jurisdiction)* (No 2).[14] Such a jurisdiction has been described as "a safety net to protect vulnerable adults subject to coercion or undue influence", the purpose of which is, "aimed at enhancing or liberating the autonomy of a vulnerable adult whose autonomy has been compromised by a reason other than mental incapacity." Clearly, any orders made under the inherent jurisdiction must be both necessary and proportionate. If the court were to find that BD did have the capacity to make decisions concerning residence and/ or contact, there is some authority that a protective regime could be imposed on her through the use of the inherent jurisdiction if that was the only way in which her interests could be safeguarded, i.e. determining for her own protection that she should live in residential care away from her family members: see Parker J in *NCC v PB & TB*[15] at paragraph 121. In any event the court under the inherent jurisdiction could at the very least make an injunction under its own motion to prevent BD's mother in particular from coming into contact with her.

Discussion/learning points

BD could benefit from the appointment of an Independent Advocate who could help her to express her views and wishes whilst minimising the possibility of influence or acquiescence. She could also benefit from individual sessions with a clinical psychologist to assist her to make sense of, and cope with the effects of, the historical abuse and her relationships with her family in general and with her mother in particular.

The difficulty arises when a vulnerable adult expresses the wish to return to a harmful situation. What status should their views have? Whilst under section 4 of the Act a major consideration is the individual's past and present wishes and feelings, and the beliefs, values and other factors which the individual would be likely to consider if he had the capacity to do so, the individual circumstances of the particular person and the circumstances of the particular case play an important role. The closer to the borderline of capacity a person is, the more weight may be attached to their wishes and feelings, whilst always striving to avoid the temptation to engage in paternalistic decision-making.

---

14 (CA) [2012] 3 WLR 1439
15 [2014] EWCOP 14

References

Department for Constitutional Affairs. (2007). Mental Capacity Act 2005: Code of Practice. Retrieved from www.gov.uk/government/publications/mental-capacity-act-code-of-practice

Owen, A. L. & Wilson, R. R. (2006). Unlocking the riddle of time in learning disability. *Journal of Intellectual Disabilities*, *10*(1), 9–17.

Series, L., Fennel, P., Doughty, J. & Mercer, A. (2017). *Welfare cases in the Court of Protection: A statistical overview*. Cardiff University & Nuffield Foundation. Retrieved from http://sites.cardiff.ac.uk/wccop/files/2017/09/Series-Fennell-Doughty-2017-Statistical-overview-of-CoP-Key-findings.pdf

6 Capacity to make and revoke a will (testamentary capacity)

Dr Tracey Ryan-Morgan

With Alex Troup

Introduction

> The population in 2016 was at its largest ever, at 65.6 million and projected to reach 74 million by 2039. While it is growing, improvements in healthcare and lifestyles mean the population is getting older; in 2016 in the UK, 18% of people were aged 65 and over, and 2.4% were aged 85 and over.
>
> (Office for National Statistics, 2018)

Jovanovic and colleagues (2008) refer to epidemiological data which confirm that "medical comorbidities aggregate with ageing". The principal appears to be that although adults in the UK are living longer, most people will have at least one medical condition that affects their physical or mental integrity as they age. Figures suggest that up to two thirds of the general population have not made a will, although figures vary considerably with age. Whilst only 6 per cent of those aged 16–24 have a will, up to 82 per cent of those aged 75 or over have one (Humphrey et al, 2010).

Not all wills are made by those who are elderly or infirm, but, as Nicholas Strauss QC pointed out in *Walker v Badmin*,[1] most testators *are* elderly. A survey was carried out in 2014 by Lightspeed Research for the charity Will Aid, which surveyed 2,250 people aged 25 to 84 from England, Wales, Scotland and Northern Ireland. The findings make interesting reading (Lightspeed Research, 2014):

- Forty-eight per cent of adults say they have written a will (an increase of 4 per cent and the highest percentage of people saying they have written a will since the survey was first run in 2006);
- The greatest increase in percentage of people writing a will in the younger age group (aged 25–34) where the percentage has doubled, up from 11.6 per cent in 2013;
- However, it is only in the over-55 age group where a significant majority has made a will.

The legal context

The legal test for testamentary capacity is that set out in *Banks v Goodfellow*,[2]

> It is essential that a Testator shall understand the nature of the act and its effects; shall understand the extent of the property of which he is disposing; shall be able to comprehend and appreciate the claims to which he ought to give effect; and, with a view to the latter object, that no disorder of mind shall poison his affections, pervert his sense of right or prevent the exercise of his natural faculties – that no insane delusion shall influence his will in disposing of his property and bring about a disposal of it which, if the mind had been sound, would not have been made.

Although the quotation above is expressed in terms of what the testator "shall" understand, it is well established that the test is concerned with the testator's *capacity* to understand, rather than his actual understanding.[3]

In general, a testator must satisfy the *Banks v. Goodfellow* test when the will is executed. But where a testator's capacity has deteriorated between giving instructions and executing the will, the so-called rule in *Parker v. Felgate* provides that the testator will still have capacity if he satisfied the *Banks v. Goodfellow* test when giving instructions for the will, provided that (a) the will is drafted in accordance with his instructions; and (b) at the time of execution he is capable of understanding, and does understand, that he is executing a will for which he has given instructions.[4]

Whilst the MCA (2005) provides the framework for the cases presented in this book, it was held in *Walker v Badmin*[5] that the *Banks v Goodfellow* test remained the correct and only test for testamentary capacity. The Judge, Nicholas Strauss QC, identified the following three main differences between the common law *Banks v. Goodfellow* test and the statutory test set out in the MCA (2005):

i)   The burden of proof: The MCA (2005) contains at section 1(2) a presumption of capacity, whereas at common law the burden of proof rests initially on those seeking to propound the will to prove capacity[6].
ii) The MCA (2005) requires the person making the will to be able to understand all of the information relevant to the decision. This may arguably require more of the testator than the *Banks v Goodfellow* test, which concentrates on whether the will correctly represents the testator's intentions and his appreciation of the claims to which he ought to give effect.

2 (1870) LR 5 QB 549, 565
3 *Hoff v. Atherton* [2004] EWCA Civ 1554; [2005] WTLR 99
4 *Parker v. Felgate* (1883) 8 PD 171, as approved in *Perrins v. Holland* [2011] Ch 270
5 [2015] COPLR 348. A similar conclusion was reached as regards lifetime gifts in *Kicks v. Leigh* [2015] 4 All ER 329
6 See *Key v. Key* [2010] 1 WLR 2020 at [97]

iii) The combined effect of section 3(1) and section 3(4) MCA (2005) is that a person will not have capacity unless he is able to understand, use and weigh information as to the reasonably foreseeable consequences of the choices open to him; whereas under the *Banks v Goodfellow* test, the testator does not need to understand the reasonably foreseeable consequences of the will.[7]

Nicholas Strauss QC preferred the test in *Banks v Goodfellow* because (among other things) it sets a relatively low threshold so as not to deprive elderly persons of the ability to make wills in their declining years. The decision in *Walker v. Badmin* was recently followed in *James v. James*.[8] Both cases are however first instance decisions, and Court of Appeal guidance is needed on this issue.

The Law Commission has provisionally proposed that the test in the MCA (2005) should be adopted for testamentary capacity in place of the *Banks v. Goodfellow* test, but this proposal is yet to be implemented.[9]

The "Golden Rule"

The "Golden Rule" was explained by Templeman J in *Re Simpson* as follows:

> in the case of aged testator or a testator who has suffered a serious illness, there is one golden rule which should always be observed, however straight-forward matters may appear, and however difficult or tactless it may be to suggest that precautions be taken: the making of a will by such a testator ought to be witnessed or approved by a medical practitioner who satisfies himself of the capacity and understanding of the testator, and records and preserves his examination and finding.[10]

The courts have repeatedly emphasised that compliance with the Golden Rule does not operate as the validity of a will. It is merely a statement of good practice which is designed to avoid, or at least to minimise, disputes.[11]

Statutory wills

The court has power under section 18(1)(i) MCA (2005) to make a so-called "statutory will" for a person who lacks testamentary capacity ("P"). Whether the court makes such a will, and if so upon what terms, depends upon an assessment of P's best interests, applying the factors set out in section 4 of the MCA (2005).

---

7 As illustrated by *Simon v. Byford* [2014] WTLR 1097, where the testatrix was held to satisfy the *Banks v. Goodfellow* test despite being unable to understand that a gift of shares in a family company may result in deadlock between the shareholders

8 [2018] EWHC 43 (Ch)

9 Law Commission Consultation Paper 231, entitled "Making a will"

10 (1977) 121 SJ 224

11 See e.g. *Key v. Key* [2010] 1 WLR 2020, at [8]

P's wishes and feelings will always be a significant factor to which close regard must be paid, but the weight to be attached to them will be case-specific and fact-specific.[12] It has been suggested that P's Best Interests may include being remembered for having done "the right thing", although this has been criticised on the basis that it is the court, not P, who decides on the terms of a statutory will; and in any event it may be difficult to apply in disputes involving family members with differing views as to what would be the right thing to do.[13]

The medical approach to assessing testamentary capacity

Shulman, Cohen and Hull (2005, pp.67–68) conclude that

> many cases of challenges to Testamentary Capacity involve complex and subtle issues that call for a need to go beyond the traditional Bank – vs – Goodfellow criteria. Lawyers and expert assessors need to ensure that they take into account the capacity to appreciate the consequences of executing a Will especially in suspicious circumstances where there has been a radical change to a Will in the context of . . . a significant medical/neurological condition.

It is argued, therefore, that an assessment of testamentary capacity is both task and situation specific. If there are no "suspicious circumstances" (Shulman et al, 2005) then the assumption of competence can prevail. However, when implications of the making of the will, such as the consequences of certain decisions, are substantial then questions should be asked as to the level of retained or residual cognitive (including executive) abilities.

In addition, Shulman and colleagues (2005) refer to case law in England and Wales which has "suggested that the more serious the decision, the higher the threshold for competence. '*Seriousness*' related to Testamentary Capacity may refer to the extent of departure from previously expressed wishes or the extent to which the normal beneficiaries are excluded" (p.68).

They also argue that "the threshold for Testamentary Capacity should be higher in complex and conflictual environments that call for probing and documentation." The authors refer to the question at the material time being phrased not as "is an individual competent" but "is he/she competent to do X in the context of Y" (Shulman et al, 2005, p.68).

Shulman and colleagues (2005) remind that expert assessors have the opportunity to describe patterns of behaviour associated with disease processes to the court. The role could be in detailing medical conditions that may have relevance to testamentary capacity, such as delusional beliefs about the self or others as part

---

12   *In re M (Statutory Will)* [2011] 1 WLR 344. See also *Aintree University Hospitals NHS Foundation Trust v. James* [2014] AC 591, at [51]
13   *Re G(TJ)* [2011] WTLR 231, at [53]

of a diagnosable illness or detailing aspects of organically-driven behaviours that may reasonably follow a cerebral event such as a head injury or stroke, "experts must consider intellectual functioning, overall health and physical condition as well as whether the signs and symptoms of mental disorders do (or do not) reach the level of destroying Testamentary Capacity" (Jovanovic et al, 2008, p.490). However, it is made clear by Shulman and colleagues (2005, p.68) that

> the mere presence of such a disorder is not sufficient to declare the testator incapable, task-specific competencies may vary even when a mental disorder is evident. Cognitive issues such as memory and orientation as well as executive brain function, such as the capacity for abstract thinking, impulsiveness and social judgement need to be carefully explored and documented.

Roked and Patel (2008) refer to language capacity as being a clear and consistent predictor of testamentary capacity in patients with Alzheimer's disease, whilst Han and colleagues (2000) attempt to predict the annual rate of cognitive decline in Alzheimer's disease using the Mini Mental State Examination (MMSE, Folstein, Folstein & McHugh, 1975). The MMSE was widely used until relatively recently when it became subject to copyright and has been replaced in common test usage with other, more robust, freely available measures of cognitive ability in the elderly (such as the ACE-III or the MOCA). However, the MMSE will commonly be seen in historical medical records for many years to come and familiarity with its weaknesses (Simard, 1998; Kim & Caine, 2002) is essential in cases where it has been used as a proxy test for capacity.

Jovanovic and colleagues (2008) report research findings which indicate that testators experiencing organic mental disorders are "significantly more likely to be incapable than testators without those disorders" (p.490).

PROSPECTIVE TESTAMENTARY CAPACITY

Case 1: CA

Presenting question/problem

This is the case of a young adult male, who has moderately severe cerebral palsy as a result of a birth accident. Legal action for the negligent care at his birth had resulted in a significant financial settlement. He has marked communication difficulties and is physically disabled, being dependent upon others for all of his physical care needs. He is cared for by his father and is estranged from his mother. There have been a number of instances where his mother has allegedly attempted to access his considerable financial resources for personal gain. An initial assessment of his testamentary capacity indicated that he lacked the ability to draw up a will but that there was scope to maximise this. This case describes the work that was undertaken to enable CA to successfully draw up a valid will.

Background to the case

Clinical issues

CA has severe communication difficulties. He is unable to communicate verbally other than by making non-specific noises at different volumes. He is unable to articulate words or sounds that could approximate words. He is also limited in his use of facial expression or gesture due to the severity of his cerebral palsy. However, his father and step-mother know him and his behaviours so well that they are often able to infer meaning from his sounds and gestures, checking these out with him to ensure that they have correctly understood him. This level of mutual understanding was critical to proceeding with the assessment.

Family/social context

CA lives with his father and step-mother. He is electively estranged from his birth mother as she had physically abused and neglected him when he had been in her care as a child. As he entered into early adulthood and had been living with his father for some time, his mother had turned up unannounced at CA's day service and attempted to make contact with him for the purpose of accessing his settlement monies. Although the matter was dealt with appropriately by all concerned, including a report to the local Safeguarding service, CA had thereafter refused to re-engage with the day service due to fear that his mother may find him again. An injunction was taken out against CA's birth mother, to which she responded by preventing CA from having access to his much-loved sister (who lived with his birth mother). This enforced estrangement continues.

Psychological/neuropsychological matters

CA experiences mood swings which manifest behaviourally. For example, if upset or distressed he will refuse food or personal care. He can become physically combative if particularly agitated. Neuropsychologically, he has been assessed over time as having low average cognitive function rather than the expected moderate to severe cognitive dysfunction often associated with severe cerebral palsy.

Assessment and rationale

The purpose of the assessment was to ascertain CA's level of understanding in the context of satisfying the legal test for drawing up a will. The assessment comprised unstructured interview, structured interview and selected neuropsychometric tests.

The unstructured interview was carried out in the solicitor's office with CA's father present but not in his line of sight (therefore, theoretically, unable to influence CA's answers to questions). The questions were focused on CA's present level of decision-making/choices on a day-to-day basis. For example, does he choose his own clothes, meals, activities? Questions were also posed to assess CA's experience of money. Does he carry or have access to his own money? It was established that he had previously had a bank card and had been taught to memorise his own PIN number when in college so that he could be supported to access money (when with his support workers) to make small purchases of his own choosing.

The structured interview was drawn together from BILD resources and consisted of pre-prepared questions on topics of day-to-day access to, and use of, money. There were also questions designed to tap into CA's general fund of knowledge about banks, different types of account, different types of bank card, credit, debit and loan arrangements as well as the value of numbers, concepts relating to amounts and currency values.

In terms of neuropsychological assessment, the following tests were selected and administered to CA:

- the Matrix Reasoning Subtest of the Wechsler Abbreviated Scales of Intelligence – to provide an approximate level of cognitive function (non-verbal).
- the Picture Naming Subtest of the Repeatable Battery for the Assessment of Neuropsychological Status – to give an indication of visual recognition and naming of everyday objects.
- the Story Retelling Subtest of the Cognitive Linguistic Quick Test – to assess immediate recall and recognition for verbally presented material.

CA was also assessed in terms of those elements of testamentary capacity that people making a will must understand:

- the nature of the will and its effects (the understanding that they will die and who they want to have their 'property');
- what they have to leave in the will (realise and recollect the extent of the property there is to dispose of); and
- to be aware that there are people who would normally have a claim on that person's estate – even if they intend to leave them nothing.

The results of the assessment suggested that CA retained the capacity to make basic testamentary dispositions *but* did not have a grasp of the nature and extent of his material assets. It also indicated that although able to make choices on a daily basis with regard to key aspects of his life, CA did not have sufficient knowledge of, or responsibility for, his finances at that time. At this stage, in agreement with himself, his father and his solicitor, the decision was made to take all practicable steps to maximise his potential for capacitously drawing up a will.

In order to maximise CA's mental capacity to make a will it had to be established that he understood, and retained, sufficient information over time about a number of concepts related to making a will. These concepts were considered thematically as follows:

- quantity, numbers and money;
- networks of family and friends;
- the size and extent of his "estate" (including his treasured possessions);
- the concept of death; and
- the concept of a will.

Repetition of the contents of these assessments was central to determining that CA had retained the information over time to establish consistent understanding.

CA was provided with a review sheet (Mencap, 2007) to take home with him after each session which gave him the opportunity to provide feedback. The review sheet consisted of three questions:

- one thing he had learnt;
- one thing he still wanted to know; and
- one thing he may do differently now.

This sheet would be completed with the support of his father and brought along to subsequent appointments.

This piece of work has been published (Rees & Ryan-Morgan, 2012).

Opinion/outcome

As a result of the assessment and subsequent skills-based and knowledge-training work undertaken with CA, he was successfully able to draw up a valid will, over several appointments and with ongoing support. The Code of Practice which accompanies the MCA (2005) exhorts the practitioner to maximise an individual's potential for capacitous decision-making along the following lines:

- Does the person have all of the relevant information that is needed to arrive at a decision?
- If there are alternatives, have all of these been presented to them?
- Has the information required been presented in the most appropriate way for that individual?
- Are there times of day when the individual's level of understanding might be better or worse and has this been taken into account?
- Are there locations where the individual might feel more comfortable or at ease in considering the information needed to make the decision?
- Is it possible to postpone the decision until capacity might improve (such as when the individual is physically or mentally recovered from an illness)?
- Is there anyone close to the individual who can help them to make a choice or express a view (such as assisting with communication)?

Whilst it may not always possible or practicable to undertake such an extensive piece of work, where it *is* appropriate, it can be seen that this can make a significant difference to an individual's autonomy, independence and self-determination.

Legal commentary

This is a good example of a testator, who would otherwise lack testamentary capacity, acquiring such capacity as a result of being given suitable assistance and explanation.

Arguably, there is a distinction between the role of such assistance and explanation at common law and under the MCA (2005).[14] At common law, it seems that a testator who requires assistance or explanation in order to understand the relevant matters set out in the *Banks v. Goodfellow* test will lack capacity unless such assistance or explanation is in fact given. So, for example, Gibson LJ stated in *Hoff v. Atherton*[15] that:

> It is a general requirement of the law that, for a juristic act to be valid, the person performing it should have the mental capacity **(with the assistance of such explanation as he may have been given)** to understand the nature and effect of that particular act. (emphasis supplied)

In contrast the MCA (2005) provides at section 1(3) that a person is not to be treated as unable to make a decision unless all practicable steps to help him (such as explanations) have been taken without success. This suggests that a testator would have testamentary capacity if he would be able to understand the relevant matters with an explanation, even if that explanation was not in fact given.

In the present case this distinction is immaterial because a suitable explanation was in fact given. To minimise the risk of subsequent challenge it would be prudent for the medical practitioner to witness the will and for a copy of the medical assessment to be kept with the will, in accordance with the Golden Rule.

Discussion/learning points

At the outset, the referral had been for an assessment only. At no point was it suggested either by the instructing solicitor or by the family of CA that work could or should be undertaken to maximise his decision-making powers. However, it quickly became apparent that, with a programme of targeted learning and assistance to understand the key concepts around death, personal assets and the role and function of a will, CA could arrive at a point where he would have achieved testamentary capacity. It was extremely encouraging that the idea to undertake this work with CA received immediate support from all parties and was able to proceed with relative ease. The Law Commission has asked whether there should be a supported decision-making scheme to help adults to make a will.[16]

---

14 The argument is advanced in detail in an article by Alexander Learmonth in the *Trusts Quarterly Review*, Vol. 13, 2015, at p.4

15 [2005] WTLR 99. Although c.f. *Kicks v. Leigh* [2015] 4 All ER 329 at [27] and [195] which appear to suggest otherwise, although *Hoff v. Atherton* does not appear to have been cited

16 Law Commission Consultation Paper 231, entitled "Making a will"

Were such a scheme to be enacted, it would provide a framework within which such support would be the rule rather than the exception.

Case 2: CB

Presenting question/problem

This is the case of a 20-year-old lady who had received a traumatic brain injury as a young child. Throughout her developmental period she had been in receipt of support services in the context of significant family breakdown and had developed risky behaviour patterns in adolescence which persisted and which were placing her in danger, in terms of her entering into abusive or exploitative relationships and being coerced into illegal acts. Her solicitor wished to establish whether or not she retained the capacity to make a will due to her vulnerability and her extensive estate. This exercise was repeated at regular intervals as her life circumstances changed, for example, when she settled down to live with a long-term partner and when she entered into motherhood in her late twenties.

Background to the case

Clinical issues

CB had a traumatic brain injury in 2000 at the age of 5. Her GCS score at the time of the accident was 6/15 although this is noted at 5/15 in Accident and Emergency notes and, subsequently, dropped to 3/15. A CT scan reported general cerebral oedema with left frontoparietal contusions a right thin subdural haematoma and skull fractures. By the time of discharge from hospital the cerebral oedema (swelling) had reduced. Early sequelae of the head injury included temper tantrums and flair ups, tics, bed wetting, language and communication problems, rigid and routinised behaviour, behaviour problems at school and slowed processing. A later CT scan noted that the oedema had resolved although there was a widening of the sulci (indicating atrophy) particularly at the left sylvian fissure. There was obviously significant cerebral injury to the left temporal and frontal lobes. More recent brain scans indicated that there is localised atrophy affecting both frontal lobes, more extensively on the left side, with additional evidence of generalised cerebral atrophy consistent with the sequelae of a traumatic brain injury.

In early adulthood, CB was noted to be impulsive, disinhibited and vulnerable. She frequently associated with others who would take advantage of her inability to weigh up risk. She began to smoke and take drugs, allowing relative strangers to move into her home. She would struggle to engage with support staff or with rehabilitation programmes in the community, particularly with respect to structured domestic, leisure and vocational activities.

Family/social context

CB's mother has longstanding problems with alcohol which mean that she has only ever been able to offer intermittent, and somewhat unreliable support to her daughter. CB and her sister have a volatile relationship and there is evidence of both mother and sister seeking monies from CB for large purchases for themselves. CB has evidence that her sister has stolen from her in the past as well as having a partner who attacked CB on one occasion when drunk.

Between the several assessment periods, CB appeared to mature quite considerably in terms of her behaviours and approach to life. She settled into a long-term relationship with a partner who was supportive of her needs following brain injury. She currently has two children with this partner and they have bought a home and have a strong and supportive relationship.

Psychological/neuropsychological matters

There is clear and unequivocal evidence of brain injury in this case. Whilst in the developmental years CB experienced a range of cognitive and behavioural problems, she has reached maturity with an average level of cognitive functioning but has significant executive dysfunction, referred to by some in the published literature as frontal lobe paradox. Essentially, this means that CB can "pass" neuropsychometric tests designed to assess executive functions but, in daily life, she struggles with decision-making, retaining key information, weighing up important considerations and making judgements which draw on past experiences. She cannot consider more than one issue at a time and that can only be done in small, sequential steps, with support and direction.

Assessment and rationale

The purpose of each assessment was to ascertain CB's level of understanding in the context of satisfying the legal test for drawing up a will. Each assessment comprised unstructured and structured interviews of CB without her partner so as to mitigate the possibility of influence.

Time 1 – on this occasion, CB was one year into her relationship. She was living with her partner. He had his own business as a builder. CB had a financial deputy which afforded a layer of protection. CB had been adamant that she wished to contribute more to the household and an arrangement was arrived at where her partner would be paid for a certain number of hours of care for her each week which would then be channelled into the costs of running the home.

The following structured and unstructured interviews were carried out with CB:

- What is a will?

  "What you give to people when you die."

- How/When does a will work?

    "When you die, don't know how it works."

- What do people use a will for?

    "It's about who you're going to leave your house to and all that."

- If you could write a will, what:

    o   Could/Would it say?

    "Don't know."

- What can you give others in a will?

    o   (Money – different accounts, physical assets – jewellery; art work; furniture; property – house/holiday home)

    "Nothing." CB seemed unable to make the connections between the different items which were discussed with CB as part of the definition of an estate.

- Who would / might you mention in your will?

    CB lists names of selected family members here – excluding her mother and sister.

- Why them and why not others?

    "Cause nobody else deserves any."

- Would everyone in your family be happy with this?
- Who wouldn't be happy with this and why not?

    "Grandparents would not be happy but they have not been truthful with me."

- What do others think you should do?

    o   (Family, friends, boyfriend)

    "My Mum wants me to buy her a house for her and her partner to live in and for me to rent a house for myself."

- Who is in your family?

    Following lengthy discussions, a genogram was drawn up and referred to throughout to provide a visual reminder of the extended family and connections.

- Why do you think you should make a will?

    "Don't know."

- What would happen if you do not make a will?

    "I suppose everything would go to my mum and sister."

The interview continued to discuss recent events in CB's life and her understanding of the same. CB felt disappointed that at the time there were people in her life who had not been honest with her.

During the assessment CB appeared to come across as insightful but this was only superficial. She had an unrealistic or idealised view of her present and future. She lacked insight into the possible risks and pitfalls in her life and responded when these were pointed out to her with "I don't really care anyway."

It was clear in relation to the present assessment of testamentary capacity that CB did have some understanding of the matters set out in the *Banks v. Goodfellow* test but that this level of understanding was superficial and incomplete. Her motivation tended to fluctuate considerably, and her decision-making could be impulsive. She had a history of relationship cycles with the key figures in her life who were either in favour and engaged with her or out of favour and cut off from her. These cycles had been observed on several occasions within her extended family.

Time 2 – on this occasion, CB had remained with her longstanding partner and they had had a child together. CB wanted to draw up a will which made provision for her child.

The following structured and unstructured interviews were carried out with CB:

- What is a will?

   "When you die you leave money, house, whatever to whoever you want."

- How/When does a will work?

   "When you die it lets you have an opinion about what you want."

- What do people use a will for?

   "To stop people you don't want from getting hold of your stuff."

- If you could write a will, what:
   o Could/Would it say?

      "Leave specific things to specific people . . . leave everything to my son."

- What can you give others in a will?
   o (Money – different accounts, physical assets – jewellery; art work; furniture; property-house / holiday home)

      "House, money, car – I don't have any valuable jewellery."

- Who would/might you mention in your will?

   "My son."

- Why them and why not others?

   "Because I've already helped my family lots and they still keep asking. I don't know who to trust."

- Would everyone in your family be happy with this?

  o   Who wouldn't be happy with this and why not?

      "I recognise that I can't please everyone or meet everyone's expectations. I expect them all to be disappointed."

- What do others think you should do?

  o   (Family, friends, boyfriend)

      "Probably leave stuff for them."

- Who is in your family?

      The same genogram that had been previously drawn up was updated to reflect changes and referred to throughout to provide a visual reminder of the extended family and connections.

- Why do you think you should make a will?

      "To make sure that my son is looked after."

- What would happen if you do not make a will?

      "I suppose everything would go to my mum and dad."

It was clear from the present interview that CB has increased her understanding of the issues surrounding the making of a will since the previous assessment. It was also clear that CB retains sufficient information concerning the nature and content of will making and the implications of the same and was able to demonstrate this at interview during the present assessment.

CB retains testamentary capacity and was in a position to draw up a will at this point in time. She clearly understands both the act and effect of making a will as well as the extent of her present estate in principle. She is fully cognisant of the possible claims of others but is clear in her own mind as to how she wishes to dispose of her assets after her death. Whilst the severe traumatic brain injury and its legacies are permanent and whilst CB is vulnerable to the whims of her relatives, she has continued to mature both personally and neuropsychologically since the previous assessment.

Time 3 – on this occasion, CB continued in her relationship with her long-standing partner and they had had a second child together. CB wanted to revisit her will so as to make adequate provision for her children. The solicitor wished to ensure that she retained testamentary capacity.

There had been a change in CB's circumstances since the previous assessment, in that she and her partner had bought a new house together and have lived there since the end of 2015. In the summer of 2016, CB gave birth to her second child, a daughter. More recently, CB's partner has sold his business and is now employed as full-time nanny in order to support CB who was struggling to cope with two young children. CB has less contact with her immediate family than previously, but relationships remain largely unchanged. CB is more settled generally. She appears more insightful into the ins-and-outs of family dynamics and more balanced in her decision-making around the same. CB is clear that she wishes to include her new daughter in her will but also wishes to make some changes which she has decided on without the influence of others and which she will discuss in detail with her solicitor. The present assessment confirmed that CB takes no regular medication and that there have been no significant changes to her health status since the previous assessment.

At this stage an updated genogram was confirmed with CB.

CB needs to understand the nature of a will, its effects, the extent of her assets and needs to recall all of that information in order to formulate her wishes as to what she wishes to leave to whom and for this to be encapsulated in the legal document (the will).

CB retains a full understanding both of the nature of the will, the nature and extent of her assets, the effect of making the will on those persons who may have a reasonable claim to be beneficiaries and the genogram was used for this purpose. It was also possible to ascertain that CB is free of delusions and is presently not under the influence of any individual seeking to bring pressure to bear on her decision-making in respect of her testamentary dispositions. It is also noted that she is clearly able to express her wishes in terms of the disposition of her assets.

CB retains testamentary capacity and is in a position to draw up a revised will at this point in time. She has the requisite understanding despite the legacies of her brain injury, and this is due to the thorough work of her deputy in providing her with relevant information to maximise her capacity in terms of decision-making but also in terms of the maturity of both her brain injury and her outlook on life generally. CB is well supported but not suggestible and is clear in her own mind. Although the legacies of the severe traumatic brain injury are permanent CB is now in a position to adapt to these in a way which enables her to retain her decision-making capacity in respect of drawing up a will.

Opinion/outcome

The outcome, over the three time periods, is that CB reached a point where she attained testamentary capacity in spite of a significant legacy of her severe brain injury and a complex family network of relationships which were not always to her benefit. Testamentary capacity was reached by means of spontaneous brain maturation, psychological maturation, support from a steady life partner, support from her deputy and reflections on achieving motherhood.

Legal commentary

This is an example of a testator whose capacity changes over time. Both at common law and under the MCA (2005), testamentary capacity is time-specific and can therefore fluctuate. It seems clear that CB did not satisfy the *Banks v. Goodfellow* test at Time 1, not least due to her inability to understand the extent of her estate. Even if she had understood the relevant matters, she was apparently unable to make a decision as to what her will should say.

In *Key v. Key*[17] a testator suffering from affective disorder caused by bereavement was found to lack testamentary capacity. Whilst it was not possible to point to a conspicuous inability by the testator to satisfy one of the distinct limbs of the *Banks v. Goodfellow* test, it was held that he nevertheless lacked testamentary capacity due to his inability to exercise the decision-making powers required of a testator. To the extent that this conclusion involved a slight extension of the *Banks v. Goodfellow* test, it was necessitated by the greater understanding of the mind now available from modern psychiatric medicine. Arguably the same applied in the present case at Time 1.

The ability to use and weigh up the relevant information is an explicit part of the capacity test under section 3(1)(c) of the MCA (2005).

On the other hand, it appears that CB had acquired testamentary capacity at Times 2 and 3, with the aid of appropriate assistance in the form of the genogram. The assessor was rightly alive to the possibility of undue influence and took appropriate steps to minimise this risk by seeing CB alone, in the absence of her partner, and by expressly considering whether her decisions are the product of her own free will.

Discussion/learning points

The initial assessment of capacity had demonstrated clearly that the CB's brain had yet to reach full maturity. This process, which normally occurs by about age 21 in adulthood, is delayed in those who experience a brain injury in childhood, often until the late twenties. In the early years of her twenties, she displayed what is often referred to by neuropsychologists as the dissociation between knowing and doing. In other words, the individual is in possession of the concrete knowledge which is pertinent to the situation in hand but lacks the requisite ability to apply that knowledge in a way which facilitates effective weighing up and consideration of potential consequences. However, by her later twenties, when she had reached greater maturity and was more settled and consistently supported, CB became more able to apply experience to her decision-making and to seek advice where she was unsure.

Case 3: CC

Presenting question/problem

CC was diagnosed with multiple sclerosis ten years previously. Due to deteriorating mobility she moved to a nursing home within two years. CC had a psychiatric history including several hospital admissions on a voluntary basis

17 [2010] 1 WLR 2020

and one formal admission under a section of the Mental Health Act. Her primary diagnosis was depression, but she often displayed quite psychotic features including suspiciousness of others and believing that people are talking about her. She frequently stopped taking the medication which was prescribed to keep her symptoms under control. The referral came from her solicitor who had drawn up a will with her, following her instruction, but who was increasingly concerned after several follow-up visits to finalise the will that CC may not have retained testamentary capacity.

Background to the case

In 2015, a consultant psychiatrist with a special area of practice in mental capacity assessments, recorded the opinion on the CoP3 form that CC has cognitive impairment associated with multiple sclerosis and mental illness and is therefore unable to make any decisions for herself in relation to property and finances. The psychiatrist also notes that CC's executive function is markedly impaired, that this appears to be a longstanding difficulty and that she also appears to have cognitive impairment which may progress.

A second psychiatrist, also specialising in assessments of mental capacity, reported in 2017 that CC has impaired functioning of the mind in the form of neuropsychiatric sequelae to her multiple sclerosis incorporating impaired executive functioning and memory impairment. The psychiatrist, who had been asked to assess her ability to make decisions to refuse medical treatment, concluded that,

> On the balance of probabilities however – and given that I think CC has damage to the area of the brain associated with the ability to make reasoned judgements – I have a reasonable belief CC lacks capacity to make informed health decisions.

It was also noted at the time, that CC does not reliably retain information provided to her about her treatment.

Clinical issues

CC was maintained on a combination of antidepressant and antipsychotic medication but unilaterally decided to withdraw from the psychotropic medication regime around 2005. However, there are indications in the GP notes that her refusal to take her medication may go as far back as early 2002. It is understood that CC has been monitored in the interim, through outpatient review and day hospital attendance. She is currently under the care of a community psychiatrist and she has a social worker, who is a member of the local Community Mental Health Team.

There are specific concerns concerning CC's oral intake and her weight. It is not believed that CC experiences a formal psychiatric eating disorder, a clinical opinion which was reached in early 2015.

Family/social context

CC had been widowed for many years and estranged from her son and his family for many more. The current will had been drawn up in early widowhood but had recently been revised based on a reconnection with her family. There is a son, a daughter-in-law and two adult grandsons. CC no longer owns her own home, having been accommodated in care homes for many years. She has no social network or living siblings.

Psychological/neuropsychological matters

CC has a long history of suspicion of others, their motivations and behaviours. She has a similarly lengthy history of discordance with medical opinion and non-compliance with medical treatment. It is noted that previous assessments of capacity have included significant efforts to provide CC with relevant information in order to maximise her capacity to make the decisions in question, but she has been unable, or unwilling, to take such information on board and use it to inform her understanding. For example, when assessed previously in respect of her refusal to eat and her plummeting weight (68 kg to 44 kg over one year), she was combative when presented with evidence. When told that her weight was lower than was healthy, she started a discussion about how weight is measured. When asked about her dietary intake, she reported to dislike carbohydrates (there was no evidence of this in care home records). When it was explained to her that low body weight can result in muscle being harvested to meet the body's needs, she reported that obesity would put more of a strain on the body. Her beliefs were entrenched, and she would not brook any counter-arguments.

Assessment and rationale

CC was assessed at her care home with her consent although she was suspicious of the reason for the assessment, and who had organised it, from the outset.

CC was asked about her son, she reported that he was 57 in the same month as the assessment, she could not recall his name or that he was married. She was unable to confirm where he lived but thought it may have been some 100 or so miles away and although she reported that he travels a lot with his work, she was unable to describe what he did for a living. It appears from the convoluted conversation that there is infrequent contact between CC and her son, despite their recent reconnection. She was asked if her son had any children and reported that there are three adult grandsons whose names she could not provide.

CC was asked how long she had lived at the present care home and she was unable to give any indication. When asked if this was years or months, she could not estimate but felt it was months (in fact, it had been over ten years). She reports having lived in the region since the 1970s. She reports having been a children's nurse in the south east prior to her marriage.

CC was asked about her health and felt that she is generally in good health and never had any major health issues. She did not disclose any psychiatric history despite questioning and did not disclose her diagnosis of multiple sclerosis. She was asked about her eyes as she appeared to be struggling to focus. She said that she had never had any surgery before but 10 minutes later reported that she had undergone eye surgery about 10 years ago at a local hospital. She was unable to give any further information or detail.

CC was then asked about her assets in the context of drawing up a will. She reports that she is aware of the amount of money she has but would not disclose this at interview as she did not trust me. It is possible that she was suspicious of being asked but it is equally possible that she is unaware of the extent of her assets. She is aware that there is a financial advisor who works for the home manager and owner at her current care home who visits approximately once a year and gives her a statement but then said, "I don't know how it works." She took some considerable time to remember the name of the financial advisor but had no means of contacting her independently.

The interview with CC was followed up with telephone interviews with her IMCA and with her social worker. The IMCA had met with CC approximately six times over several months and had been strict in terms of the boundaries of her conversations with her. The IMCA's impression was that CC had been largely consistent in terms of wanting to bequeath her assets to her son but was aware that there were concerns regarding his ability to manage the same sagely as he had several failed businesses and a bankruptcy behind him.

The social worker noted that CC has been very reluctant to admit mental health issues and to engage with services. She has been involved professionally for approximately one year and has had a number of conversations with CC which she estimates to be about five. The social worker confirmed that there are three grandsons but there is only sporadic contact as they were estranged for a very long time. She estimates the contact has only recommenced over the last five years. Her impression is that whilst CC appears to be clear about what she wants to put in her will at each appointment she does forget appointments that have happened with professionals. The social worker related an event at which she had met with CC on one particular day and on the following day CC was unable to remember the appointment or the fact that the social worker had attended at all.

It was noted throughout the assessment that CC had an "odd" manner in that she did not adhere to the usual turn-taking in social conversation, would frequently talk over the other person or interrupt with a tangential comment. She was also noted to halt speech on occasion and wink conspiratorially with a passing carer, putting her finger to her lips as she did so. She has been heard talking loudly in her bedroom and mewing like a cat on occasion.

Opinion/outcome

CC does understand the nature of a will and does have some understanding of the people who may have reasonable expectation to benefit under her will. However, the concern is that she does not appear to understand the full extent of her estate or the process by which that information may be provided to her. Similarly, there is a concern that there is a disorder of mind in the form of the neuropsychiatric sequelae to multiple sclerosis which have been noted in detail in recent psychiatric assessments in the context of mental capacity.

There is also the concern about the potential effect of influence against the backdrop of some fluctuation in her presentation. It appears from the interview, from the presentation of staff at the outset of the assessment at the care home and from conversations with CC's IMCA and social worker, as well as information contained within psychiatric reports, that there is a longstanding backdrop of suspiciousness on the part of CC which is easily brought to the fore. This is a lady who, although appears to have robust opinions, has sufficient gaps in her memory, sufficient impairments of brain as a result of her multiple sclerosis and a sufficient longstanding history of suspiciousness of others for her to be readily vulnerable to influence, whether intended or not.

CC lacks the necessary testamentary capacity at this stage and would benefit from the protections provided by a statutory will. She has expressed a relatively consistent view as to what her wishes are which could easily be encapsulated within a statutory will.

Legal commentary

The fact that CC's earlier will was made before her recent reconnection with her family, and that CC now wishes to make a new will in favour of her son, suggest that it would be in her best interests to apply for a statutory will. The Court of Protection is likely to give considerable weight to CC's wishes, given that (a) whilst she may not satisfy the *Banks v. Goodfellow* test, the degree of her incapacity appears to be close to the borderline, (b) her views have been expressed consistently and (c) her wishes appear readily capable of being implemented and accommodated within the court's overall assessment of her best interests.[18]

The concerns regarding the son's ability to manage CC's assets sagely, given his failed businesses and previous bankruptcy, may lead the Court of Protection to provide for him in the statutory will by way of either a protective trust[19] or a fully discretionary trust.

Discussion/learning points

This is an interesting case where the lack of capacity is less to do with the psychiatric symptoms, which are readily evidenced in assessment, but more to do with the wider context of an inability to clearly, objectively understand, or hold on to,

---

18 These all being relevant factors in determining the weight to be given to P's wishes and feelings: see *In re* M (*Statutory Will*) [2011] 1 WLR 344, at [35]

19 See s.33 of the Trustee Act 1925. The beneficiary under a protective trust has a life interest until such time as he goes bankrupt or tries to dispose of his interest, at which point a discretionary trust arises for him and his family

key information in order to make an informed choice. Suspiciousness, whether founded in fact or constructed within the mind, renders all involved in the will-making process vulnerable, from the person, to the solicitor, to the beneficiaries. The possibility of influence and suggestion calls for the protection which is provided by a statutory will.

RETROSPECTIVE TESTAMENTARY CAPACITY

There are particular difficulties inherent in the retrospective challenging of testamentary capacity. Effectively, the primary source of evidence is not available as the person is no longer living. Therefore, "the expert must interpret the data from multiple sources" (Shulman et al, 2005, p.64) and finds themselves in the strange juxtaposition where the challenge is a legal one, but the evidence considered by the courts in such challenges is typically clinical in nature. In *Hawes v. Burgess* the Court of Appeal cautioned against placing too much reliance on a retrospective assessment of testamentary capacity, saying "The court should be cautious about acting on the basis of evidence of lack of capacity given by a medical expert after the event, particularly when that expert has neither met nor medically examined the testatrix . . ."[20]

Case 4: CD

Presenting question/problem

This is the case of a woman who struggled to cope with the sudden death of her husband in middle-age and relied heavily upon her adult sons to continue the family business. She was unexpectedly diagnosed with terminal cancer several months after being widowed and died within a few short weeks. Her will which, unbeknown to her children, had been drawn up between her diagnosis and death, disinherited them (and her parents) in favour of an estranged sister. The estate was considerable comprising money, a profitable business and a large family home. The sons were challenging the will on the grounds that their mother lacked the requisite capacity at the time of the will and had been susceptible to undue influence from the estranged sister. There were no contemporaneous attendance notes available from the solicitor. An assessment of CD's testamentary capacity at the time of the will was requested by the sons' solicitor.

Background to the case

Clinical issues

CD was noted to be struggling after her husband's sudden death in April of the year that she died. It is clear from entries in the medical records that the deceased had been significantly emotionally affected by the sudden loss of her husband earlier in the year and had visited the GP on several occasions to discuss the same and was, according to GP records, in receipt of bereavement counselling. It is more likely than not that having visited the GP for bereavement counselling as recently as mid-September, the deceased, at time of writing the will, would have been seeking to address the cumulative effects of the sudden loss of her husband and her grief reaction to the same as well as to her own personal reaction to a probable diagnosis of terminal cancer. Thus, it is unlikely that there was an *exacerbation* of background stress or depression but most likely to be a *continuation* of the same low mood and distress which is clearly recorded throughout medical records from April, in relation to the most recent episode. This background of psychological turbulence will certainly have rendered the deceased's decision-making abilities vulnerable to influence.

Family/social context

CD had been estranged from her sister (and brother-in-law) for many years. The exact cause of the relationship breakdown was not clear. CD had three sons who lived with or near her and provided significant support to her both personally and in terms of keeping the family business going following the sudden death of their father earlier in the year. It is understood that the sister and brother-in-law accompanied CD to *their* solicitor's offices and sat in on the will-making appointment with her. The will was drawn up in a single appointment.

Psychological/neuropsychological matters

Contemporaneous medical records attest to CD being "very distressed" on 22 November (doctor's report), "very tearful and distressed" on 29 November (doctor's letter of 12 December) and was "terribly upset, confused and kept mixing things up" on 30 November, according to the witness statement of the eldest son. The will was made on 24 November, **in between these dates.**

CD was noted, by her parents, on 30 November to be "confused". It is improbable that an individual who had been psychologically distressed on the 22nd would have recovered sufficient psychological composure to make a will on 24th and then return to being "very tearful and distressed" on 29 and 30 November.

The distress appears related to the tentative, and later evidenced, diagnosis of terminal cancer of the colon. It suggests a level of disturbance or distress which could interfere with the decision-making processes involved in drawing up a will. The court might also wish to consider in connection with this, that the palliative care consultant who visited the deceased at her sister's address in the days leading up to her death, commented that "she remains in denial about the severity of her illness and says she is a fighter and is hoping for chemotherapy in the new year." Whilst denial is a commonly recognised step in bereavement and grief reactions, it is more likely than not (based on the evidence provided) that the deceased did not actually believe she was going to die.

Assessment and rationale

Psychological theories of decision-making have indicated that if the decision "problem" (such as making a will, for example) is framed in different ways to the individual who is undertaking the decision, that individual's perceptions of the decision "problem" will be altered. Research has clearly shown that an individual will make their decision based on the way in which the information under consideration is placed before them.

In a seminal paper, two eminent psychologists, Tversky and Kahneman (1981) posed identical scenarios to two different groups of decision-makers where each scenario had exactly the same outcome. However, the way in which the information in each scenario was presented to the two different groups dictated their choices and each group made a completely different choice based on their assessment of gains and losses, as presented in the wording of the scenario. The authors labelled this the "framing effect" of decision-making.

Opinion/outcome

Based on the information provided, it is likely, on balance of probabilities, that the decision-making of the deceased was impaired and susceptible to influence at the time when she executed the will due to her observed and reported level of distress and apparent confusion.

Legal commentary

The effect of CD's bereavement and her distress about the cancer diagnosis on her decision-making powers, coupled with the surprising decision to disinherit her sons in favour of her estranged sister, point towards a lack of testamentary capacity. This is compounded by the striking failure on the part of the solicitor who drafted the disputed will to follow the Golden Rule or even to keep a contemporaneous attendance note of his meeting with CD. In those circumstances the burden of proof is likely to shift to the sister to prove testamentary capacity, and she may struggle to discharge that burden.

The fact that the sister and brother-in-law arranged for the will be to be prepared by their own solicitor, and sat in on the meeting at which the instructions were given and the will was executed, is likely to give rise to alternative claims based on either undue influence[21] or lack of knowledge and approval.[22]

---

21 The legal principles applicable to undue influence claims relating to wills are helpfully summarised in *Re Edwards* [2007] WTLR 1387, at [47]
22 As to which see *Gill v. Woodall* [2011] Ch 380

Discussion/learning points

Clearly, any challenge to a will that is made retrospectively is heavily reliant upon objective and contemporaneous records, both medical and legal. The court will take into account retrospective assessments of testamentary capacity by suitably qualified experts, but only as part of the wider evidence. As was stated in *Key v. Key*,

> the issue as to testamentary capacity is, from first to last, for the decision of the court. It is not to be delegated to experts, however eminent, albeit that their knowledge, skill and experience may be an invaluable tool in the analysis, affording insights into the workings of the mind otherwise entirely beyond the grasp of laymen, including for that purpose, lawyers and in particular judges.

Case 5: CE

Presenting question/problem

This is the case of an elderly spinster who had died of a dementing illness, leaving all of her estate to a relatively new carer, disinheriting her family who had been closely involved in supporting her in the last years of her life. The family launched a challenge to the will and an assessment was requested of her testamentary capacity at the material times to both revoke and destroy an earlier will and to make a new will. The specific instruction was to establish whether or not CE:

a)   was able to know and approve the contents of her will in the light of her medical condition; and
b)   at what point in time did she lose testamentary capacity, if at all?

Her final will was made two months before her death.

Background to the case

Clinical issues

From perusal of medical records, it became apparent that CE had experienced a series of unexplained falls, over a 5-year period. There was no evidence in the notes of depression but there was evidence of increasing confusion and disorientation latterly. However, there was no specific diagnosis made and no formal cognitive assessment, such as a Mini Mental State Examination (MMSE) as is usually done in primary care at first point of contact. CE was being treated for longstanding hypertension, which can exert a cerebral effect, particularly in the white matter of the frontal lobes, but there was no documented evidence to support this possibility.

Family/social context

CE had several key figures in her life who were mentioned in various wills. There had been a will two years before her death, which had made her best friend's daughter the principal beneficiary (Ms A.). However, this had been destroyed and replaced by a will a year later. This second will is alleged to have reduced an existing (but modest) bequest to her nephew, Mr B., after she become angry that he had removed papers from her home without her consent. No copy of the second will was ever found and its existence is disputed by some family members. The final will, which is the subject of the dispute, was made two months before her death. The principal beneficiary was still Ms A. but now her nephew (Mr B.) was excluded and two new beneficiaries, Mr and Mrs C. (her cleaner and her husband), were now bequeathed an almost equal share to Ms A.

It is also noted as being of key relevance that nine months before her death, CE was admitted to hospital following a further fall and Ms A. was removed from the notes as her next-of-kin, being replaced by Mr and Mrs C. There was no evidence of a falling out with Ms A. anywhere in the records.

Psychological/neuropsychological matters

There were numerous anecdotal reports of CE being forgetful, falling, being confused and disorientated (sometimes failing to recognise familiar people) with impaired recollection of recent events (such as visits from friends) along with increasingly frequent repetitive questioning. These reports are confirmed from several sources. However, at the same time, both the nephew (Mr B.) and the solicitor who drew up the final will dispute such accounts.

There is no evidence in primary care (GP) records of depression or cognitive decline in the time period during which the three wills were drawn up. Ms A. reports in her statement that she had tried to get CE reviewed by a psychogeriatrician but that this had been blocked by Mrs C. This is disputed by Mrs C.

Assessment and rationale

In the case of assessment of retrospective testamentary capacity, it is not possible to obtain information from the primary source as they are deceased. All other sources of information are, therefore, secondary or even tertiary, which has implications for the reliability of the same.

In this instance, assessment involved a detailed review of GP and hospital records, a review of statements by all key witnesses, including the views of the instructed solicitor. The solicitor did not make contemporaneous notes of the meeting with his client to discuss the will and it emerged that CE had not actually instructed the solicitor personally, but a note had been prepared, in the handwriting of Mr C., purporting to come from CE and the final will had been drawn up on that basis.

Opinion/outcome

Counsel in the case had suggested that if the final will of CE was declared invalid, then she would, technically, have died intestate as she had explicitly instructed her solicitor to destroy each will on the preparation of a subsequent version. However, legal issues are to be decided by the court and do not lie within the remit of this assessment.

There are three key considerations in the formation of the following opinion:

a   Past medical history
      There is no clinical evidence to indicate the presence of cognitive decline in CE in the available records, at any material time.
b   Golden Rule
      The Golden Rule was not followed, but this is merely a rule of good practice. The fact that it was not followed is not in itself evidence of testamentary incapacity.
c   State of mind at the time of making final will
      There is no evidence to indicate that CE was of anything other than sound mind at the time of making the final will. It is clear from statements submitted to the court that there are those who suggest the changes made in the final will from the former will are questionable.

The final opinion is that there is no robust, reliable or convincing evidence to prove that CE lacked testamentary capacity at the time of drawing up her final will, two months before her death. There is no medical evidence to suggest that she did not know or approve the contents of her will. Likewise, there is no medical evidence, such as a formal diagnosis of cognitive decline, which would have impacted on her decision-making ability at the material time.

Legal commentary

Whilst the evidence suggests that a claim based on lack of testamentary capacity may face difficulties, the possibility of a claim based on lack of knowledge and approval (or even undue influence) would merit further investigation. This is particularly so if the solicitor's role was merely to draft the will on the basis of the written instructions prepared by Mr C., and did not extend to overseeing its execution. Compare, for example, *Poole v. Everall*[23] where a will prepared for a testator by his carer, by which he disinherited his partner, family members and charities in favour of the carer, was set aside on the ground of lack of knowledge and approval in circumstances where the only evidence that the testatrix understood the will came from the carer herself.

23 [2016] WTLR 1621

Discussion/learning points

The main learning point of this case is not to fall into the trap of assuming that because a person is elderly and makes significant changes to their will that it naturally follows that they have lost testamentary capacity. Best practice would dictate that solicitor who is instructed to draft a will should ask about previous wills and about the rationale behind any sudden or significant changes. Having said that, a testator is entitled to make a will which is unfair or capricious. As stated in *Boughton v. Knight*, a testator with testamentary capacity "may disinherit . . . his children and leave his property to strangers to gratify his spite, or to charities to gratify his pride."[24]

Case 6: CF

Presenting question/problem

This is the case of an elderly lady who, following a diagnosis of dementia and with several other health problems, made a number of wills over a short period of time, disinheriting various family members in turn. A retrospective assessment of her testamentary capacity at the time of each will was requested. She died, aged 86.

Background to the case

Clinical issues

There is a history of serial TIAs (transient ischaemic attacks) dating from age 59 to 70 with several subsequent bouts of unexplained dizziness against a backdrop of hypertension. Clinically, this is suggestive of a vascular component to CF's presentation. There may well be cerebral implications.

The first recorded indications of observed and reported confusion occur when CF is 74. The first recorded indications of memory decline occur at the age of 76. Between the ages of 76 and 80 there are several references to CF experiencing either depression or low mood.

The first reference to dementia as a diagnosis is when CF is 78. Unfortunately, the full Mini Mental State Examination (MMSE) is not administered and at no point in the medical notes is there any clarity about which form of dementia has been diagnosed. The first full MMSE to be administered, according to records, is when CF was 81. However, there is a problem with the scoring. According to published scoring criteria (Folstein et al, 1975) it is not possible to gain half a mark on any item. In the notes, half a mark has been awarded for the incomplete (and inaccurate) reproduction of the intersecting pentagons. The correct mark for this item should be zero, thus reducing the overall score to 19. Given the lack of contemporaneous information recorded on the form at the time of

24 (1873) LR 3 P&D 64

the administration of the MMSE at this time, it is not possible to check the scoring of other items. The next full MMSE score in the notes is 13/30 and this was carried out one year prior to CF's death.

Family/social context

CF had no siblings or close relatives of her generation still living. She had five nieces and nephews, three in one family, two in another.

Psychological/neuropsychological matters

The initial will made when CF was 71, which left equal shares to the five cousins, appears to have been made during a time where a picture of vascular-based symptoms was already beginning to emerge:

Age 59 – vertigo sudden onset left horizontal nystagmus TIA 2/52.

Age 60 – TIA 2/52 (TIA two weeks ago)

Age 71 – **First will made**

Age 72 – Still dizzy neuro NAD

Age 75 – BP elevated patient unsure of prescription or medication since July 1996

Age 75 – Patient misunderstood information to recommence medication

Age 76 – Depressed. (*Depression is not uncommon in the early [prodromal] stages of dementia as the patient often has preserved insight.*)

Age 76 – Dizzy and sick today

Age 77 – Patient reported a deterioration in short-term memory – otherwise well

Age 77 – CF's sister-in-law attends alone and reported that she was concerned about CF's level of confusion

Age 78 – Feeling depressed

Age 78 – CF attended and reported a one-year history of deteriorating memory but no other symptoms

Age 78 – "Memory loss" entered on to haematology result sheet (as a reason for referral)

Age 78 – Review Mini Mental State Examination – aware of date of birth, orientated TPP, aware of Queen but not PM or own home address. Unaware of which month of the year. Short-term memory loss – **early dementia**

Age 79 – Sudden loss of memory for today only

Age 79: **Amended will** (changed to include a £10,000 legacy to CF's son and to reduce the five cousins' entitlement to £10,000)

Age 80 – Headache – possible diagnosis of TIA for current and previous episodes

Age 80: **Amended will** (This will maintained the £10,000 legacy to her son, excluded one of the cousins, but left £10,000 each to the remaining four cousins)

Assessment and rationale

The MMSE is a brief structured test of mental status and is purported to assess global cognitive function. Specific test items assess:

- orientation
- word recall
- attention and calculation
- language abilities
- visuospatial abilities.

However, the MMSE is not completely objective in that:

- It takes no account of race or ethnicity;
- It takes no account of age, therefore, scores decline with advancing age irrespective of cognitive function;
- It takes no account of educational level, scores are elevated in individuals with high level pre-morbid educational achievement;
- It does not directly assess executive function which is altered in the early stages of Alzheimer's dementia;
- It may lack sensitivity to early signs of dementia; and
- It is subject to practice effects with repeated administration.

The MMSE still remains a widely used, well-validated and reliable tool for screening for evidence of cognitive decline, however, it cannot substitute for a thorough diagnostic assessment. Sensitivity (accuracy in identifying individuals with dementia) and specificity (identifying those who do not have dementia) within the MMSE are both good.

There has been a significant amount of research undertaken on what is known as the average rate of progression or average rate of change (ARC) in the Alzheimer's variant of dementia. There is general agreement that this lies between 2.9 and 3.7 points decline on MMSE scores per year (Han et al, 2000). However, there can be considerable individual variation in this.

Opinion/outcome

It is clear from medical records that CF's GP considered that from the age of 75 onwards, there was convincing evidence of deteriorating cognitive function. This GP had attended CF 79 times over a 7-year period and can, therefore, be considered to have sufficient familiarity with the person to form a robust opinion. There is consistent evidence of confusion, memory loss and depression, all of which would have exerted an appreciable effect on decision-making on the part of CF.

Opinion is, therefore, that there was sufficient compelling evidence that CF lacked the requisite testamentary capacity for the two amended wills, made at the ages of 79 and 80.

Legal commentary

Whilst the MMSE test may be a useful indicator of cognitive decline, it is not a test of testamentary capacity and should not be treated as such. For example, in *Burns v. Burns*[25] a testatrix was held to have testamentary capacity in 2005 despite scoring only 19/30 on an MMSE test in 2003.

The court would draw its conclusion on CF's testamentary capacity based on an assessment of all the evidence, including that of the solicitor who drafted the two later wills (assuming that they were professionally drafted). The Court of Appeal in *Burgess v. Hawes*[26] emphasised that the evidence of an experienced independent solicitor should not be too readily upset by retrospective medical evidence. However, the evidence of such a solicitor will be worthless if it is not based upon a proper assessment and accurate information.[27]

Discussion/learning points

This case is the embodiment of the exhortation of Shulman and colleagues (2005) that close scrutiny needs to be brought to bear in cases where there is a radical change to a will in the context of a significant neurological condition. In this case, the radical change was the removal of one of five cousins who had been included on an equal footing in previous wills going back over a period of almost ten years with no explanation given.

Bibliography

British Medical Association and The Law Society. (2010). *Assessment of Mental Capacity: A Practical Guide for Doctors and Lawyers (3rd Ed)*. London: The Law Society.

Department for Constitutional Affairs. (2007). Mental Capacity Act 2005: Code of Practice. Retrieved from www.gov.uk/government/publications/mental-capacity-act-code-of-practice

Folstein, M. F., Folstein, S. E. & McHugh, P. R. (1975). Mini Mental State: a practical method for grading the cognitive state of patients for the clinician. *Journal of Psychiatric Research*, *12*(3), 189–198.

---

25 [2016] WTLR 755
26 [2013] WTLR 453
27 See *Ashkettle v. Gwinnett* [2013] WTLR 1331, at [43]

Han, L., Cole, M., Bellavance, F., McCusker, J. & Primeau, F. (2000). Tracking cognitive decline in Alzheimer's disease using the Mini-Mental State Examination: A meta-analysis. *International Psychogeriatrics, 12*(2), 231–247.

Humphrey, A., Mills, L., Morrell, G. (NatCen), Douglas, G. & Woodward, H. (Cardiff University). (2010). Inheritance and the family: Attitudes to will-making and intestacy (August). Cardiff: National Centre for Social Research & Cardiff University.

Jacoby, R. & Steer, P. (2007). How to assess capacity to make a will. *British Medical Journal, 335,* 155–157.

Johnson, G. (2017). Sharp and Bryson v Adam and Adam & Others [2006] EWCA Civ 449. Retrieved from www.cascaidr.org.uk/2017/03/23/sharp-and-bryson-v-adam-and-adam-others-2006-ewca-civ-449/

Jovanovic, A.A., Jovovic, S., Milovanovic, S. & Jasonvic-Gasic, M. (2008). Medical reasons for retrospective challenges of testamentary capacity. *Psychiatra Danubina, 20*(4), 485–493.

Kenward v Adams. (1975). *The Times,* 29 November.

Kim, S. Y. H. & Caine, E. D. (2002). Utility and limits of the Mini Mental State Examination in evaluating consent in Alzheimer's disease. *Psychiatric Services, 53,* 1322–1324.

Lightspeed Research. (2014) Wills: The facts and figures. Retrieved from www.infolaw.co.uk/partners/wills-the-facts-and-figures

McCarten, J. R., Rottunda, S. J. & Kuskowski, M. A. (2004) Change in the Mini-Mental State exam in Alzheimer's disease over 2 years: The experience of a dementia clinic. *Journal of Alzheimer's Disease, 6*(1), 11–15.

Mencap. (2007). *Making sense of money: A training pack for people with a learning disability.* Mencap, FSA & Citizens Advice Bureau.

Newby, H. & Ryan-Morgan, T. (2013). Assessment of mental capacity. In Newby, G., Coetzer, R., Daisley, A. & Weatherhead, S. (Eds.), *The Handbook of Real Neuropsychological Rehabilitation in Acquired Brain Injury* (pp. 179–207). London: Karnac.

Office for National Statistics. (2018). Overview of the UK population. Retrieved from www.ons.gov.uk/peoplepopulationandcommunity/populationandmigration/populationestimates/articles/overviewoftheukpopulation/november2018

Rees, S. J. & Ryan-Morgan, T. (2012). An exercise for maximising capacity in decision making. *Journal of Social Care and Neurodisability, 3*(2), 69–76.

Roked, F. & Patel, A. (2008). Which aspects of cognitive function are best associated with testamentary capacity in patients with Alzheimer's disease? *International Journal of Geriatric Psychiatry, 23,* 552–553.

Ryan-Morgan, T. (2005). The Mental Capacity Act 2005 and clinical neuropsychology. *APIL PI Focus Special Issue on Medicine, Ethics and Clinical Injury Claims, 15*(6), 14–16.

Shulman, K.I., Cohen, C. & Hull, I. (2005). Psychiatric issues in retrospective challenges of testamentary capacity. *International Journal of Geriatric Psychiatry, 20,* 63–69.

Simard, M. (1998). The Mini Mental State Examination: Strengths and weaknesses of a clinical instrument. *The Canadian Alzheimer Disease Review,* December, 10–12.

Sullivan, K. (2004). Neuropsychological assessment of mental capacity. *Neuropsychological Review, 14*(3), 131–142.

Tversky, A. & Kahneman, D. (1981). The framing of decisions and the psychology of choice. *Science (New Series), 211*(4481), 453–458.

7 Capacity to enter into a sexual relationship/capacity to marry

Dr Tracey Ryan-Morgan

With Abigail Bond

> The intention of the Act is not to dress an incapacitous person in forensic cotton wool but to allow them as far as possible to make the same mistakes that all other human beings are at liberty to make and not infrequently do.[1]

There is perhaps no other context in which it is more important to guard against protectionism than where consent to sexual relations or consent to marriage are concerned. Both are areas of private life of the utmost sensitivity and the court should be extremely cautious before it holds that a person is incapable of making such decisions for themselves. The practical consequences of a declaration that a person lacks the relevant capacity can be widespread. For example, where a person lacks capacity to enter into sexual relations, the local authority may have to undertake very close supervision of the individual to ensure that the opportunity for sexual relations is removed.[2] However, in both contexts, the court's jurisdiction upon a declaration of a lack of capacity is expressly limited: under section 27(1)(a) and (b) of the MCA (2005) consent to marriage and consent to have sexual relations cannot be given on that person's behalf.

The functional test for capacity

The "functional test" for capacity is set out by section 3(1) of the MCA (2005) which provides that a person is unable to make a decision for himself if he is unable

> (a) to understand the information relevant to the decision; (b) to retain that information; (c) to use or weigh that information as part of the process of making the decision; or (d) to communicate his decision (whether by talking, using sign language, or any other means)."

---

1 Hedley J in *A NHS Trust v P* [2013] EWHC 50 (COP) at para. 10
2 per Sir Brian Leveson P in *IM v LM & Liverpool CC* [2014] EWCA Civ 37

Section 3(4) provides that the "information relevant to the decision" includes information "about the reasonably foreseeable consequences of (a) deciding one way or another, or (b) failing to make the decision."

In addition, the Code of Practice at paragraph 4.16 explains that:

> It is important not to assess someone's understanding before they have been given relevant information about a decision. Every effort must be made to provide information in a way that is most appropriate to help the person to understand. Quick or inadequate explanations are not acceptable unless the situation is urgent . . . Relevant information includes:

- the nature of the decision;
- the reason why the decision is needed;
- the likely effects of deciding one way or another or, making no decision at all.

The test for capacity to consent to sexual relations

Pre-MCA (2005) case law

Paragraph 4.33 of the Code clarifies that the Act was not intended to replace the pre-existing common law tests for capacity and that the new definition of capacity was in line with those tests. The common law test for capacity to consent to sexual relations was considered in *X City Council v MB, NB and MAB*.[3] Munby J (as he then was) agreed with the submission that the ability to choose whether to engage in sexual relations should not be one which is beyond that of the person of average intelligence, does not require any degree of expert advice to aid understanding, and that it was unhelpful in this context to refer to the "more complicated" common law test for consent to medical treatment as set out in *Re MB (Medical Treatment)*.[4] Whilst that did not mean the test in *Re MB* was irrelevant, he clarified that such a "refined analysis" was probably not necessary where the issue was as simple as the question of whether a person had the capacity to marry or the capacity to consent to sexual relations.

Pre-Act case-law also drew parallels with the test for capacity to marry (see below) in holding that capacity to consent to sexual relations is "issue specific", i.e. it is a question directed to the nature of the activity rather than to the identity of the sexual partner. In *Re MM (An Adult)*,[5] a case decided when the Act was on the statute book but had not yet been brought into force, Munby J (as he then was) explained

3 [2006] EWHC 168
4 [1997] 2 FLR 426
5 [2007] EWHC 2003

A woman either has the capacity to consent to "normal" penetrative vaginal intercourse, or she does not. It is difficult to see how it can sensibly be said that she has the capacity to consent to a particular sexual act with Y whilst at the same time lacking capacity to consent to precisely the same sexual act with Z . . . capacity to consent to sexual intercourse . . . does not depend upon an understanding of sexual intercourse with a particular person. Put shortly, capacity to consent to sexual relations is issue specific: it is not person (partner) specific.

Post-MCA (2005) case-law

Post-Act case-law has focused on an apparent conflict in some of the authorities as regards two issues: the extent to which the evaluation of capacity to consent to sexual relations involves the need to consider whether the individual is able to "use or weigh" the relevant information; and the conclusion that capacity to consent to sexual relations is "issue" and not "person" specific. Both issues have now been resolved by the Court of Appeal in *IM v LM, AB & Liverpool City Council*.[6]

In *D Borough Council v B*,[7] Mostyn recognised that although it was difficult to think of an activity more person-and-situation-specific than sexual relations and marriage, it did not follow that capacity to either marry or consent to sexual relations was spouse or person specific, and suggested that there had perhaps been a conflation of capacity to consent to sex and the exercise of that capacity.

The degree to which a person needs to be able to "use or weigh" relevant information in this context was considered by Hedley J in *A Local Authority v H*[8] in a case concerning an adult with mild learning disabilities, atypical autism and a full-scale IQ of 64, who had demonstrated an early and deep degree of sexualisation. He observed that:

> This is a difficult concept in the context of human social relations since choices are generally made rather more by emotional drive and instinct than by rational choice. Of course, there is a rational element that has been for most people assimilated into instinct and the control of emotional drive . . . what is at issue here is whether the person is able to deploy the general knowledge set out above into a specific decision-making act.

In *IM v LM, AB & Liverpool City Council*[9] Sir Brian Leveson P, Tomlinson LJ and McFarlane LJ expressed concern that the terminology that had developed in this field ("person specific", "act specific", "situation specific", "issue-specific") meant that there was a risk of losing sight of the fact that all decisions, whatever

6 [2014] EWCA Civ 37
7 [2011] EWHC 101 (Fam) 36
8 [2012] EWHC 49 (COP)
9 [2014] EWCA Civ 37

their nature, need to be evaluated under the structure of the MCA (2005) and that whereas in some circumstances, having understood and retained relevant information an ability to use it will be critical, in other circumstances the need to weigh competing considerations will be paramount. The Court of Appeal held that the ability to use and weigh information is unlikely to loom large in the evaluation of capacity to consent to sexual relations.

What "information" is "relevant to the decision" in the context of capacity to consent to sexual relations?

In *IM v LM, AB & Liverpool City Council*[10] the Court of Appeal reiterated the need for a practical limit on what needs to be envisaged as reasonably foreseeable consequences so as to not to divorce the notional decision-making process attributed to the protected person from the actual decision-making process undertaken on a daily basis by persons of full capacity, which is "largely visceral, owing more to instinct and emotion than analysis." Specifically, the Court of Appeal considered that it was wrong to introduce into the test for capacity to consent to sexual relations the question of whether a person was able to recognise the non-specified health risks to herself or to the foetus in becoming pregnant, or that the foreseeable outcome of the pregnancy might be that she may not be able to have care of or even contact with the baby. The Judge below had, therefore, not erred in finding that LM had capacity to consent to sexual relations on the basis that she understood the rudiments of the sexual act, she had had children before, and that she had a basic understanding of the issues of contraception and the risk of sexually transmitted diseases.

In *London Borough of Southwark v KA*[11] Parker J resisted the request to specify more precisely what needed to be understood, stating instead that the tests for capacity in respect of sexual relations and marriage are neither high nor complex, and reminding herself that individuals of full capacity rarely engage in intellectual debate with each other before entering into sexual relations. She identified the "core information" as: (i) the mechanics of the act; (ii) that sexual relations can lead to pregnancy; and (iii) that there can be health risks caused by sexual relations, and added as "fundamental" to having capacity rather than as "information" as to the nature of the act, that "P knows that she/he has a choice and can refuse." KA understood and retained the understanding of the need for consent of himself and his partner. That he believed that pregnancy would always result from sexual intercourse, or that he believed gestation to be a very rapid process, did not affect the fact that for him it was a foreseeable consequence of sexual intercourse. Nor was the fact that he was under the misapprehension that pregnancy could only occur within marriage sufficient to displace the presumption of capacity.

---

10   [2014] EWCA Civ 37 at para. 80
11   [2016] EWCOP 20

A decision that a person has the capacity to consent and engage in sexual relations may not necessarily be the end of the matter. In *A Local Authority v TZ*[12] notwithstanding a finding that TZ had such capacity, Cobb J found that he lacked the capacity to decide whether any individual with whom he may wish to have a sexual relationship is safe: as a result of his autism and learning disabilities he lacked the ability to interpret subtle details in a person's verbal and non-verbal communications, and was unable to recognise anyone who might cause him harm. An appropriate educational and care package was therefore required.

The test for capacity to marry

Much of what has been said above with regard to the test for capacity to consent to sexual relations also applies to the test for capacity to marry. There is a helpful aide-memoire set out in *London Borough of Southwark v KA*[13] as follows:

- Marriage is status specific rather than person specific;
- The wisdom of the marriage is irrelevant;
- P must understand the broad nature of the marriage contract;
- P must understand the duties and responsibilities that normally attach to marriage, including that there may be financial consequences and that spouses have a particular status and connection with regard to each other;
- The essence of marriage is for two people to live together and to love one another;
- P must not lack capacity to enter into sexual relations.

In *Luton Borough Council v SB and RS*[14] RS lacked the capacity to marry since, partly as a result of his "concrete thinking" arising from his particular combination of disabilities, he had no grasp of the role of husband and wife or of mutuality, reciprocity and the capacity for compromise as the indivisible components of marriage. Further, in view of the disabilities which prevented him from weighing and evaluating essentially abstract concepts, there was no real prospect of him gaining the capacity to consent to marriage or sexual relations (it being considered that sex education work might have the consequence of further sexualising him).

Case 1: DA

Presenting question/problem

DA is a 24-year-old young gentleman who was born at full term with a normal delivery but has a long history of developmental delay and learning difficulties.

---

12 [2014] EWHC 973
13 [2016] EWCOP 20
14 [2015] EWHC 3534

He has a diagnosis of lobar holoprosencephaly (HPE), with partial fusion of his frontal lobes. Medical opinion is that were DA to become a father himself the chance of his having a child with HPE could be high. His parents were seeking legal "consent" for their son to be surgically sterilised in order to completely remove the risk of him becoming a parent to a disabled child. This had yet to be discussed with him. An assessment was sought of his sexual knowledge and understanding as well as his reasoning ability within this context.

Background to the case

Clinical issues

DA is supported by local learning disability services. He attends day services and has an appointed social worker. He has a weekly timetable of activities including daily living responsibilities and hobbies. He is supported to refer to, and learn, his timetable to maximise his independence. He cannot undertake any activity without support but is able to contribute to decisions each day such as what he eats, what he wears and when he goes to bed. He receives regular support from a community occupational therapist within the community support team and has, in the past, been treated by a specialist speech and language therapist.

Family/social context

DA lives in a group home with other adults with learning disabilities, supported by a 24-hour staff team. He visits his parental home one weekend per month and has supportive parents.

DA has a range of valued relationships in his life but gets on particularly well with one of his fellow tenants, an adult male, as they share many of the same interests, including gaming on the computer. DA has other male friends whom he spends time with at the statutory day service, but staff are unaware of any particular female friends.

Staff note that DA has expressed a desire to be "gay" but when this was explored with him by staff during a person-centred planning process, DA's understanding of "gay" was that this involved "going out with boys" and appeared to have a non-sexual meaning to him. There has been no formal sexual education provided to DA from within the statutory service provision he receives.

Psychological/neuropsychological matters

DA presents as a friendly, easy-going person who enjoys the company of others. There is evidence on record of DA having received unwelcome sexual attention from a male service-user at a previous residence. Staff spent time with him to provide support for him to express himself assertively in such situations and say "no" when such attentions are not wanted. However, staff also formed the view that DA does not have any real understanding of what may be appropriate or inappropriate social/sexual behaviour in himself or others and that this lack of knowledge may render him vulnerable to either receiving or giving unwelcome sexual attention. To date, there is no evidence that he has developed any sexual identity or preferences or that, to the knowledge of staff, he has engaged in any sexual activities.

Assessment and rationale

It was decided to confirm DA's level of cognitive functioning to inform the level of understanding and to establish at what level to pitch the assessment. It was also considered critical to assess DA's level of social and consequential reasoning as well as his knowledge of, and attitudes towards, sexual matters. Finally, it was considered important to establish DA's ability to identify emotions in others as this is the first step in reciprocal social relationships.

The assessments included the Wechsler Abbreviated Scale of Intelligence (WASI) which classified his Full Scale IQ as being in the region of 49–57, which is approximately commensurate with 0.1 per cent of the general population.

DA, therefore, meets the first criterion for a diagnosis of learning disability in that he has an impairment of intellectual functioning.

DA was also assessed using the Adaptive Behaviour Assessment System II (ABAS-II) which provides a comprehensive, norm-referenced assessment of adaptive skills for individuals. The scores indicate that, generally, DA is performing at "borderline" or "extremely low" level across all skill areas and that this is below what would be expected of his age peers within the general population. However, he demonstrated three areas of *relative* strength in the domains of "home-living", "leisure skills and social activities", and "social skills". "Home-living" is defined as the skills needed for the basic care of the home setting, including cleaning, property maintenance, repairs, food preparation and performing chores. "Leisure skills" include the need for engaging in, and planning, leisure and recreational activities, including playing with others, engaging in recreation at home, and following rules and games. "Social skills" include the need to interact socially and get along with other people, including having friends, showing and recognising emotions, assisting others and using manners.

Under the General Adaptive Composite (GAC), which represents a comprehensive and global estimate of a number of skill areas, DA obtained a score of 56–62 (95 per cent level of confidence), which is classified as being within the extremely low range of functioning

With reference to the WHO (1992) criteria for learning disability, DA's scores indicate that it is highly likely that he would struggle with many aspects of day-to-day life without substantial support, most notably in the areas of community use, communication, functional academics, health and safety, self-care and self-direction.

DA therefore meets the second criterion for the diagnosis of learning disability reflected in the descriptor, "severe impairment of adaptive functioning".

The British Ability Scales (BAS) Social Reasoning sub-test was administered to DA as this tool provides a useful means of assessing an individual's level of reasoning, although only the first four items were able to be administered to DA since the language used in the last three vignettes was too complex for him to understand. DA scored consistently at level 1 which is indicative of an individual who responds relevantly but only in terms of *immediate* reactions or consequences and without further elaboration or the ability to grasp situations or actions from the perspectives of others. In summary, DA expresses limited consequential reasoning.

The Sexual Attitudes and Knowledge Assessment (SAK) was used to evaluate DA's attitudes, knowledge and skills in the four main areas of:

1   understanding relationships,
2   social interaction,
3   sexual awareness and
4   assertiveness.

This was administered to DA who was asked to respond to a series of questions, each accompanied by a picture (line drawing). The results suggest that DA has very limited understanding of relationships, social interaction, sexual awareness and assertiveness skills.

A range of 18 coloured line drawings of facial expressions, known as Emotional Expression Widgets, were presented to DA in order to assess his ability to identify and name emotions. The range of emotions was from the simple (including "sad" and "angry") to the more complex (such as "frustrated", "confused" and "confident"). DA's responses to these 18 items suggested that he has a very limited range of emotional recognition. He correctly identified worried, angry, upset, sad and happy (with prompting) but was unable to identify more complex emotions from the coloured line drawings available.

Observations during assessment

DA engaged with the assessment and appeared relatively eager to please. Since he demonstrated a limited understanding of expressed language, short, concrete, simple sentences with as few information-carrying words as possible were used in order to maximise his potential for comprehension and expression.

Opinion

DA is functioning in the "moderate" learning disability range of cognitive functioning with extremely limited adaptive behaviour skills when compared to the general population. He is only able to use a fairly concrete level of social reasoning at the "immediate consequences" level (roughly equivalent to whether he views something as "bad" or "good") and is unable to evaluate from other perspectives or to extrapolate general principles and consequences. His limited range of recognition and labelling of human emotions means that he may be vulnerable in certain social situations since he may not be able to read the non-verbal cues and social interactions of others.

It is clear from DA's answers on the Sexual Attitudes and Knowledge question-naire, his knowledge of body parts, which was assessed during interview, and his limited understanding of emotional expression, that he has a need for sexual (and relationship) education in order to build up appropriate skills and equip him to deal with unwanted sexual attentions. Whilst relationship and sexuality skills are usually developed through a learning process taking place over a person's life-time, DA has not been able to acquire them. This is most likely due to the dissociation between "knowing" and "doing" (Teuber, 1964) which exists in individuals with compromised intellectual function. It is often the case that an adult with learning disability may be able to demonstrate that they possess the concrete knowledge of the information (such as the requirements to understand the mechanics of the sex act, that sex may lead to pregnancy or involve health risks and that an individual has the right to refuse sex) yet lack the ability to *apply* that information at the required time in a specific situation where a decision is needing to be made.

DA would best be assisted by being provided with a detailed individual pro-gramme of sexual education, which includes aspects of sexual relationships including consent, assertiveness, sexual expression, and also encompasses issues such as privacy and rights. (There is a myriad of information and resources avail-able on the British Institute of Learning Disabilities website which can be easily obtained and incorporated into his care planning.) He would also require ongo-ing support so that he can be assisted to apply the concrete knowledge in the requisite situations in order to both exercise freedom of judgement (if he has the capacity to do so) or to keep himself safe (if he lacks the same).

Legal commentary

It is clear that the question of capacity to consent to sexual relations cannot properly be determined until steps have been taken to assist P to acquire that capacity by providing him or her with sex education in accordance with the pro-vision of section 1(3) of MCA (2005). It is of course difficult to predict whether a court will find that DA has capacity to enter into sexual relations after an appropriate programme of sex education has been provided to him and reassess-ment will be needed at that stage. As set out in the introduction to this chapter, an understanding of the core relevant information in respect of sexual relations involves understanding (a) that P knows he or she has a choice and can refuse; (b) the mechanics of the act; (c) that sexual relations can lead to pregnancy; and (d) that there are health risks caused by sexual relations. If DA understands the mechanics of sexual intercourse, understands that both parties need to consent, and understands even only on a very rudimentary level that the consequences of sex may be pregnancy and ill-health, he is likely to have capacity. The pre-sumption in favour of capacity is unlikely to be rebutted if DA understands the need for contraceptive protection yet struggles to retain knowledge of how he could protect himself and his partner, and/or if he struggles to understand and weigh up that serious ill-health may result from unprotected sex. There is some suggestion in the case-law, obiter, that pregnancy need not be considered where P is gay although the point has not yet had to be decided (see *London Borough of Southwark v KA*):[15]

> I take the view that KA, a young man, needs to have an understanding, if not a sophisticated one, that pregnancy is a foreseeable consequence of het-erosexual relations. It is beyond the scope of this judgment to decide whether pregnancy is a foreseeable consequence, and therefore needs to be under-stood, by other individuals, for instance by reason of sexual orientation, age, or particular physical characteristics.

Discussion/learning points

The learning points from this case are that an individual about whom concerns are (rightly) expressed in terms of sexual identity, relationships and choices, ought first to be provided with a formal, appropriately targeted programme of education so that any assessment of decision-making can be based on the individual adopt-ing an informed position. In this case, DA had not received any such instruction or support, yet consideration was apparently already being given to sterilisation as a means of protecting a non-sexually aware or active individual. This is an overly protective approach, albeit springing from a position of concern for his welfare. Sexual risk management is a feature of many such cases and it is clear that the approach to each needs to be as individual as the person being assessed and sup-ported. The law should be protectively, not paternalistically, applied.

Case 2: DB

Presenting question/problem

DB is a 20-year-old woman with a lifelong learning disability. An assessment of this young woman's ability to consent to sexual activity was sought by the police, in the context of criminal charges having been brought against a local man accused of having non-consensual sexual relations with her.

Background to the case

Clinical issues

DB was assessed as having experienced global developmental delay as a child. At the age of two, the health visitor had expressed concern about DB's general development, as well as her development of speech and hearing. A speech and

---

15 [2016] EWCOP 20 at para. 63

language therapy assessment found that she required assistance in class and was noted to display a reduced vocabulary for her age with difficulties in sequencing and reasoning. She attended special educational needs schools. She was treated for primary enuresis, but health services struggled to engage her mother and family in the necessary treatment regime.

Family/social context

DB first came to the attention of the local authority following an NSPCC referral. The NSPCC had received an anonymous call to their helpline raising concerns that DB's sister had been sexually abused by their half-brother and that her mother was verbally abusive towards her eight children. All of the children were placed away from the family and their names were placed on the Child Protection Register under the categories of Neglect and Sexual Abuse. Records contained the following entry, "This family is extremely chaotic, loud and aggressive . . . DB remains unkempt, misses school a great deal and remains extremely vulnerable." A family support worker recorded that one-to-one work with DB (then aged 13) was focused on hygiene, sex education and relationships.

The chronology of the family history:

- family moves to Wales;
- family moves to Southampton;
- DB referred to SSD – poor cleanliness and enuresis plus allegations of physical abuse by sibling;
- frequent instances of physical marks and bruising noted by school;
- Child Protection investigation;
- subsequent Child Protection investigation;
- family moved to East Wales;
- family moved to West Wales;
- NSPCC referral regarding sexual abuse of sister and allegation of abuse of DB both by half-brother XX;
- mother arrested for neglect. Children removed by Police Order;
- DB on Child Protection Register: Neglect and Sexual Abuse;
- charges against XX dropped;
- DB removed from Child Protection Register;
- DB re-registered on Child Protection Register under category of Neglect;
- DB alleges kissing with XX in his car;
- respite care began;
- brief work done with DB on "Good touch and bad touch". During same visit, DB was sexually inappropriate with her social worker;
- referral made to clinical psychologist for assessment;
- appointment offered by Positive Behavioural Intervention Service (PBIS);
- reference to family having failed to attend 4 appointments with PBIS;
- speech and language therapy assessment: "DB experiences considerable difficulties with both receptive and expressive language. She is likely to struggle

to follow instructions and produce both spoken and written work in class . . . an up-to-date Educational Assessment is required"; and

- DB has informed two girls at her respite placement that she has been raped by her brother. DB has also told a support worker that she has the same boy-friend as her sister and this person is thought to be a married man living in the same village. Subsequently DB was interviewed by police. DB was consid-ered to have "a very limited understanding of the consequences of her actions and as a result places herself at risk of manipulation and potential harm".

Psychological/neuropsychological matters

It became clear from the case papers that DB has been emotionally and physically at risk for most of her childhood and early adult life and had spent brief periods in care and in respite away from her family. She was clearly considered to be psychologically and physically vulnerable in the context of global developmental delay and inadequate parenting.

Assessment and rationale

The clinical assessment framework provided by Murphy and O'Callaghan (2004) is useful in evaluating capacity to consent to sexual relationships even though it extends well beyond the legal test for this. The following areas are included:

1 basic sexual knowledge (e.g. of body parts, sexual relations and sexual acts);
2 knowledge and consequences of sexual relations including sexually transmitted diseases and pregnancy;
3 an understanding of appropriate sexual behaviour and the context for this;
4 an understanding that sexual contact should always be a matter of choice;
5 the ability to recognise potentially abusive situations; and
6 the ability to show skills of assertion in social and personal situations and to thereby reject any unwanted advances at the given time.

Whilst it is recognised that the scope of this assessment exceeds the requirements of the specific legal test for assessment of capacity to consent to sex, when applied it provides rich information about any gaps in knowledge or understanding which can then form the basis of a remedial education and skills-training programme.

A structured clinical interview was developed covering each of those main areas. This was administered to DB and her responses are summarised as follows.

DB shows a limited and concrete understanding of complex matters regarding sexual behaviours and sexual activities. She is unable to explain the terms rape or sexual assault but is aware at a superficial level that a person can say no if they do not want to do something. However, when pressed for an example of the last time she had said no when she did not want to do something, she was unable to recall and give an account. DB is aware that sex can lead to "a baby and diseases" but was unable to elaborate further. When asked "who you can and cannot have sex with" DB's answer was "your boyfriend", when asked the difference between men and women she replied, "don't know", although when prompted replied, "men drink more". When asked about contraception and shown pictures of different kinds of contraception she was only able to identify a condom and birth control pill. She is aware that you are able to obtain such items from a chemist or a doctor. Interestingly, when posed a series of scenarios about being pressurised into sex or sexual activities with a boyfriend that she may not wish to do, DB replied that she would tell either the police or an "adult". She is, in the eyes of the law, an adult herself.

The Sexual Attitudes and Knowledge Assessment (SAK) was also administered to DB. The results indicated that DB has a limited understanding of relationships, sexual awareness and assertiveness. As is frequently the case with someone with a learning disability, there is a superficial veneer of knowledge which is rarely invoked in practice, since by reason of the learning disability they are usually not able to apply the concrete knowledge that they have acquired in the situation-specific circumstance, also referred to as a failure in adaptive behaviour.

In order to assess DB's level of cognitive functioning, the WASI was administered. This is a standardised psychometric assessment of level of cognitive functioning. DB's results indicated that she is functioning in the IQ range of 49–57, which is commensurate with the lowest 0.1 per cent of the general population and is at a level of more than three standard deviations below the average. This is an extremely low IQ which would be considered to represent "moderate" learning disabilities. Given the profile of scores this is consistent with an individual who has experienced developmental delay across the broad range of cognitive function.

The ABAS II is an assessment of an individual's adaptive behaviour system which provides a comprehensive norm-referenced assessment of adaptive skills for individuals from birth to 89 years. The results of the ABAS II contribute to a complete assessment of the daily functional skills of an individual. This was administered to DB's sister as collateral informant. The results indicate that, generally, DB is functioning within, at best, the bottom 3 per cent but generally, overall, in the bottom 0.5 per cent of the population in relation to her adaptive behaviour skills. Most of her scores lie around two standard deviations from the mean, with some even lower, suggesting that she has compromised adaptability skills within the context of daily living. This adds to her level of vulnerability.

The Gudjonsson Suggestibility Scale (form 1) was developed specifically to objectively measure the vulnerabilities of individuals to give "factually correct" accounts when interviewed. Specifically, it is able to measure the degree to which, if at all, an individual is vulnerable to suggestion if interpersonal pressure is applied or negative feedback given by the person asking the questions. The scales are particularly applicable to the context of police interviewing, but they can be usefully applied to any interview situation including clinical practice. The scales give a reliable measure of an individual's verbal memory recall. This test was administered to DB and the results indicate that DB's memory functioning is *below* that of a non-forensic population with intellectual disabilities and that she is significantly susceptible to both leading questions and negative feedback during questioning. Her total suggestibility score is significantly above the mean for her population subgroup, adding to her vulnerability within the context of legal proceedings.

The British Ability Scales (BAS) Social Reasoning sub-test was also administered to DB as it is a particularly good test of an individual's level of consequential reasoning. It presents a series of crude moral dilemmas about which specific opinion-questions are asked. DB's abilities, as measured by this test, generally lie around the level of *immediate* consequences only. Individuals who respond in this format often talk about the punishment or a reward which one person will get or if a proposed action is simply "good" or "bad". Overall, this suggests that her ability to reason consequentially is impaired relative to her peer group.

Observations during assessment

Throughout the assessments DB needed significant prompting to stay on task and to elaborate on previously given responses. Her comments were generally concrete in nature and open questions were used as far as practicable in order to encourage her to elaborate. She appeared to experience difficulty in following and understanding task instructions and her speech was noted to be disfluent on occasion. She presented with a very open and friendly demeanour and complied with all that was asked of her.

Opinion

It is clear that by virtue of DB's moderate learning disability there is a permanent impairment of functioning sufficient to satisfy the diagnostic test under the MCA (2005). The assessment demonstrated that she experiences difficulties with comprehension, with memory, with executive skills (which include decision-making and problem-solving) and with communication. DB was clear during the assessment interview that she had said "no" to the alleged perpetrator, but that "he talked me into it". The application of the Murphy and O'Callaghan (2004) criteria led to the following observations:

1 Basic sexual knowledge.

DB does have basic sexual knowledge. Whilst this is fairly superficial, it is likely that this has been achieved through the educational efforts of the social services over time, who provided one-to-one intervention around sex and relationships to DB in recent years. She will also have gained some knowledge through (alleged) inappropriate sexual behaviour with a sibling as a minor.

2 Knowledge of the consequences of sexual relations including sexually transmitted deceases and pregnancy.

DB has partial knowledge of sexual relations including STDs and pregnancy, but this knowledge is concrete and superficial with significant gaps, for example, "you can't get pregnant unless you have sex in bed".

3   An understanding of appropriate sexual behaviour in the context of this.

The assessment indicates that DB has a non-experiential understanding of appropriate sexual behaviour which would probably have been obtained during the educational interventions provided by the local authority. She is aware of the simple difference between "public" and "private" but occasionally got confused as to who she was able to have sex with and where. This is likely to reflect both her difficulty with understanding complex concepts such as the difference between public and private locations or public and private behaviours. Her moderate level of learning disability precludes her from grasping these distinctions at an abstract, conceptual level.

4   An understanding that sexual contact should always be a matter of choice.

DB does appear to have an understanding that sexual contact should always be matter of choice. However, her knowledge is non-experiential and when pressed through deeper questioning of more complex concepts around this issue she struggles to adapt her responses flexibly, suggesting that the complex concept of choice is one that is only partially grasped by her. In addition, her own account regarding the alleged offence is that she attempted to express a choice by saying "no" but that she was pressurised into a choice she did not wish to make.

5   The ability to recognise potentially abusive situations.

The SAK involves a set of clearly line drawn vignettes being presented with concrete examples of potentially abusive situations. As with all her other responses DB was able to give a superficial account of what she felt to be appropriate and what she understood to be wrong. DB is unlikely to be able to formulate how to respond behaviourally to the same in specific situations which require analysis of risk at an abstract level of consequential reasoning.

6   The ability to show skills of assertion in social and personal situations and to reject any unwanted advances at the given time.

Based on all of the assessment information reported above, within social and personal situations in which DB would be alone she is unlikely to be able to assert herself appropriately to any unwanted advances. By her own account in relation to the present allegations she was able to be "talked into it".

Legal commentary

In *IM v LM*[16] the Court of Appeal clarified that whereas the Court of Protection looks "forward" in considering the general capacity to give or to withhold consent to sexual relations, the focus of the criminal court is on the person-specific and time-and-place-specific occasion when that capacity is deployed, and consent has been either given or withheld. The issue of consent in the criminal context falls

16   [2014] EWCA Civ 37

to be evaluated with respect to that particular event. However, the fact that a person either does or does not consent to sexual activity with a particular person at a fixed point in time, or does or does not have capacity to give such consent, does not mean that it is impossible for a court assessing capacity to make a general evaluation which is not tied down to a particular time, partner and place (Sir Brian Leveson, P, at paragraph 76).

Conversely, even if a person has sufficient understanding of the information relevant to making a decision, she might nonetheless be unable to make an autonomous choice as to whether to agree to sexual touching. The issue arises in the criminal sphere under section 30(1) of the Sexual Offences 2003 Act, which provides that

(1) a person (A) commits an offence if—

(a) he intentionally touches another person (B),

(b) the touching is sexual,

(c) B is unable to refuse because of or for a reason related to a mental disorder, and

(d) A knows or could reasonably be expected to know that B has a mental disorder and that because of it or for a reason related to it B is likely to be unable to refuse.

(2) B is unable to refuse if –

(a) he lacks the capacity to choose whether to agree to the touching (whether because he lacks sufficient understanding of the nature or reasonably foreseeable consequences of what is being done, or for any other reason), or

(b) he is unable to communicate such a choice to A.

Whether or not DB has sufficient understanding of sexual relations and their consequences is not necessarily the critical issue when considering an offence has been committed under section 30. Even if she had sufficient understanding to make a decision, she might by reason of, say, an irrational fear or confusion of mind arising from her "mental disorder", have been unable to choose or to communicate her choice at the relevant time[17].

For the Court of Protection undertaking a general evaluation of a person's capacity to consent to sexual relations *in the future*, a "rudimentary" understanding of the ability to choose, the mechanics and consequences can suffice. However, where, as here, further probing in this area suggests that P is merely parroting the words "baby and diseases" rather than demonstrating even a basic understanding of possible consequences, the presumption of capacity would be likely to be rebutted.

17 R v C [2009] UKHL 42

Discussion/learning points

It is clear that in utilising the tools available to the clinician to assist the courts in assessing capacity to consent to sex, their scope often exceeds the specific requirements of the legal test. However, this cannot be considered a weakness of approach. The clinician often has more than one imperative when assessing a vulnerable adult in relation to their capacity to consent to sex. The obvious driver is to inform the court in relation to the specific information required as per statutory guidance. However, the clinician may also find it necessary to identify clear gaps in knowledge and experience the continued absence of which renders the adult vulnerable and, potentially, at risk of harm, thus indicating areas for intervention in terms of psychoeducation and skills training quite separate from the legal processes at play. Once the intervention is delivered, a further assessment may be warranted to see if the adult in question may now have gained an appropriate level of understanding. However, the difference between "knowing" and "doing" can be vast and merely delivering knowledge to the vulnerable adult may be insufficient to keep them safe whilst still maintaining an appropriate level of autonomy.

Case 3: DC

Presenting question/problem

This 30-year-old man has a history of learning disability, schizophrenia and drug misuse. Before being taken into care for his own protection, DC had been a male prostitute. His current care home manager expressed a genuine concern about his ability to understand the risks of unprotected sexual activity, in the context of DC engaging in risky sexual behaviours with other (vulnerable) residents. Local safeguarding services started a process of investigating his sexual vulnerability both as potential victim and potential perpetrator. As far as could be ascertained at the outset, DC had never engaged in heterosexual activity.

Background to the case

Clinical issues

DC has the diagnoses of learning disability and schizophrenia. DC is said to have no medical needs beyond his current mental health issues. He has not been tested for HIV or hepatitis although he does claim during interview that he has been diagnosed with HIV.

Family/social context

DC's parents separated when he was 6 years old and he was raised by his mother along with three siblings. When aged 8 he was taken into care and from age 9 onwards he began stealing from his mother. Schooling appeared difficult for DC, although this is reported to have been for behavioural reasons and he was moved to a school where his particular needs could be met. Following school, he was introduced by an older boy to the lifestyle of male prostitution and he worked in this regard for some time.

In the early 2000s DC served a 3-month prison sentence for robbery and has smoked cracked cocaine, although there is no recorded evidence of drug-taking since he was released from prison. DC moved to the local area in the mid 2000s and remains relatively settled. He is visited every six months by his social worker from his original area of residence.

Psychological/neuropsychological matters

DC is reported by staff at the supported living project to occasionally exhibit challenging behaviour and has difficulty controlling his anger at times. He also presents with symptoms of anxiety. He complies with his medication regime largely because he is prompted by staff to do so.

Assessment and rationale

Clinical objectives for the assessment included the following, which are all required to inform the assessment of an individual's capacity to consent to a sexual relationship:

- assessment of DC's level of cognitive function;
- assessment of DC's adaptive skills; and
- assessment of DC's sexual knowledge and attitudes.

A pre-prepared structured interview was administered to DC. The interview schedule covered topics such as:

- knowledge of the difference between public and private places;
- knowledge of possible consequences of sexual activity (eg: health risks, pregnancy);
- knowledge of who one can and cannot have sex with and when;
- knowledge of the concept of non-consensual sex;
- knowledge of risks associated with sexual activity with strangers;
- knowledge of sexual differences and sexual health.

Results of this interview with DC indicated that he has some basic knowledge of sexual matters. For example, he is aware that a condom should be used in sex and can prevent pregnancy and that condoms can be bought in a shop. He also appears aware of the contraceptive pill and was able to confirm that this "stops ladies getting pregnant".

Records indicate that DC has frequently claimed that he has been raped (and there is evidence indicating that he probably has been raped in the past by a male), he was unable to explain the concept of rape other than to confirm his understanding that "it's horrible". He was similarly unclear about either mastur-bation or homosexuality, seeing them both as "bad". He had no independent understanding which was consistent with the ideas of public and private in terms of where it is appropriate and acceptable to have sexual relations.

Generally, DC had a superficial grasp of the concepts of good and bad within his knowledge of sexual matters, but no consistent clear framework for under-standing deeper issues or consequences around sexual behaviour. The Sexual Attitudes and Knowledge assessment (SAK) was administered and the results indicate that he has significant gaps both in terms of understanding relationships and interacting with others and in the areas of sexual awareness and assertiveness in relationships. This gives a clear indication as to where further educational work is required in order to promote DC's choice to be sexually independent.

The WASI is a standardised brief measure of an individual's level of cognitive functioning. It was administered to DC. Unfortunately, it was not possible to derive a reliable IQ score due to DC's poor effort and reduced motivation during test participation. However, qualitative observations of his performance during the overall assessment noted that DC experiences:

- poor reasoning ability;
- concrete thinking;
- impaired problem-solving skills; and
- impoverished verbal abilities.

Overall, the clinical *impression* is that DC is most likely functioning at a level of mild learning disabilities. This would support his longstanding diagnosis.

The ABAS II provides a comprehensive, norm-referenced assessment of adaptive skills for individuals. It can be used to document an individual's strengths and limitations across a broad range of adaptive skills. It was admin-istered to the manager at DC's residence who was present for the assessment. The results of the ABAS II indicate that DC is generally functioning at the extremely low level of adaptive behaviour skills when compared to the general population. This is consistent with an individual with a learning disability. One particular area of *relative* strength for DC is that relating to self-care although it should be stated that his score here is still more than two standard devia-tions below the mean and is therefore considered to be extremely low for the general population. This particular domain refers to the skills needed for per-sonal care including eating, dressing, bathing, grooming, toileting and hygiene. It is understood from interview with the home's manager that although DC possesses skills in this regard, he consistently lacks the ability to apply them without prompting by support staff.

Observations

DC was able to maintain an appropriate level of eye contact although certain of his social behaviours were overly familiar. He appeared significantly demotivated and required significant prompting and a break after a brief period of questioning in order to motivate him to return to complete the assessment. This is consistent with documented evidence which describes DC's consistently lacking motivation.

Opinion

In evaluating capacity to consent to sexual relationships, six key areas were assessed during the present assessment and an opinion is given in relation to these below.

1   Basic sexual knowledge. DC is assessed as having very basic sexual knowledge in terms of body parts, sexual relations and sexual acts. However, gaps were identified in this knowledge in relation particularly to homosexual relationships and masturbation.
2   With specific regard to DC's knowledge of the consequences of sexual relations, he appeared to have no knowledge of sexually transmitted diseases, although he had heard of AIDS but was unable to describe what this was. He believed that he was HIV+ but there was no documentary evidence to support this. DC confirmed that he had very rudimentary knowledge in relation to pregnancy, although this was not tested in detail as frequently during the assessment, he appeared to want the questioning to end.
3   Questioning relating to DC's understanding of appropriate sexual behaviour and the context for this suggests that there are significant gaps in his knowledge. It took significant prompting and suggestion in order to obtain satisfactory answers as to the difference between public and private places in relation to the appropriateness of sexual behaviours.
4   DC appeared to have a very basic understanding that sexual contact should always be a matter of choice, although it is not clear that he would adhere to this knowledge if put under pressure as staff indicate that he can be vulnerable to suggestion.
5   It is not clear from the present assessment that DC has the ability to recognise potentially abusive situations, or the knowledge of what to do in such situations in order to extricate himself. He had been raped in the past and this raises the concern that he may place himself in risky situations where it may not be possible to maintain his own safety.
6   In terms of DC's ability to show skills of assertion in social and personal situations and to thereby reject any unwanted advances at the given time, there is no evidence to suggest that he is sufficiently protected in that regard through use of his personal resources, without support.

It was noted from the assessment that DC is only able to use a concrete level of reasoning, appears unable to generate ideas to solve problems and has impoverished communication abilities. It is clear from DC's answers to the Sexual Attitudes and Knowledge (SAK) questionnaire, that his knowledge is patchy at best. This represents an area of significant development needs for DC.

The MCA (2005) defines capacity as when an adult can only be considered incapable of making a particular decision if he or she has an impairment of or disturbance in and functioning of the mind or brain (whether permanent or temporary) *and* he or she is unable to understand, retain, weigh up information and communicate a decision. It can be seen when applying this two-stage test of mental capacity to DC that his scores on the psychometry and interview reported above confirm that he does have an impairment of, and disturbance in, the functioning of mind or brain and that this is permanent. The cognitive assessment reports that he is functioning at a level where he has only partial understanding of information, is unlikely to retain all that information, may only be able to perform limited mental operations on that information and see the consequences of it and may have questionable communication abilities in that regard. From the assessment above, therefore, it is interpreted that within the confines of the MCA (2005), DC does not presently enjoy the capacity to make decisions around sexual activity and behaviours.

Legal commentary

The court would need to be satisfied before determining whether or not DC had capacity to consent to sexual relations that all practicable steps to help him to do so had been taken without success, i.e. has there been appropriate intervention in the form of a programme of sex education targeted in accordance with his cognitive abilities and learning needs? As with DA, it is also relevant to note here that there is some suggestion in the case-law, albeit obiter, that pregnancy need not be considered where P is gay although the point has not yet had to be decided (see *London Borough of Southwark v KA*:[18]

> I take the view that KA, a young man, needs to have an understanding, if not a sophisticated one, that pregnancy is a foreseeable consequence of heterosexual relations. It is beyond the scope of this judgment to decide whether pregnancy is a foreseeable consequence, and therefore needs to be understood, by other individuals, for instance by reason of sexual orientation, age, or particular physical characteristics.

Discussion

Like all other competencies, relationship and sexuality skills are developed through a learning process that takes place over one's lifetime. It is important to get a balance of what people with learning disabilities might want out of personal relationships with others. Starting sexuality and relationship education early builds up appropriate skills before problems can occur, such as having to deal with unwanted

18 [2016] EWCOP 20 at para. 63

sexual attentions from others, as it involves the acquisition of skills and strategies that allow the individual to assert their rights and freedoms safely. Individuals with a learning disability often have limited social experiences which can result from living within a care environment. Typically, care environments for people with learning disabilities are protective rather than facilitative. This can be beneficial in terms of protecting an individual who has been sexually exploited or is at risk of being so but can also appear overly-paternalistic if not applied sensitively.

Case 4: DD

Presenting question/problem

This is a case of a 40-year-old lady, DD, with learning disability and a history of having been sexually abused as a young adult when living in a previous (supported) residential home. The Police sought a further assessment of her ability to consent to a sexual relationship and of her level of vulnerability to a person in a position of responsibility over her as allegations of further abuse (with her as victim) had been made in relation to her current care home manager where, paradoxically, she had been removed for her safety.

Background to the case

Clinical issues

It had been ascertained from medical records that DD was mildly hydrocephalic during her development period and that the label of "mental retardation" had been applied as well as that of "educational difficulties". There was a diagnosis of epilepsy at age 15 and at the time an EEG a recording had been abnormal. She had attended special schooling throughout her formal developmental period.

Family/social context

According to the documents provided DD was, between the mid-1990s and late 2000s, a victim of systematic sexual abuse at the care home where she was placed by a remote local authority on the basis that she had previously been sexually abused in her area of origin, in a similar setting. The defendant is the registered manager (and co-owner, along with his wife) of the current care home which is a residential unit for vulnerable adults with learning disabilities and mental health issues.

Psychological/neuropsychological matters

During the second of the two assessments, DD was interviewed about her sexual knowledge. She asked if there might be any counsellors she could go to talk to as she feels she has not had the opportunity to talk about what happened to her. She feels that she is unable to visit her GP to ask for advice in this regard as she is concerned about confidentiality and is under the impression that the GP would inform the owners of the care home.

Assessment and rationale

For the first of the two assessments, DD was accompanied throughout by a female police officer of the Public Protection Unit at the local police station. For the second of the assessments, the same police officer delivered DD for the interview and returned at the close of the interview to engage in discussion. This was to allow DD to speak freely and confidentially in the interview.

Initially, DD was very reluctant to engage in the assessment or even respond verbally to questions. She asked for a pen and paper and wrote answers down, initially, but did begin conversation and eye contact as she felt able to trust the process. During the first of the two assessments, eye contact was relatively poor. By the second assessment DD was more comfortable even though the subject matter was more intrusive and distressing for her. She was able to speak freely, to volunteer information verbally and to maintain good eye contact.

DD described a wish to go back to college and is upset that this has also been disrupted by being removed from the residential placement. Generally, DD describes herself as feeling "fed up" and she was tearful throughout the second half of the assessment. She wants to talk about what happened to her in relation to the alleged sexual abuse but becomes upset whilst doing so. She reports that she has no difficulty remembering what happened, but that she tries to forget it because it is so distressing. DD feels as though she has lost out as she is now cut off from her former home and the people she knew who worked and lived there. She confirmed that some former staff had promised to be in contact with her and have not been able to do so and she is seeking further contact with one of the residents who is wheelchair bound and would need transport and assistance to visit DD in her current (interim) residence.

In terms of outlook, DD doesn't feel that things are going to get any better for her and she reports feeling let down by support services, feeling that "nobody cares". She no longer wishes to stay where she is presently living but is concerned that the present charges will not go ahead against the alleged perpetrator and feels "very down" about that.

To respond to the framework suggested by Murphy and O'Callaghan (2004), a structured clinical interview was developed. This was administered to DD at the second assessment appointment. Her responses indicate that DD is aware that she can say "no" if she does not want to do something but considers that on the occasions relating to the allegations in question, she was too frightened to say so. She is aware that sex can lead to babies and that you are not supposed to have sex in cars but that it is ok to do so in bedrooms. She considered that people have sex in order to keep the relationship going and that individuals may continue to do this even when they don't want to. In terms of sexually transmitted diseases, she was able to name AIDS but was unable to respond to further questioning in regard of checking out her understanding of the same. She was able to identify three types of contraception, although she felt that the pictures of contraceptive methods and devices shown to her were related to periods and were not necessary to prevent pregnancy.

DD was aware that contraception is available either from her doctor or from a health clinic but became uncomfortable when asked to define the word "rape" and declined to answer further. When asked whether or not it was ok to have sex with someone who is not sure or who wishes to say "no", she said that she recognised this was not acceptable but that it can occur whether or not somebody says "no". Her actual words were "no but they still do with me".

The Sexual Attitudes and Knowledge Assessment (SAK) was administered to DD. The results indicated that there are significant gaps in DD's knowledge. She scored relatively highly on the assertiveness questions of this measure, yet when these matters were interrogated more deeply during the structural clinical interview reported above, it is clear that although DD is aware that she is able to say no, in relation to the allegations specifically made against the alleged perpetrator, her opinion is that she felt unable to say no out of fear. There is a clear discrepancy between her body of knowledge and her ability to apply the same, sometimes referred to as a dissociation between "knowing" and "doing" (Teuber, 1964) noted as a particular feature associated with compromised cognitive function.

The WASI was administered as a standardised psychometric assessment of level of cognitive functioning. DD's results place her level of functioning in the IQ range of 54 to 62. This places her in the bottom 99.8 per cent of the population. This corroborates what has been gleaned from her medical records in terms of her developmental difficulties which have remained throughout. Her true level of cognitive function may be somewhat below this as on the administration of the tests, DD required *significant* prompting and may have been inadvertently assisted to achieve a higher than expected score in that regard in order to maintain her participation in the process.

This level of cognitive functioning places DD in the category of "moderate learning disabilities". It can be said that DD has a disability or disorder of the mind or brain, which is permanent and which results in an impairment or disturbance of mental functioning.

In order to assess DD's level of suggestibility and her ability to apply consequential reasoning to situations, the Gudjonsson Suggestibility Scale (Form 1) and the British Ability Scales (BAS) Social Reasoning sub-test were administered.

The Gudjonsson scales were developed specifically to measure the vulnerabilities or proneness of people to give erroneous accounts when interviewed. DD's results on this assessment indicate that she is experiencing particular difficulty with recall of verbally presented information and when pressed to recall this (as per test instruction) is inserting some distortion and fabrication (collectively considered as confabulation) in order to replace gaps in memory. Her scores are in line with the norms drawn from a non-forensic population with intellectual disabilities.

This indicates that DD would be vulnerable to suggestion at interview. This applies to both police and clinical interviews but could also be considered in the context of those with a significant interest in the outcome of this case being able to persuade her of a given recollection of facts which favours the defendant.

DD's abilities lie between the two lowest levels of reasoning that the test is able to measure. DD's level of consequential reasoning lies between her being only able to grasp one side of a problem to focusing on the punishment or reward in the context of a specific problem situation. She is unable to extrapolate from experience and apply abstract concepts more broadly.

Observations during assessment

During the assessments reported above it was noted that DD attempted to formulate and implement strategies throughout the psychometric aspects of the assessment but often failed to apply these successfully without assistance. When she found a task difficult, she would withdraw verbally and place her hand over her eyes or face until the subject or task was changed, thus indicating her refusal or inability to participate in the task or discussion in hand. As the assessment progressed this was also interpreted as her being uncomfortable with the subject matter in hand and a degree of sensitivity was fostered in order to adapt for her.

Opinion

As reported above in the assessment section, Murphy and O'Callaghan (2004) indicated that the following criteria ought to be considered in order to develop a clinical opinion that an individual has the capacity to consent to sexual relationships:

1   Basic sexual knowledge.
    It is clear that DD does have a basic sexual knowledge in terms of body parts, sexual relations and sexual acts.
2   Knowledge of the consequences of sexual relations including sexually transmitted diseases and pregnancy.
    It is clear from the assessment reported here that DD has *incomplete* knowledge of the consequences of sexual relations.
3   An understanding of appropriate sexual behaviour and the context for this.
    It is clear from the assessment reported here both from the psychometry, the structured clinical interview and the observations undertaken, that DD does have an understanding of appropriate sexual behaviour and the context for this.
4   An understanding that sexual contact should always be a matter of choice.
    It is clear that DD understands that sexual contact should be a matter of choice but by her own account in relation to herself, felt unable to apply that theoretical choice as she was overcome by fear of the consequences of saying no.
5   The ability to recognise potentially abusive situations.
    It is clear from the responses to the assessments administered to DD that she does have limited ability to recognise potentially abusive situations and has a partial (theoretical) knowledge of how she would behave during the same. In practice, she reports that fear would prevent her from acting according to her wishes.

6   The ability to show skills of assertion in social and personal situations and to thereby reject any unwanted advances at the given time.

DD has a partial theoretical knowledge of how to assert herself in sexual situations in terms of unwanted advances but has made it clear that she felt unable to do so in relation to the alleged sexual abuse by the alledged perpetrator, through fear.

DD's own personal account is that she was not consensual in the context of the allegations against the alleged perpetrator and that within the context of the Sexual Offences Act (2003) she was not in a position to give that consent.

Recommendations

Given the current context of significant losses to DD, which have been the unfortunate sequelae to the allegations against the perpetrator, it is clear that she has needs which are not presently being met. She has effectively lost her home, friendship with her fellow residents and contact with those members of staff at her former home with whom she felt comfortable. Where she is presently accommodated, she is unable to access her college, a regular activity she enjoyed. DD herself has verbalised the need that she has yet to receive targeted psychological counselling in relation to the actions against her detailed in the present allegations. Her current needs are not being met and there are duty of care issues here which need to be considered carefully.

DD has a social worker in the local authority in the area she previously resided. However, DD should be provided services from a *local* learning disability service where she can access the full range of support services in order to assist her to deal with the distress she is experiencing in relation to the (alleged) sexual abuse. She should be able to access clinical psychology for psychological assistance and distress and in relation to the alleged sexual offences against her. She should be able to access appropriate nursing and medical care and support within the same team. She should also be able to access a local key worker (care co-ordinator) and social worker in order to assist with issues such as accommodation, living support, attendance at college and review of benefits.

Legal commentary

As discussed following case DB (above), in *IM v LM*[19] the Court of Appeal clarified that whereas the Court of Protection looks "forward" in considering the general capacity to give or to withhold consent to sexual relations, the focus of the criminal court is on the person-specific and time-and-place-specific occasion when that capacity is deployed, and consent has been either given or withheld. The issue of consent in the criminal context falls to be evaluated

19   [2014] EWCA Civ 37

with respect to that particular event. However, the fact that a person either does or does not consent to sexual activity with a particular person at a fixed point in time, or does not have capacity to give such consent, does not mean that it is impossible for a court assessing capacity to make a general evaluation which is not tied down to a particular time, partner and place (Sir Brian Leveson, P, at paragraph 76).

Discussion/learning points

A difficult professional dilemma emerged during the present assessment. In order to assess DD fully in the context of the criminal allegations made by her, the interview had, by definition, to be comprehensive and thorough, exploring difficult areas for DD and pursuing particular lines of questioning. However, this meant requiring DD to open up and discuss matters of a distressing nature from her immediate and distant past and to explore her losses in the context of the allegations. This had to be carried out in the full knowledge that no therapeutic work could be provided to assist her to address the painful recollections, despite her specifically requesting "counselling". The most that could be provided was strongly worded recommendations that clinical psychology services, within the local learning disability team, ought to be provided to DD as a matter of urgency to prevent her feeling "punished" for disclosing the (alleged) abuse.

Case 5: DE

Presenting question/problem

This is a case of a 35-year-old gentleman who had experienced a severe brain injury several years earlier as a result of an accident. Since his head injury, he had married impulsively, against the advice of family and legal support and the union was annulled after a few days. The annulment was argued on the basis that he had been coerced to marry on the grounds that his "wife" was pregnant and if he did not marry her, she would prevent him ever having contact with his child. It emerged immediately after the wedding that his new wife was not, in fact, pregnant and an immediate annulment was sought.

He had since settled down into a long-term relationship and expressed a wish to marry again. His lawyer requested an assessment of his capacity to marry, in the light of his finances being protected by a Court Appointed Deputy.

Background to the case

Clinical issues

At the time of the original brain injury, DE's GCS was 4/15. His initial brain imaging on admission had shown blood in each occipital horn as well as several areas of intraparenchymal haemorrhage. His intracranial pressure was monitored by neurosurgeons using an ICP bolt and he was managed conservatively. He was later diagnosed with diffuse axonal injury, which is indicative of widespread, permanent brain damage. DE also presented with post-traumatic epilepsy for which he remains medicated, although his seizures are relatively well-controlled.

Family/social context

DE had married his first wife under pressure and from the false belief that she was pregnant with their child. He was told by his partner that if he did not marry her, she would prevent him having contact with their child, when born. DE describes their relationship as "based on sex" and was aware that he "did not love her" at the time but felt pressurised into marrying her.

DE is well-supported by his mother and sisters. They are a family with strong mutual bonds. DE's current partner has lived with him for several years. She is fully aware of his difficulties following his brain injury and works with him and his family to support him as needed.

Psychological/neuropsychological matters

DE had been assessed by neuropsychologists several years previously as part of his personal injury claim and the data were a matter of record. There are significant neuropsychological legacies to the injury, notably in terms of dysexecutive functioning, which are central to present considerations. However, it was considered essential to re-assess his functioning across a range of domains in order to obtain a more up-to-date view of his abilities and challenges as well as directly assessing his level of insight into the issues surrounding the proposed marriage.

Assessment and rationale

DE's general cognitive function was assessed in order to establish his level of understanding, reasoning and ability to make decisions. Similarly, problem-solving tests were selected on the basis of measuring DE's ability to weigh up information and select and implement solutions from a range of possibilities. Finally, it was considered critical to assess DE's memory function in order to obtain an understanding of his ability to take on board new information as part of the decision-making process under assessment.

Results indicated that DE was functioning in the low average range of general cognitive functioning, which places him at around the 25th to 50th centiles. This means that he is functioning in the third quartile of the general population. He also performed at this level on the problem-solving tasks which were presented to him (Problem-Solving sub-test of the Kaplan Baycrest Neuropsychological Assessment battery; Key Search sub-test of the Behavioural Assessment of Dysexecutive Syndrome battery). His scores indicated that he retained an ability to solve everyday problems but that he would do better with prompting, for example, to wider considerations and alternative possibilities.

In terms of memory function, DE was assessed by means of the BIRT Information and Processing Battery (BMIPB) Story Recall, Figure Recall and List Learning sub-tests. He clearly struggled to take new information on board, whether presented verbally or visually to him. On average, he performed at lower than the bottom 2 per cent of the general population. His strongest skill was remembering visually presented information but even this was no better than the lowest ten per cent of the population. Clearly, this level of memory ability has implications for decision-making.

DE was also interviewed in respect of his decision to marry his partner. He reported that he had learned much from the experience of his first marriage. He reports that he has learned how not to be "walked over" and that his "opinion does count". He understands that being married means being together, doing things together but also having time apart to see one's own friends.

He understands that marriage can mean having children but is also aware that his fiancée is now past child-bearing age. DE has two sisters who each have children and he enjoys spending time with his nephews and nieces. His fiancée has two adult children with whom DE has regular, positive, contact.

When asked for potential reasons why he might not marry, DE commented that his fiancée is "always right" and that this might get worse when they are married but this was said with humour which indicated that this is not a significant barrier. He also indicated that he believes that it is "normal" for couples to argue and he confirmed that he and his fiancée will argue approximately once a month. He tends to end arguments by offering to make his partner a cup of tea, drawing a line under whatever the disagreement was about. He feels that this works well and contributes to their, relatively, quiet life together.

When asked about the difference between marriage and co-habitation, DE was of the view that he wanted to marry his fiancée so that he could have a "wife" and be able to call her "Mrs DE". He is of the view that marriage brings a closeness that co-habitation does not.

DE is keen to point out that this relationship is quite different from that he enjoyed with his former wife. He reports that, "I never loved my first wife the way that I love my fiancée".

DE accepts the possibility that he may be easily influenced but is similarly of the view that if he knows what he wants he will, "stick to his guns".

When asked about the different roles and responsibilities that are inherent within a marriage, DE clarified that he takes responsibility for the garden, some hoovering and cooking whereas his fiancée takes care of the remainder of the cleaning, cooking and washing. His expectations of the marriage include that he has, "someone to call mine, my wife" and admits that he experiences feelings of jealousy if he sees his fiancée talking to another man.

DE was asked about his current level of decision-making. He reports that he does not choose his own clothes as he has been made aware that he rarely chooses clothing appropriate to the weather or situation. However, he does choose his meals and mealtimes. He also chooses which football team to support and confirmed that he attends "home" matches frequently.

Opinion

Within the context of the MCA (2005), it is clear that DE meets the conditions for the Stage One test, in that he has impairment of his brain in the context of the material decision as to whether or not to marry.

With respect to Stage Two:

- There is evidence that DE is able to *comprehend and understand* the key requirements, roles and responsibilities for marriage and the reciprocal obligations for both parties. DE indicates a clear understanding of the roles, responsibilities and reciprocal obligations which is coupled with wisdom from previous experience. He has approached this (proposed) marriage more cautiously and with a considered view, having taken the time to ensure, through cohabitation, that the decision to marry is right for him at this time.
- With regard to *memory*, at the present time, although DE has been demonstrated to display marked memory deficits, he does have a good recollection of the requirements of a matrimonial partner and also of his previous negative experiences of marriage which he is keen not to repeat.
- Current assessment results indicate a degree of flexibility in thinking which, when optimised, would certainly enable and empower him to make a capacitous decision regarding matrimony. He has the ability to spontaneously consider the range of options and alternatives to marriage, albeit in concrete terms.
- DE's *communication* skills are impaired by dysarthria yet he is able to make his views known.

In considering all of the information available, it is my opinion that, on balance of probabilities, he does retain sufficient decision-making capacity to do so. This opinion is drawn up in the context of consistent cognitive incapacities over time since the index accident and injury. However, DE has been able to reflect and consider his present circumstances in a way that he did not appear to do at the time of his first marriage. He is able to apply the benefit of experience and form a clear view as to his wishes should the proposed marriage fail.

Legal commentary

It is agreed that the presumption of capacity will not be rebutted in this case. The commentary on the legal test for capacity to marry is set out at the beginning of the chapter.

Discussion/learning points

The key learning point here is about not setting the bar higher for a person with a brain injury than it would be set for non-injured member of the population. The emphasis is on achieving a balance between protecting a vulnerable adult whilst not preventing them from enjoying the mutual benefits of a positive, reciprocal relationship that marriage can provide.

References

Murphy, G. H. & O'Callaghan, A. (2004). Capacity of adults with intellectual disabilities to consent to sexual relationships. *Psychological Medicine, 34*(7), 1347–1357.

Teuber, H. L. (1964). The riddle of the frontal lobe function in man. In J. M. Warren & K. Akert (Eds.), *The frontal granular cortex and behaviour* (pp. 410–458). New York: McGraw-Hill.

World Health Organisation. (1992). *The ICD-10 Classification of mental and behavioural disorders: Clinical descriptions and diagnostic guidelines*. Geneva: World Health Organisation.

8   Capacity to make a lifetime gift

Dr Tracey Ryan-Morgan

With Alex Troup

This chapter focuses on the capacity to make a lifetime gift (otherwise known as an *inter vivos* gift). Testamentary gifts have already been considered in Chapter 6 above. There is a third category of gift, known as a *donatio mortis causa* (or death-bed gift), which refers to a gift made in contemplation of death, but these are not addressed in this Chapter.[1]

The *Re Beaney* test

The common law test for capacity to make a lifetime gift is set out in *Re Beaney*.[2] The Judge indicated that "the question is whether the person making it was capable of understanding the effect of the deed when its general purport has been fully explained to him." It follows that the test is one of *ability* to understand, rather than actual understanding; and that the nature and extent of any explanation given to the donor forms a crucial part of the test.

As regards the degree of understanding required, the Judge explained that:

> The degree or extent of understanding required in respect of any instrument is relative to the particular transaction which it is to effect. In the case of a will the degree required is always high. In the case of a contract, a deed made for consideration or a gift inter vivos, whether by deed or otherwise, the degree required varies with the circumstances of the transaction. This, at one extreme, if the subject matter and value of a gift are trivial in relation to the donor's assets a low degree of understanding will suffice. But, at the other extreme, if its effect is to dispose of the donor's only asset of value and thus, for practical purposes, to pre-empt the devolution of his estate under his will or his intestacy, then the degree of understanding required is as high as that required for a will, and the donor must understand the claims of all potential donees and the extent of the property disposed of.

---

1 For the requirements which need to be satisfied in order to make a valid *donatio mortis causa*, see *King v. Chiltern Dog Rescue* [2016] Ch 221
2 [1987] 1 WLR 770

If the donor makes a series of gifts over a relatively short period of time, then the *Re Beaney* test should be applied to the course of conduct as a whole, rather than to the individual gifts.[3] Otherwise one would end up with the absurd situation that the test for capacity to make the last gift would be higher than that for the first, since the donor's assets would by then be reduced by the value of the earlier gifts.

The burden of proof lies on the person alleging incapacity, although if that person can establish a *prima facie* case that the donor lacked incapacity then the burden will shift to the defendant to prove otherwise.[4]

As with testamentary gifts,[5] there is an ongoing debate over whether the common law test set out in *Re Beaney* has been replaced by the statutory test set out in the MCA (2005). In *Kicks v. Leigh*[6] it was held that the *Re Beaney* test is still the correct test to apply. However, this is only a first instance decision and Court of Appeal guidance is required on this issue.

Again, as with testamentary gifts,[7] it has been held that the rule in *Parker v. Felgate* applies to lifetime gifts *mutatis mutandis*. This can be useful where a donor's capacity significantly deteriorates between giving instructions for a gift and the making of the gift. In such circumstances the donor will still have capacity if he satisfied the *Re Beaney* test when giving instructions, provided that (a) the gift, when made, accords with his instructions and (b) at the time of the gift the donor is capable of understanding, and does understand, that he is making a gift for which he has given instructions.

If it is found that a purported gift is made at a time when the donor lacked capacity, there is an unresolved legal debate over whether the gift is void or voidable.[8] The distinction can be important in practice since if the purported gift is voidable, rather than void, then a defendant seeking to uphold the gift can rely upon equitable defences such as delay and acquiescence; and further the gift may be affirmed if the donor regains capacity.

Attorneys and deputies

Where a person lacks capacity to make a gift, an attorney under a Lasting Power of Attorney (LPA)[9] or a deputy appointed by the Court of Protection may make gifts on their behalf, albeit that their powers to do so are strictly limited. If the attorney or deputy wishes to make a more extensive gift which falls outside their limited powers, then they should apply to the Court of Protection for authority to do so.

3 See *Gorjat v. Gorjat* [2010] EWHC 1537 (Ch); 13 ITELR 312, at para 136
4 See *Williams v. Williams* [2003] WTLR 1371, 1383
5 See Chapter 6, above
6 [2015] 4 All ER 329
7 See Chapter 6, above
8 See *Sutton v. Sutton* [2009] EWHC 2576 where the point was left undecided
9 The same also applies to attorneys acting under Enduring Powers of Attorney (EPA). As from 1 October 2007 it has not been possible to create a new EPA, although existing EPAs remain valid. See s.66 of, and Sch.4 to, the MCA (2005)

As regards an attorney under an LPA, their limited power to make gifts is set out in section 12 of the MCA (2005) as follows:[10]

(1) Where a lasting power of attorney confers authority to make decisions about P's property and affairs, it does not authorise a donee (or, if more than one, any of them) to dispose of the donor's property by making gifts except to the extent permitted by subsection (2).
(2) The donee may make gifts

  (a) on customary occasions to persons (including himself) who are related to or connected with the donor, or
  (b) to any charity to whom the donor made or might have been expected to make gifts, If the value of each such gift is not unreasonable having regard to all the circumstances and, in particular, the size of the donor's estate.

(3) "Customary occasion" means

  (a) the occasion or anniversary of a birth, a marriage or the formation of a civil partnership, or
  (b) any other occasion on which presents are customarily given within families or among friends or associates.

Further guidance is found in the Code of Practice which accompanies the MCA (2005) at paragraphs 7.40 to 7.42 (pp.126–127). This emphasises the need to take into account the size of the donor's estate, so that, for example, it would not be reasonable to buy expensive Christmas gifts if the donor was living on modest means and had to do without essential items in order to pay for them. The attorney must also take into account any other limitations or restrictions specified in the LPA itself, as well as the donor's own wishes and feelings to decide whether the proposed gift would be in the donor's best interests.

As regards deputies, they have no statutory power to make gifts at all. Instead, their power to make gifts will be set out in the order of the Court of Protection appointing them as deputy, and such orders routinely include gift making powers in identical terms to section 12, above.

Case 1: EA

Presenting question/problem

This is a case of a 75-year-old lady with a medical history of serial strokes who had, in effect, given away her home to a distant relative (without considering the reasonable entitlement of closer family) whilst still living in her house.

---

10 The equivalent (but not identical) power of an attorney under an EPA to make gifts is set out in para 3(3) of Sch.4 to the MCA (2005)

The result was that she (effectively) became homeless. An assessment was requested of her ability to enter into such an arrangement, given her health problems and the resulting consequences of her actions.

Background to the case

Clinical issues

EA has a lifelong learning disability. She has a social worker and was looked after by her mother in the family home. EA's mother frequently expressed concerns to their GP about how EA would cope when she passed away and what provision could be made for her. There are numerous entries in the medical notes of EA suffering from depression and stress to the point where she felt she could not cope. The relationship with her mother was somewhat strained.

Family/social context

EA's mother had signed the house over to EA *inter vivos* to ensure that her daughter would be provided for after her death. However, a week before the mother's death, EA moved out of the family home and signed the house over to her widowed sister-in-law. She signed a deed of gift which had been drawn up by a solicitor who did not know her or her family circumstances. The gift, effectively, left EA without a home of her own. EA is married, and her husband is still living in co-habitation with her. She was married at the time of the deed of gift.

Psychological/neuropsychological matters

EA had voluminous social work records which document, consistently, and over a lengthy period of time, her inability to understand, use or manage money. She had no concept of amounts of money in terms of income, what money must be used for (to discharge bills) or how much things cost.

Assessment and rationale

The concern was expressed at the outcome that EA had entered into the deed of gift without any real understanding of the nature of the transaction, its consequences or who else may have moral claim to the property upon her death.

Several years after the transaction, a detailed psychological assessment was proposed to formally, and objectively, assess EA's capabilities. She struggled to co-operate, not because she was oppositional in behaviour but because she experienced difficulty processing and responding to task, and test, instructions from the outset. She was only able to complete four out of 14 proposed tests selected to allow a robust assessment of her general cognitive functioning. The results of the four completed tests were brought into question in terms of their validity due to her compromised receptive language skills.

At the time of this assessment, there was no evidence of formal mood disorder or cognitive decline due to an underlying degenerative process. There was no significant medication which could have affected EA's performance and no significant health issues which might have compromised her ability to fully participate in the assessment. The conclusion was drawn that her clinical presentation was consistent with that noted in historical medical records. EA has a lifelong learning disability.

Opinion/outcome

A diagnosis of learning disability, based on the World Health Organisation (1992) definition on the basis of global developmental delay and a deficit in adaptive behaviours before the age of 18 years, requires that in order to meet the first criteria for learning disability, a person's IQ should be at 70 or below (Department of Health, 2001).

The average IQ for the general population is 100. Standard units of measurement away from this average are expressed in the form of a "standard deviation". It is accepted, when discussing general cognitive function, that a standard deviation is equivalent to 15 and that two or more standard deviations away from the average (i.e., 100) is considered to be "abnormal". Therefore, the maximum IQ that a person can have and still be eligible for the diagnosis of learning disability is 70. An IQ of 70 is equivalent to functioning in the bottom 2 per cent of the general population.

There is no record that has been made available for the purpose of this report to indicate that EA has undergone cognitive testing at any time since 1964. However, Community Learning Disability Teams, which comprise specialist nurses and social workers typically have widely accepted eligibility criteria which make explicit reference to IQ as the first criteria. It is unlikely that EA will have been given social work support from within the local authority if she did not meet this eligibility criterion.

An IQ of 70 or below is, in my view, incompatible with the complex cognitive skills required to formulate the decision to "give away" one's home. Individuals with a learning disability typically have impoverished skills of consequential reasoning. There is no reason to consider that EA was atypical in that regard.

There is no evidence in the current bundle that the solicitor ensured that EA was capable of understanding the gift or its implications, as referred to in the *Re Beaney* test. For example, it would be expected that the potential consequences to herself and significant others would have been explored. Similarly, it would be expected that a range of perspectives would have been generated in order to ensure understanding of the implications as well as recollection of information previously given in relation to the assignment. None of this is present in the attendance note and it is assumed that, therefore, this was not done.

It is, therefore, my view, on the balance on probabilities, that EA did not have the capacity to enter into a deed of gift at the material time.

Legal commentary

At the outset, it may be said that it was unfortunate that EA's mother decided to give her the family home outright, rather than creating some kind of trust to allow a suitable third party to manage the property as trustee and to protect EA from her own folly.

On the face of it, the fact that EA gave away her property, without any obvious explanation, at a time when she was suffering from a learning disability, and apparently without proper advice from her solicitor, does strongly suggest a lack of capacity. In those circumstances the burden of proof would probably shift to the sister-in-law to prove capacity.

Nevertheless, in order to reach a final view on EA's capacity to enter into the deed of gift, it would be necessary to investigate:

(1) the nature and extent of EA's other assets, in order to determine the degree of understanding required in order for EA to make a valid gift of the property in accordance with the *Re Beaney* test;
(2) the precise terms of the deed of gift, including in particular whether it imposed any obligations on the sister-in-law to allow EA (and her husband) to remain living in the property and if so upon what terms; and
(3) what (if any) moral claims the other family members had upon the property;
(4) what evidence could be given by others, including in particular the solicitor and EA's husband.

There may be other causes of action to consider. One obvious possibility is a claim to challenge the gift on the ground of undue influence. Whilst there is no evidence of actual undue influence, a presumption of undue influence would arise if (a) there was a relationship of trust and confidence between EA and the sister-in-law, and (b) the gift called for an explanation.[11] If such a presumption did arise, then the burden would lie on the sister-in-law to rebut it by showing that EA entered into the transaction of her own free will.

Another possibility is a professional negligence claim against the solicitor. It is arguable that, by analogy with the so-called Golden Rule which applies in cases of testamentary capacity,[12] the solicitor in the present case should have obtained medical evidence before proceeding with the gift. However, the case of *Thorpe v. Fellowes Solicitors LLP*[13] serves as a salutary warning. In that case the defendant solicitors were sued, unsuccessfully, for allowing their client to sell her property when she suffered from dementia. The Judge held that a solicitor is only required to make inquiries about a client's capacity to enter into a transaction if there are circumstances such as to raise doubt, and went on to say that "there is plainly

11 See *Royal Bank of Scotland v. Etridge (No.2)* [2002] 2 AC 732
12 See Chapter 6, above
13 [2011] PNLR 13

no duty upon solicitors in general to obtain medical evidence on every occasion when they are instructed by an elderly client just in case they lack capacity."

Discussion/learning points

The solicitor in the present case should plainly have considered EA's ability to understand the gift and its implications in accordance with the *Re Beaney* test and should have kept a clear attendance note of his findings. He should also have advised EA fully as to the consequences of the gift so as to rebut any presumption of undue influence. It would also have been prudent to obtain contemporaneous medical evidence as to EA's capacity to enter into the gift, by analogy with the so-called Golden Rule which applies in testamentary capacity cases. His failure to take any of these basic precautionary steps represents a serious omission on his part.

If the conclusion is that the EA lacked capacity to make the gift, then the next question will be whether she has capacity to litigate (as discussed in Chapter 10, below). If not, then it may be necessary to apply to the Court of Protection for the appointment of a deputy to pursue any litigation as litigation friend on EA's behalf.

Case 2: EB

Presenting question/problem

This is the case of a lady who, at the age of 70, gave away her home to a distant relative and his step-children who were of no blood relation. Her medical history indicated severe developmental delay, psychiatric illness throughout her life and serial parasuicide. Evidence also emerged that the main beneficiary of the gift had also assaulted her on several occasions. A retrospective assessment was requested of her ability to enter into such an arrangement, given her health problems and the resulting consequences of her actions for herself.

Background to the case

Clinical issues

EB had a longstanding psychiatric history which included numerous admissions for depression and self-harm. Records appeared to indicate that the self-harm was often a response to situations she could not cope with, including widowhood and parenting her two sons. Assessment of her general cognitive function in her early adulthood indicated that she was functioning in the learning disability range, that is, her IQ was below 70.

Ten years before the deed of gift was entered into, EB had a stroke which led to a left hemiparesis. There were pyramidal signs indicating brain stem involvement.

Family/social context

EB was widowed in her late twenties. By that time, she had two sons. Her mother lived with her until her death. Both sons demonstrated worrying psychiatric symptoms during their childhood and the dominant dynamic between family members was aggressive, threatening and manipulative. At one point, all three generations were being concurrently treated by local psychiatric services. EB would frequently present at her GP's surgery with signs of having been assaulted by one of her two sons, including scratches, black eyes and visible bruising. Assaults were also witnessed by third parties.

Within the medical records, there is significant evidence of longstanding health difficulties on the part of EB, including cardiac issues, type II diabetes, stroke, high blood pressure and stress. There is a consistent pattern throughout EB's medical records of her failing to attend scheduled appointments. This was so problematic at one stage that the GP had to exert significant effort to persuade several hospital consultants, across different specialties, to keep offering EB appointments because of concerns as to her health. There is no clear reason given for her serial non-attendance.

Psychological/neuropsychological matters

Throughout records, EB was frequently described in psychiatric terms as anergic, morose, irritable, depressed, neurotic, easily-manipulated (by her mother and both of her sons) and consistently refusing of all offers of assistance or treatment.

Opinion/outcome

Without any indication that her decision represented a longstanding intent, or a reasoned decision, EB entered into a deed of gift with an estranged brother's son and his step-children (who were not related by blood to EB). The estranged brother's son had not been involved in EB's life to any significant extent for many years.

Reference to *Re Beaney* would indicate that the threshold for decision-making by EB in her wish to gift her home (to a person outside of her immediate family) should be on a par with the legal test for testamentary capacity because it would essentially consist of her giving away her entire estate.

The test for capacity to make a will is set out in *Banks v. Goodfellow*[14] and, in summary, requires that the testator should be capable of understanding the nature of a will, the extent of his assets, the moral claims on his estate, and that he should be free from any insane delusion which may influence his will.

Shulman and colleagues (2005, pp.67–68) conclude that

> many cases of challenges to Testamentary Capacity involve complex and subtle issues that call for a need to go beyond the traditional Bank – vs – Goodfellow

14 (1870) LR 5 QB 549, 565. For a full discussion please refer to Chapter 6

criteria. Lawyers and expert assessors need to ensure that they take into account the capacity to appreciate the consequences of executing a Will especially in suspicious circumstances where there has been a radical change to a Will in the context of. . . a significant medical/neurological condition. ().

In addition, the authors refer to case law in England and Wales which has " suggested that the more serious the decision, the higher the threshold for competence. '*Seriousness*' related to Testamentary Capacity may refer to the extent of departure from previously expressed wishes or the extent to which the normal beneficiaries are excluded" (p.68).

It is argued, therefore, that an assessment of testamentary capacity is both task *and* situation specific. If there are no "suspicious circumstances" (as described by Shulman et al, 2005) then the assumption of competence can prevail. However, when circumstances at the time of making the will, such as the consequences of certain decisions, are substantial then questions should be asked as to the level of cognitive (including executive) abilities. Executive abilities refer to the key elements of decision-making including reasoning, predicting potential consequences, weighing up costs and benefits, forming judgements, organising one's thoughts and demonstrating mental flexibility.

It has been established in the medical records that EB had a low IQ (below 70). There is significant evidence of her vulnerability throughout her adult life and a history of significant influence by her mother. There is also evidence of psychiatric ill health throughout her records from the 1960s up to her death in the early 2000s.

An IQ of 70 or below is, arguably, incompatible with the complex cognitive skills required to formulate the decision to "give away" one's home. Testamentary capacity has been described as, "an advanced activity of daily living (a complex capacity) and is mediated by higher cognitive functions including frontal/executive functions" (Royall et al, 2002, in Shulman et al, 2005). Such activities are acknowledged to be different from household activities of daily living. Individuals with a learning disability typically have impoverished skills of consequential reasoning, working memory, concept-formation and mental flexibility as these are considered to be the higher-order functions associated with an IQ within the normal (or superior) range. There is no reason to consider that EB was atypical in that regard. These skills are considered to be critical to drawing up a will or deed of gift.

There is significant evidence throughout the medical records of EB relying on others to a significant degree, most particularly her mother until her death, for direction and support. This is a consistent behaviour evidenced with an adult with a learning disability.

In EB's medical records, there is evidence of a longstanding history of psychiatric disorder which extended throughout adulthood. There is a significant reference to EB sharing a *folie à deux* with her youngest son for which she was prescribed an antipsychotic medication (Olanzepine).

The attendance notes of the solicitor who prepared the deed of gift were not available. It would have been essential at the material time for the solicitor to demonstrate that EB was capable of understanding the deed of gift as required by the *Re Beaney* test. For example, it would be expected that the potential consequences to herself and significant others would have been explored. Similarly, it would have been expected that a range of perspectives would have been generated in order to ensure her understanding of the implications as well as to test her recollection of information previously given in relation to the deed of gift. She would have needed to demonstrate a clear understanding of the permanence of the gift.

Jovanovic and colleagues (2008) argue that "the evidence for challenges to Wills, based on a lack of Testamentary Capacity, can be substantially dependent upon expert medical assessment." The authors refer to the person (EB) having to appreciate the legal binding nature of the legal document as well as understanding its personal, legal, social and financial implications for the future.

Jovanovic and colleagues (2008) refer to "several pathophysiological mechanisms mediating between mental status and body functions so that several medical conditions can present with psychiatric symptoms in impaired mental capacity."

There are significant gaps in knowledge which cannot be gleaned from the medical records provided and these relate to questions as to the following:

1   EB's ability to manage her own finances independently on a day-to-day basis over a significant period of time;
2   Whether or not EB was in receipt of any day-to-day support with living skills, at what level and from what date;
3   Whether she was fully aware of the implication of the deed of gift;
4   Why the deed of gift appeared to exclude her sons who appear to be completely dependent upon her;
5   Whether there is any statutory service support to EB on the basis of her identified health and mental needs; and
6   Whether the solicitor who drew up the deed of gift was able to fully satisfy himself that EB had considered all implications and ramifications gift at the material time.

"Forensic experts must consider intellectual functioning, overall health and physical condition as well as whether the signs and symptoms of mental disorders do (or do not) reach the level of destroying Testamentary Capacity" (Jovanovic et al, 2008, p.490). To summarise, there are significant factors at play including:

1   EB's lifelong learning disability;
2   Apparent lifelong dependence on others for direction and support;
3   Longstanding history of psychiatric disorder extending through adulthood and which, frequently, required psychotropic medication or admission to psychiatric hospital;
4   Complex (and dysfunctional) interpersonal relationships and inter-dependencies within the family; and
5   Cerebro-vascular event, in the context of complex health co-morbidities.

All of these factors give rise to a robust question as to the assumption of mental capacity at the time of drawing up the deed of gift.

Shulman and colleagues (2005) argue that

> the mere presence of such a disorder is not sufficient to declare the testator incapable, task-specific competencies may vary even when a mental disorder is evident. Cognitive issues such as memory and orientation as well as executive brain function, such as the capacity for abstract thinking, impulsiveness and social judgement need to be carefully explored and documented.

There does not appear to be any evidence in the available evidence that any of this assessment was undertaken at the time of the drawing up of the deed of gift. Shulman and colleagues also argue that "the threshold for Testamentary Capacity should be higher in complex and conflictual environments that call for probing and documentation." The authors also refer to the question at the material time being phrased not as "is an individual competent" but "is he/she competent to do X in the context of Y".

EB lacked the requisite capacity to enter into the deed of gift at the material time.

Legal commentary

As with Case 1 (EA), this is a case in which the available evidence strongly suggests a finding of incapacity, with the result that the burden will probably shift to the beneficiary to prove capacity, although no final conclusion can be drawn without further details of EB's assets at the time when the gift was made, the provisions of the deed of gift, the other moral claims upon EB's estate, and, critically, the solicitor's file (including any attendance notes). It would also be prudent to investigate whether there are grounds for challenging the deed of gift on the alternative ground of undue influence.

Discussion/learning points

This is a case where the gaps in the evidence are such that any conclusion as to EB's capacity can only be provisional. It is likely that the capacity assessment will need to be reviewed when the further evidence is obtained including, in particular, the solicitor's file and attendance notes.

References

Department of Health. (2001). *Valuing people: A new strategy for learning disability for the 21st century.* Retrieved from https://assets.publishing.service.gov.uk/government/uploads/system/uploads/attachment_data/file/250877/5086.pdf

Jacoby, R. & Steer, P. (2007). How to assess capacity to make a will. *British Medical Journal, 335*, 155–157.

Jovanovic, A. A., Jovovic, S., Milovanovic, S. & Jasonvic-Gasic, M. (2008). Medical reasons for retrospective challenges of testamentary capacity. *Psychiatra Danubina*, *20*(4), 485–493.

Shulman, K. I., Cohen, C. & Hull, I. (2006). Psychiatric issues in retrospective challenges of testamentary capacity. *International Journal of Geriatric Psychiatry*, *20*, 63–69.

World Health Organisation. (1992). *The ICD-10 classification of mental and behavioural disorders: clinical descriptions and diagnostic guidelines*. Geneva: WHO.

9 Capacity to consent to medical treatment (not considered life-saving)

Dr Tracey Ryan-Morgan

With Paul Sankey and Andrew Hannam

Section 37 of the Mental Capacity Act (2005) makes the following provision for "serious" medical treatment (by an NHS body):

(1) This section applies if an NHS body—

   (a) is proposing to provide, or secure the provision of, serious medical treatment for a person ("P") who lacks capacity to consent to the treatment, and

   (b) is satisfied that there is no person, other than one engaged in providing care or treatment for P in a professional capacity or for remuneration, whom it would be appropriate to consult in determining what would be in P's best interests.

(2) But this section does not apply if P's treatment is regulated by Part 4 or 4A of the Mental Health Act.

(3) Before the treatment is provided, the NHS body must instruct an independent mental capacity advocate to represent P.

(4) If the treatment needs to be provided as a matter of urgency, it may be provided even though the NHS body has not been able to comply with subsection (3).

(5) The NHS body must, in providing or securing the provision of treatment for P, take into account any information given, or submissions made, by the independent mental capacity advocate.

(6) "Serious medical treatment" means treatment which involves providing, withholding or withdrawing treatment of a kind prescribed by regulations made by the appropriate authority.

(7) "NHS body" has such meaning as may be prescribed by regulations made for the purposes of this section by—

   (a) the Secretary of State, in relation to bodies in England, or

   (b) the National Assembly for Wales, in relation to bodies in Wales.

The key issue centres around assessment of competence (capacity) to consent or refuse serious medical treatment and, in those cases where capacity is in question, how can best interests be decided, and, by whom?

This is an over-simplification, of course. The picture is complicated by several issues.

First, there is the confluence of individual autonomy (which typically has primacy), medical necessity (which can, on occasion, trump autonomy) and the legal imperative to protect those who retain competence but wish to make decisions that may be judged as irrational or, even, harmful to themselves. An interesting aside to this is offered by Rumley (2005) who is concerned that, "as medical science and treatments have advanced, in many respects the line between life and death has become blurred. The capacity to prolong biological life sometimes sits uneasily alongside quality of life issues" (p.10). Second, the person may have made an Advance Decision (to refuse treatment). Third, the person may have fluctuating capacity for a decision that may not wait.

Advance Decisions do not have to be in writing unless the person wishes to refuse life-sustaining treatment. It is understood that the decision cannot include a refusal of pain relief, food, drink, warmth or nursing care. Similarly, it cannot make a demand for particular treatments. Most specifically, it cannot make a demand for assisted death and cannot be used to refuse treatment for a mental disorder that comes under the jurisdiction of the Mental Health Act (2007).

There may cases of individuals facing medical treatment where capacity may wax and wane. An example of such fluctuating capacity might be found in a person in post-traumatic amnesia (PTA) who would not be reliably competent to consent due to the nature of PTA. This is where continuous memories may not yet be laid down following an insult to the brain and may last for several hours, days, weeks or even months. However, if asked to consent by a clinician unaware of this post-brain injury condition, the person may present with a veneer of competence and, wrongly, be judged to retain capacity to consent to medical procedures. There are many other examples of fluctuating capacity where there is an underlying serious medical condition, including the effects of powerful medications which affect the level of consciousness and/or an individual's ability to think clearly.

The scope of consent is admirably discussed, in journal articles and conference presentations, by David Archard, Professor of Philosophy and Public Policy at Lancaster University. He illustrates the point made here, in Chapter 3, where the framing of a decision can heavily influence the decision-maker. He talks of the opacity of consent where a person may consent to an operation described as "life-saving" but may decline the same operation when described in terms of the level of pain and debilitating period of recovery it will entail. Similarly, he distinguishes between consenting to a procedure but not to the possible side-effects. An example of this lies in the request to assess a person's capacity to consent to an organ transplant as a life-saving procedure. Assessment made it possible to clearly demonstrate that, despite their fluctuating cognitive function, they accepted the surgery and its risks and consented to the surgery but would not make a commitment to taking the *essential* anti-rejection medication that they would need for the rest of their life following transplantation.

In fact, the law in relation to consent, as formulated by the Supreme Court, focuses on risk. Under *Montgomery v Lanarkshire Health Board*[1] a doctor's duty is "to take reasonable care to ensure that the patient is aware of any material risks involved in any recommended treatment, and of any reasonable alternative or variant treatments." This does not mean the duty is restricted to advising of risk: to make an informed decision, patients will need to know about the benefits of different alternatives. The duty has probably been formulated in this way because the issue generating litigation tends to be where risks have materialised of which patients had not previously been advised.

Assessment of capacity to consent to medical treatment has received much coverage in the extant literature. Wong and colleagues (1999) present the reader with a clear and helpful decision-tree to assist clinicians in navigating (and evidencing) the process of assessment. Tunzi (2001) offers a structured interview in the context of proposing a "threshold" approach where the assessment is required to be more stringent in cases where the weight of the decision is heavier. Essentially, the suggestion is that there is a play-off between potential benefits and risks which should determine the depth and breadth of the assessment. This is taken up by Buchanan (2004) who reflects on the notion that the gravity of the decision should affect the threshold for determining whether capacity is retained or forfeit. However, Buchanan cites *Re B*[2] as a note of caution, "if refusal might have grave consequences for the patient, it is most important that those considering the issue should not confuse the question of mental capacity with the nature of the decision made by the patient, however grave the consequences" (p.416), which brings the reader back to the primacy of autonomy in decision-making. A legal view might be that, as a matter of law Re B must be right and Tunzi must, therefore, be wrong. Nothing in the MCA (2005) introduces the notion of different thresholds. However, in reality, it is possible that a patient with marginal capacity may be able to grasp a simpler issue with less serious consequences than a more complex one.

Wong et al (1999) had already considered this issue, pre-MCA (2005),

> an adult is presumed to have capacity to give or withhold consent until proved otherwise. This right to autonomy exists whether the reasons for making the choice are rational, irrational, unknown, or even non-existent, and regardless of whether the outcome might be detrimental to the person.
>
> (p.438)

Buchanan (2004) cogently argues against the notion of a balance-sheet of decision-making, listing pros and cons for the decision in question, on the grounds that weighing any other considerations above individual autonomy is "disrespectful" of that autonomy. A more important point is that raising the threshold for decision-making capacity, in whatever instance, automatically

---

1 [2015] UKSC 11
2 [2002] 2 All E.R. 449

increases the numbers of those who will be deemed not to retain capacity, potentially disempowering them or even rendering them vulnerable to harm.

Tunzi (2001) explores the use of a structured tool, the Aid to Capacity Evaluation (ACE), sourced at www.jcb.utoronto.ca/tools/documents/ace.pdf as a method by which clinicians can approach the assessment systematically and, importantly, defensibly.

A legally incompetent choice, where the person lacks capacity but vigorously pursues their right to make the decision in question, can lead to harm but so can going against a person's wishes, under the flag of acting in their "best interests". The case of FC below illustrates this in the context of a person refusing nutrition in an unpalatable form whilst disregarding the real risks of choking or aspirating, both of which carry the potential for significant harm and, even, risk to life.

However, Worthington (2002) reminds the reader that, "informed consent should be about moral rights . . ." (p.377). The context for these remarks is the relative merit of written over verbal consent but, the final argument is that either form of consent is only really valid if it reflects a true understanding on the part of the patient, which derives from, "the nature and quality of the interaction between patient and clinician" (p.377). The Supreme Court decision in *Montgomery v Lanarkshire Health Board* clearly places a high moral value on patient autonomy.

Once a lack of capacity, or competence, has been established, the decision is taken out of the hands of the individual. However, the treating clinician cannot always know the values, wishes and preferences of a patient. There may be no time, at point of treatment, to consult with the patient, their family or significant others. The patient may be unable to relay their views, for whatever medical reason. It could also be the case that views may be sought on behalf of the person who is incapacitated but where there are conflicting views as to how best to proceed. This is where the *process* becomes paramount (Worthington, 2002). It seems to me that there are two separate issues here. One is where a decision needs to be made urgently and of necessity. There may not be time to consult adequately but a decision must still be made in the patient's best interests. The other is where there is less time pressure, but it is difficult to establish certain information such as what the patient would want, either because the patient cannot communicate that information or because it cannot be ascertained from others (who may for instance prove impossible to contact).

This leads on neatly to the consideration of Best Interests v Substituted Judgement.

Tunzi (2001) describes substituted judgement as, "what the patient would have decided" and best interests as, "that which the surrogate judges to be best for the patient" (p.306). This is a helpful distinction as, in practice, the two are often conflated. Worthington (2002) argues that intervention by the court, acting in the individual's "best interests" merely relocates that problem of determining what is in someone's best interests further away from them, that is, from the clinic to the courtroom. Cobb, J[3] admits that there is a, "strong element of substituted judgement in the best interests' test" (paragraph 76). Worthington (2002) considers that the concept of "best interests" is an ill-defined concept, arguing that it can lead to circular thinking. Lucy Series echoes this concern, "there are a number of phrases which although they reflect legal principles, should not be trotted out as though they were magical mantras. Best interests is one of these" (p1/6 https://thesmallplaces.wordpress.com/2017/07/04/guest-post-charlie-gard-and-the-magical-mantra-of-best-interests).

The point is that, although the law uses the term "best interests", the expression poorly defines what is in fact a more complex issue.

Baroness Hale (paragraph 39 of *Aintree v James*[4]) clarified the scope of "best interests" as encompassing the widest consideration of welfare issues, including social and psychological considerations alongside the medical imperative. This is echoed by Mumby, J,[5]

> Physical health and safety can sometimes be bought at too high a price in happiness and emotional welfare. The emphasis must be on sensible risk appraisal, not striving to avoid all risk, whatever the price, but instead seeking a proper balance and being willing to tolerate manageable or acceptable risks as the price appropriately to be paid in order to achieve some other good – in particular to achieve the vital good of the elderly or vulnerable person's happiness. What good is it making someone safer if it merely makes them miserable?
>
> (paragraph 120)

Hayden, J[6] makes several interesting points in this debate about the relative merits of aspects of "best interests",

> the sanctity of life is not an absolute principle and can be outweighed by the need to respect the personal autonomy and dignity of the patient. . . .where the patient's views can be ascertained with sufficient certainty, they should be generally followed. . .or afforded great respect. . .though they are not automatically determinative.

This latter point confirms the distinction between best interests and substituted judgement. Baker, J[7] urges the focus on each individual case,

> once incapacity is established so that a best interests' decision must be made, there is no theoretical limit to the weight or lack of weight that should be given to the person's wishes and feelings, beliefs and values. In some cases, the conclusion will be that little weight or no weight can be given in others, very significant weight will be due.
>
> (paragraph 56)

4 [2013] UKSC 6
5 [2007] EWHC 2003 Fam
6 [2017] EWCOP 23
7 [2017] EWCOP 15

Specific mention is warranted here regarding cases of Clinical Assisted Nutrition and Hydration (CANH). In December 2017, the British Medical Association, General Medical Council and Royal College of Physicians issued interim guidance as a result of legal developments in this area.[8,9] Practice Direction 9E was withdrawn independent of this guidance. Further guidance from the BMA and RCP, endorsed by the GMC, is imminent. It may also be that the court issues practice guidance to replace PD9E, but this is under discussion at time of writing. At the end of July 2018, the Supreme Court[10] provided a definitive answer to the question of when it is necessary to apply to the Court of Protection for the withdrawal of CANH and when such applications are no longer necessary. The process of how to apply to the Court of Protection has now been clarified, requiring the opinion of the (experienced) treating doctor, with a second opinion from a doctor completely unconnected with the case. Where there is unanimity of opinion, there is no need to seek legal consent from the court to withdraw CANH. However, in those cases where the issues are finely balanced, or where the medical opinions differ or where there is disagreement between those who have an interest in the welfare of the patient, the court fully expects to be involved.

Case 1: FA

Presenting question/problem

FA has been identified as having contractures of both ankles which have been previously treated with stretching, splintage and botulinum toxin (Botox), apparently to little effect.

It was suggested that FA could benefit from orthopaedic surgery to both ankles, the optimum outcome of which would be for this to achieve supported standing within a mechanized standing frame.

It was established that, as the contractures had been present for some time, it was difficult to predict in advance how extensive the surgery might need to be, how protracted the recovery might be, or, what complications could arise. It was also difficult to predict what the effects of the general anaesthetic would be. There was, therefore, a significant degree of uncertainty surrounding the possible extent of the proposed clinical procedure, recovery, risks and outcomes.

FA has significant cognitive deficits as a result of his severe traumatic brain injury.

---

8   [2017] EWCOP 22
9   [2017] EWHC 2866 (QB)
10   *Re Y* [2018] UKSC 46

Background to the case

Clinical issues

At the time of his brain injury, FA's Glasgow Coma Scale score was 4/15 and he had displayed a decerebrate posture (which is commonly interpreted as an indication of severe underlying brain injury). CT scans reported small collections of blood around the brain stem, near the third ventricle in both occipital horns of the lateral ventricle plus around the under surfaces of both temporal lobes and the right temporal region. These were noted to be appearances of a severe traumatic brain injury with diffuse axonal injury and reactive brain swelling.

A further CT scan some weeks later revealed signs of atrophy, suggesting the possibility of hypoxic brain damage at the time of the accident in addition to head trauma. When this CT was repeated a month later there was further evidence of generalised brain atrophy. There were also signs of specific damage to the frontal regions of the brain and in the midbrain.

FA had been left with an inability to communicate verbally with any reliability. He was considered to be able to make his views known to staff and family that were sufficiently familiar with his vocalisations and gestures.

It was considered critical to be fully aware of the particular anaesthetic risks to FA as during previous surgeries he had experienced an adverse reaction to anaesthetic agents in the form of depressed respiratory function and had also developed complications following chest infections in the post-surgery, recovery period.

Family/social context

FA was estranged from his siblings, with the exception of one sister. His parents had passed away. He had a girlfriend from the time before the accident, but she had since married someone else. Despite this, she visited him regularly and was still an important part of FA's life.

FA was living in bespoke accommodation, designed for his living needs. He had a 24-hour care package in place and was regularly reviewed by medical staff.

Psychological/neuropsychological matters

FA's brain injury had been classified as "severe" based on key clinical indicators. There was extensive neuropathological evidence of damage to his brain and this had a detrimental effect on his cognitive and psychological functioning. There was daily evidence of him experiencing difficulties in terms of the following areas of function:

- attention;
- working memory;
- mental flexibility;
- problem-solving;
- communicating;

- understanding the concept of time; and
- understanding potential consequences to actions.

Extensive psychological assessment (using observational and behavioural methods) had established that due to FA being physically immobile and unable to reliably communicate, when he wanted to make his (negative) feelings known he would refuse food and drink and would continue to do so for several days at a time. This would frequently compromise his health and physical integrity as he would refuse support and care, including refusing to be regularly turned in bed or have his seating varied so as to protect his skin integrity.

Assessment and rationale

It was clear at the outset that FA was able to form views and to communicate these using a combination of vocalisations, physical gestures or challenging behaviours. It was considered critical to ensure that FA was in possession of the fullest information regarding the possible procedure, risks, recovery and potential outcomes.

The first step was to assist his understanding of the key issues, including the following:

- why he needs to have the procedure;
- what the procedure consists of and that the procedure would involve the use of general anaesthetic;
- any associated risk of complications related to the general anaesthetic;
- what the level of pain might be afterwards and how that might be managed;
- what possible clinical risks there are in relation to the proposed elective procedure;
- what the probability of success is of the procedure;
- what the expected clinical outcome is (supported standing within a mechanized standing frame);
- the same information in relation to alternative treatments; and
- the same information in relation to no treatment.

FA used the word "walk" on several occasions in the context of the proposed elective surgery, giving cause for concern that he may have an unrealistic understanding of the potential outcome of the proposed elective surgery. This concern was fed back to the attending physiotherapist during the assessment process.

He was assessed over several appointments to maximise his opportunities for understanding the issues and to formulate any further questions he may have in relation to the proposed treatment. He continued to believe that the proposed surgery will result in him being able to walk and ended the second appointment with the question, "when will I be able to walk again?"

Work was undertaken jointly with his speech and language therapist to develop a picture booklet with photos of the hospital, the surgeon, a hospital bed, an operating theatre, nurses, medicines and similar items. This was used over a number of appointments to assist his understanding of the key issues and also to aid his recollection by serving as a visual prompt during conversations.

In terms of assessing FA's ability to then use the pertinent information to weigh up and consider his options, the following areas were considered:

- does FA understand that he could refuse the operation; or,
- that he could agree to the operation now but later change his mind; and,
- what might happen if he did change his mind?
- does FA understand that there are significant uncertainties which are all contingent upon one another in relation to the proposed elective procedure as has been outlined by the surgeon. For example, the surgeon is unable to know in advance how extensive the surgery might need to be, what the effects of the general anaesthetic may be, how protracted the recovery might be or what complications could arise at the outset. FA would need to be able to think in the abstract, at a conceptual level, in order to fully consider these matters.

Throughout the assessment process, it was considered important to bear in mind the advice of Professor David Archard in terms of the framing of the information and questions during decision-making so as to avoid the possibility of undue influence. For that reason, all assessment appointments were conducted without family or former girlfriend present as their views were obtained separately.

Opinion/outcome

Clinical neuropsychologists adopt a functional approach to capacity assessment by looking at what an individual understands, knows, or believes they can do in the specific context at issue. The assessment also looks at the extent to which these functional abilities meet the demands for a particular situation within a given legal context. Therefore, the functional approach to capacity assessment emphasises the interaction between a person's abilities and the given situation.

The General Medical Council (GMC, 2018) guidance indicates that it is for the treating surgeon to be satisfied as to consent by the patient. The decision-maker on this issue, the surgeon, has indicated that he does not consider FA to have the capacity to consent to the proposed procedure.

It is clear that currently FA is able to make day-to-day choices from a limited and selected array, from which all potential negative consequences have been removed, and that he is effective in making such choices. It is also clear from his former girlfriend, also one of his carers (of several years standing), that FA is able to be clear in expressing his opinions about what he does and doesn't want.

It is my clinical opinion, based on all of the information provided and, on the assessment reported here, that on the balance of probabilities, FA does not have the required capacity to consent to the proposed elective surgical procedure.

Legal commentary

Mumby J in *Re* MM exhorts the following,

> the emphasis must be on sensible risk appraisal, not striving to avoid all risk, whatever the price, but instead seeking a proper balance and being willing to tolerate manageable or acceptable risks as the price appropriate to be paid in order to achieve some other good . . . what good is it making someone safer if it merely makes them miserable?
>
> (paragraph 60)

It is important that the issue FA needs to decide – if he is in fact thought to have capacity – is not formulated too narrowly in terms of one management option. The law on patient consent was set out by the Supreme Court in *Montgomery v Lanarkshire Health Board*[11] which sets out the nature of a patient's right and a doctor's duty in advising. The starting principle is that "an adult person of sound mind is entitled to decide which, if any, of the available forms of treatment to undergo." Enshrined in the law is a patient's right to choice. Choice entails being presented with alternatives. This means that, rather than being advised only about one possible treatment – in this case surgery to both ankles – the patient must be told about the range of reasonable alternatives. In every case where some form of treatment is proposed there should be at least one alternative, even if that alternative is no treatment.

The doctor is then under a duty to take reasonable care to ensure that the patient is aware of any material risks involved in any recommended treatment, and of any reasonable alternative or variant treatments. Again, the way a doctor's duty is formulated implies choice. The duty is not fulfilled by advising only as to the risks of surgery. The patient must be advised as to the risks of no surgery (or of any other reasonable alternative treatments).

A risk is material in the circumstances of a particular case if:

a)   a reasonable person in the patient's position would be likely to attach significance to the risk, or
b)   the doctor is or should reasonably be aware that the particular patient would be likely to attach significance to it.

The first test (a reasonable person in the patient's position would be likely to attach significance to the risk) aims to tread a middle line between a subjective and an objective test. A subjective test would be what this patient actually wants to know. An objective test would be what a reasonable patient would want to know. The latter is in effect a "one size fits all" approach. The Montgomery test takes the characteristics of this particular patient and filters them through the prism of what a reasonable person with these characteristics would want to know. The effect is to create a patient-centred test but not one which is not so subjective as to make life impossible for clinicians.

11   [2015] UKSC 11

The Royal College of Surgeons provides guidance to surgeons in *Consent: Supported Decision-Making: A Good Practice Guide*. Its advice is that surgeons should provide information about:

- the patient's diagnosis and prognosis;
- the right of the patient to refuse treatment and make their own decisions about their care;
- alternative options for treatment, including non-operative care and no treatment;
- advice on lifestyle that may moderate the disease process;
- the purpose and expected benefit of the treatment;
- the nature of the treatment (what it involves);
- the likelihood of success;
- the clinicians involved in their treatment. It may be sufficient to say that in relation to NHS treatment there is no guarantee that a particular surgeon will perform the procedure, notwithstanding the inclusion of this point in the guidance;
- potential follow-up treatment;
- the material risks inherent in the procedure and in the alternative options discussed; and,
- for private patients, costs of treatment and potential future costs in the event of complications.

The test in *Montgomery v Lanarkshire Health Board* applies to "an adult person of sound mind", i.e., a patient who has capacity. However, in considering whether a patient has capacity to make a decision about medical treatment it is important to consider the scope of that decision. The factors set out above indicate how wide ranging that scope is.

Discussion/learning points

The main learning points from this case are that it is essential to provide all of the pertinent information to the person who is facing the decision, but also to accept that not all information can be declared with certainly or reliability. In this case, even the surgeon was unable to give guarantees of "no risk" to FA. There is no such thing as "safe certainty" (Mason, 1983) and decisions which are made on this basis are vulnerable to scrutiny and likely to be found wanting.

Case 2: FB

Presenting question/problem

This is a case of a young adult female (FB) in residential care with a craniopharyngioma (a brain tumour derived from the remnants of the structure from which the pituitary gland is partly formed) and acquired Prader-Willi syndrome as a result. The Registered Manager of the home was seeking a capacity assessment in relation to food and unregulated intake which was resulting in significant health morbidities for FB.

Background to the case

Clinical issues

At the time of assessment, FB was morbidly obese, she weighed 28 stone (178 kg) and this reflected a steadily increasing picture over time. She experienced a range of health complications including diabetes insipidus (related to damage to the pituitary gland), hypothyroidism and urinary incontinence.

Over a long period of time, staff had spent a considerable effort in educating FB about food groups, quantities and dietary values. She had received regular support and assistance with menu planning, food shopping and preparation including information to help with portion control. Staff had also tried negotiating a "food contract" with FB which had looked well on paper but was unenforceable and failed immediately.

Family/social context

FB was due to get married to another resident in the home seven months after the assessment. Staff had tried to use the wedding as a motivator for FB to address her weight and food intake. However, it had come to light that even though extensive efforts had been made to restrict FB's access to food (locked cupboards in communal kitchens, consented room searches) FB still had relatively unfettered access to food by means of other residents sourcing it for her as a token of friendship. Indeed, her fiancé regularly bought her sweets and chocolates which he kept hidden in his room for her to access out of sight of staff. Support staff felt that FB was more cognitively able than most of the other residents and was therefore able to manipulate others into achieving her own ends.

Psychological/neuropsychological matters

It was considered critical to understand the clinical issues around FB's food behaviours from the perspective that if she did have an acquired Prader-Willi syndrome then her drive for food would be biological and not readily amenable to conscious control. (Prader-Willi syndrome is also known as hypothalamic obesity and is a failure of the hunger-satiety mechanism such that the individual is organically driven to over-eat [hyperphagia] but unable to be aware of when they are satisfied). This would have significant implications in terms of insight and clinical management.

Assessment and rationale

The assessment was predicated on the rationale proposed by Tunzi (2001) that, "certain patients may be able to decide some aspects of their care but not others" (p.300).

FB was interviewed over several appointments and observed in her home environment interacting with others around mealtimes and whilst undertaking kitchen-based activities. She denied from the outset that there was a problem with her weight or food intake and came across as childlike in manner. She was focused on her forthcoming nuptials and it was difficult to move her from this topic at times. She appeared open about what she eats and when, but became defensive when challenged about the possibility of hiding sweets and snacks in her room or of accessing "prohibited" foods through her fiancé or other residents.

The nature of her response to being challenged could be a learned behaviour, which would usually make staff desist from confrontation and close the discussion down. She demonstrated that she was aware of being watched by staff and displayed verbally challenging behaviours when staff were observed to be present, such as, "you don't like me, do you?" spoken with aggression and in a physically confronting manner. However, she would then immediately adopt a "victim" stance in order to elicit sympathy from observers, behaving as though staff had been picking on her.

Her fiancé was interviewed with her consent, although she insisted on being present. It was clear that he was less cognitively able than FB and responded to her influence at all times. He seemed eager to please FB and, within this context, it is not difficult to see how he could easily be directed by her to source whatever foods she wished.

Opinion/outcome

The starting point had to be a presumption of capacity. If capacitous, were FB's decisions (and behaviours) around food merely unwise or was she risking such a serious deterioration in health as to put her life at risk? FB's difficulties are predominantly organic in nature, and, are also perpetuated by her food-related behaviours. The craniopharyngiona has occurred as a result of a congenital condition yet FB appears to display a degree of insight in that some of her behaviours in relation to food are covert and could be said to be manipulative of others to satisfy her drive for food.

However, given that there is the diagnosis of (acquired) Prader-Willi syndrome this may provide an appropriate framework within which to understand FB's difficulties. The urge to eat and drink, and the inability to self-regulate this, in Prader-Willi is an entirely biological one and for individual professionals working with FB it is clear that the balance is really to manage the tension between the respect for her autonomy and the need for her care. The Mental Capacity Act (2005) is relevant for consideration on the grounds that, whilst FB retains capacity to consent to many aspects of her life, when it comes to food the insatiable hunger so distorts FB's thinking that it may render her incapacitated with respect to the decisions about intake. Within this argument one could defend the decision to limit access to food on the grounds that it is in FB's best interests. However, it is not clear how this would be implemented, monitored or enforced in a group home with communal areas and where FB is free to come and go at will.

Legal commentary

The issue of whether FB's decisions around food were merely unwise or were risking such a serious deterioration as to put her life at risk is not relevant to the issue of whether she has capacity. Necessity only comes into play where a patient lacks capacity. If she has capacity she is entitled to make decisions, however unwise. The more difficult issue is whether insatiable hunger distorts her decision-making so as to render her incapacitated. Whilst the professionals working with her may be uncomfortable that she is making what they regard as foolish choices, she is entitled to do so if she has capacity. There is a danger of circumventing her right to autonomy by claiming that her decisions are biologically determined and therefore not those of a person with capacity. Given the priority of autonomy and the presumption of capacity, the courts are likely to be reluctant to find that a patient's decision-making is so determined by biological necessity as to render her incapacitated.

The approach to be adopted in cases where has acquired Prader-Willi syndrome was considered in the case of *FX v A Local Authority*.[12] The proceedings commenced by application dated 16 September 2016 as a challenge to a standard authorisation which authorised the deprivation of FX's liberty at Care Home A.

The District Judge noted that the question of FX's mental capacity regarding decisions as to his welfare is to be answered by reference to the statutory framework provided by the Mental Capacity Act (2005) (MCA) and to the MCA (2005) Code of Practice. I have had at the forefront of my mind section 1 (2) of the Act which provides that "a person must be assumed to have capacity unless it is established that he lacks capacity." Thus, in determining whether FX lacks capacity the burden of proof lies with the party asserting that he lacks capacity. The standard of proof is the balance of probabilities section 2(4). In FX there was competing evidence on the question of capacity.

The District Judge considered what information P (as someone suffering from Prader Willi syndrome, PWS) needed to understand and suggested the following:

- a basic understanding that he has PWS;
- an understanding that one effect of having PWS is a need to eat which is greater than his body's need for food to remain healthy he will need to prevent himself from acting on his desire to eat; and
- if he eats in accordance with his hunger he will very substantially overeat and have severe health problems with potentially life-shortening consequences.

The District Judge was satisfied that FX understands that he has PWS and that it is an eating disorder. He has identified that he needs support when going out in the community and that he needs support with portion control. He understands that rejecting support at Care Home A caused him to gain weight. He understands that he is overweight and that this affects his health. He knows that losing weight would improve his sleep apnoea. He wishes to lose weight and he is trying to do so. He understands that staff try to help him by suggesting healthy options when out but that sometimes he rejects advice.

On that basis he concluded that FX did have capacity to make his decision about residence although he concluded that should a situation arise where there are complex decisions to be made it may be necessary to reconsider issues of capacity in light of those decisions.

Discussion/learning points

The over-riding framework for consideration in this case is section 5, MCA (2005). Although McSherry (2002) provides an interesting read, the doctrine of "necessity" is subsumed here by section 5.

Case 3: FC

Presenting question/problem

This is the case of an adult male who experienced a severe traumatic brain injury in a motorcycle accident. He has an unreliable swallow (dysphagia) and has been assessed on videofluoroscopy (VF is an X-ray which looks at how a person's swallow works mechanically) as silently aspirating anything that he tries to swallow. He is on a modified diet as a result. He has a PEG (percutaneous endoscopic gastrostomy) *in situ* which is no longer used for food but cannot be removed because he frequently refuses oral medication, resulting in it having to be administered via the PEG (against his wishes) or covertly (hidden in food and drink taken orally) according to policy. The issue is about FC's capacity to consent to life-sustaining medication and to eating a modified oral diet in order to maintain his physical health and safety. He frequently refuses both of these aspects of his care and treatment. The assessment was requested to assess his capacity to consent to compliance with life-sustaining medication (anti-epileptic drugs – AED) and to receiving a modified diet due to risks of aspiration and the implications for his health status. He has severe communication difficulties (dysarthria) and requires technical assistance to make himself understood. The assessment was jointly carried out by this author and Louise Steer, specialist speech and language therapist.

Background to the case

Clinical issues

At the time of the accident in which FC sustained his brain injury, scans indicated the following:

- sub-arachnoid haemorrhage;
- subdural haematomas; and
- haemorrhaging to the corpus callosum and basal ganglia

A range of presenting difficulties was noted post-injury, including:

- significant cognitive impairments, including executive dysfunction;
- inability to communicate other than by limited hand gesture, limited head movement and leg movement;
- inability to mobilise independently;
- double incontinence;
- severe dysphagia associated with high risk of aspiration on all oral intake
- significant frustration and de-motivation;
- post-traumatic seizures;
- complete dependence for all aspects of care; and
- significant levels of pain.

Family/social context

FC comes from a large family that have little respect for authority. The family are chaotic in lifestyle and are unreliable in terms of supporting and participating in key assessments and interventions for FC. Prior to the brain injury, FC adopted a thrill-seeking lifestyle.

Psychological/neuropsychological matters

FC frequently expressed his frustration at not being able to independently mobilise. He required assistance to move in his bed, to assume the sitting position and had to be hoisted for personal care. He would frequently behave in a way which increased his falls risk, particularly during transfers, as a means of communicating his overwhelming desire to walk again. A considerable effort was made to assist FC to understand that there was no possibility of walking independently again, but that physiotherapy intervention would aim to assist him to physically tolerate a standing frame. FC frequently lashed out at staff and refused medication and food as a means of venting his frustration.

Neuropsychologically, FC was severely compromised by his brain injury in terms of an inability to learn new information reliably, difficulty with concentrating and attending to others and problems with recall of information, despite frequent exposure to the same.

Assessment and rationale

The results of the VF were presented to FC across two separate clinical sessions with a consultant clinical neuropsychologist and speech and language therapist to aid his ability to process, understand and retain the information. He was given short, simple verbal explanations of his dysphagia and risks across the different types of oral intake consistencies. These were supplemented by visual explanations and video examples of videofluoroscopy assessment (VF) demonstrating the silent aspiration he had shown. His understanding of this information was checked in a follow-up session using a variety of binary-choice questions using single written words presented as options for him to indicate his responses.

Over the two sessions, FC showed a reliable understanding of the information presented to him about the results of his VF examination. He also communicated consistently that he wanted to choose to consume oral intake safely and follow the recommendations regarding diet, fluids and environmental modifications suggested by the VF professionals. This was considered to represent a capacitous decision on the part of FC.

There then followed a period of time with FC consuming Stage 2 thickened fluids and Texture C (thick puréed) diet as per the decision he made during the capacity assessment. The oral intake was a success and eventually the weight gain and quantities received were sufficient to withdraw his PEG feeds for nutritional purposes. The PEG remained *in situ* for the purposes of medication only on the basis that, occasionally, he would refuse his oral medication, and this would have to be administered covertly, as per local policy.

However, over time, FC presented with increasing frequencies of challenging behaviour around his mealtimes. He began to request "unsafe" foods as well as wanting to eat or drink in distracting environments (which significantly increased his risk of aspiration). At such times he would also refuse his AED medication which had been prescribed to manage his post-traumatic seizures. Detailed records were kept of each refusal.

At this time, FC received his new high tech AAC (augmented and alternative communication) device that would enable more abstract and detailed discussions regarding his knowledge, thoughts, feelings and experiences around his oral intake. It was considered appropriate to repeat the capacity assessment in light of his escalating behaviours around food and with the additional support of his new communication aid. A repeat capacity assessment would also have the benefit of considering his thoughts and feelings after experiencing a period of time consistently consuming safe oral intake.

The concern regarding the previously held-view as to his capacity to make a decision regarding his oral intake was based on the fact that his "behaviour or circumstances cause doubt as to whether they have the capacity to make a decision" (paragraph 4.35, p.56 Code of Practice).

FC's AAC was a Dynavox. This is a multi-page menu-based system with pictorial and/or single written words on a maximum of 12 tiles per page. The words programmed contained a variety of nouns, verbs and adjectives relevant to FC's everyday needs and interests. It also incorporates a keyboard for more open responses to be facilitated. FC was trained in its use and the available words, phrases and layout were tailored to his individual needs.

The repeat capacity assessment followed largely the same structure as the first, but it also explored more of FC's beliefs regarding his non-oral feeding and discharge home. It became apparent that FC thought that he would need to be consuming normal consistency oral intake and have his PEG removed prior to him being discharged home. Time was taken to appropriately challenge these erroneous beliefs and assurance was provided to him that discharge could be pursued on his current oral and nutritional intake management plan, even if no further progress was made.

Opinion/outcome

During this follow-up capacity assessment, FC was provided with repeated opportunities to demonstrate his understanding of the risks associated with normal oral intake. Each time, he indicated his belief that there were no risks involved with consuming oral intake. It is likely that this response was in line with his pre-injury approach to risk-taking but, based on the information presented, his weighing up of relevant information and communication of his wish to receive a normal oral diet, it no longer appeared that FC was making a capacitous decision about his nutritional intake given the associated risks to his health which had not changed since the first assessment of his decision-making capacity. The positive risk management approach to FC's oral intake was continued, in his best interests. The programme was placed under continual review and FC's views were routinely sought as part of this process.

The assessment had also shown that FC's intermittent refusal of his medication was not on the basis that he did not accept the rationale for treatment, or associated risks, but that he wanted to express his general frustration at his life situation and lack of ability to walk. There was no pattern to his refusals other than a clear relationship between his mood and his non-compliant behaviour. In such circumstances the clinical decision was made, and documented, to implement the covert medication policy and either administer medication via PEG or in food and drink, whichever was the least restrictive to FC on each occasion.

Legal commentary

Given that the scope of the decision as to treatment to be made by a patient with capacity includes understanding the material risks of a management option and of reasonable alternatives, it seems unlikely that FC has capacity given that he believed there were no risks of oral intake.

Discussion/learning points

Buchanan (2004) reviews the ideas that suggest that, on occasion, respecting a legally incompetent choice can lead to a degree of harm but that acting contrary to a person's expressed wishes can do even more harm. Indeed, Baroness Hale argues that considering a person's best interests has to take into account more than just their medical needs.[13] There should also be consideration of the person's

---

13 [2013] UKSC 67 para. 39

social and psychological needs as well as what the outcome of a particular intervention might be, even when it is considered to be in their best interests.

References

BMA/GMC/RCP. (2017). Decisions to withdraw clinically-assisted nutrition and hydration (CANH) for patients in permanent vegetative state (PVS) or minimally conscious state (MCS) following sudden-onset profound brain injury. *Interim Guidance for Health Professionals in England and Wales*, December.

Buchanan, A. (2004). Mental capacity, legal competence and consent to treatment. *Journal of the Royal Society of Medicine, 97*(9), 415–420.

GMC. (2018). Decision making and consent: Supporting patient choices about health and care. Retrieved from www.gmc-uk.org/-/media/ethical-guidance/related-pdf-items/consent-draft-guidance/consent-draft-guidance.pdf?la=en&hash=920B435518160455840473FA316D7BEEBDFBB332

Mason, B. (1983). Towards positions of safe uncertainty. *Human Systems, The Journal of Systematic Consultation & Management, 4*, 193–200.

McSherry, B. (2002). The doctrine of necessity and medical treatment. *Journal of Law and Medicine, 10*, 10–16.

Rumley, P. (2005). Mentally incompetent adult patients: to treat or not to treat? *Association of Personal Injury Lawyers PI Focus, 15*(6), 10–11.

Tunzi, M. (2001). Can the patient decide? Evaluating patient capacity in practice. *American Family Physician, 64*(2), 299–306.

Wong, J. G., Clare, I. C. H., Gunn, M. J. & Holland, A. J. (1999). Capacity to make health care decisions: its importance in clinical practice. *Psychological Medicine, 29*, 437–446.

Worthington, R. (2002). Clinical issues on consent: some philosophical concerns. *Journal of Medical Ethics, 28*, 377–380.

10 Capacity to enter into proceedings/ to litigate

Dr Tracey Ryan-Morgan

With Richard Stead

The issue of capacity confronts judges, lawyers and clinicians in numerous types of cases before the court. A person who lacks capacity, within the meaning of the Mental Capacity Act (2005), to conduct proceedings is known as "a protected party". In accordance with Part 2.1 of the Civil Procedure Rules (CPR) (1998), a protected party must have a litigation friend to conduct proceedings on his/her behalf, and any settlement of a claim brought by a litigation friend on behalf of a protected party must be approved by the court (CPR 21.10(1)). If a person lacks capacity and does not have a litigation friend or does not obtain the court's approval to any settlement of the claim, then the proceedings and the settlement are likely to be of no binding effect (see *Dunhill v Burgin* below). Hence the great importance in ascertaining whether any litigant lacks mental capacity to conduct the proceedings.

Judges and lawyers

It is important that all involved in litigation should be alert to the possibility of a party not having capacity to litigate. As Sir Brian Leveson said in *Dunhill v W Brook & Co*[1]: "I cannot leave the case without observing that those who act in the field of personal injury litigation should always be alert to potential difficulties about capacity when serious head injuries have been sustained."

In the 2018 *Equal Treatment Bench Book* it is stated that:

> The legal system relies on the assumption that people are capable of making, and thus being responsible for, their own decision and actions. It is therefore necessary to be able to recognise a lack of mental capacity when it exists, and to cope with the legal implication.

It is important that lawyers, who are often the first to see a party in the context of litigation, are alert to recognise the possibility of the party having a lack of capacity. Similarly, a judge may be the first person to speak to a litigant in person and it is important that a judge is also alert to the possibility of a lack of capacity. Whilst the

1 [2018] EWCA Civ 505

discovery of such a possibility might well delay proceedings and require an adjourn-ment of a hearing, it is, nonetheless, vital that the issue, once recognised, is addressed. If a lack of capacity is not recognised, then any proceedings may be of no effect.

The lawyer's or judge's concerns as to the capacity of a party may well lead to an assessment by a clinician who is most suited to make the assessment of capac-ity to litigate, and/or to the obtaining of evidence from someone who knows the individual concerned. It is not easy for a lawyer to make such an assessment without the assistance of a clinician. It is all too easy for the lawyer to be deceived by normal or, indeed, eccentric behaviour in reaching an erroneous conclusion as to capacity. Assistance can be found in *Assessment of Mental Capacity: Guidance for Doctors and Lawyers* published by the Law Society and BMA (Ruck Keene, 2015), as well as in the *Equal Treatment Bench Book* (2018), Chapter 5.

Clinicians

Clinicians often get asked to assess a patient's capacity to litigate in the context of personal injury claims or family law proceedings. It is crucial to understand the legal context for such assessments and equally helpful to grasp the rationale behind the assessment requirement. It is also essential that the clinician is aware of the specifics of the decision in question, bearing in mind the advice of Munby J[2]:

> Someone may have the capacity to litigate in a case where the nature of the dispute and the issues are simple, whilst at the same time lacking the capac-ity to litigate in a case whether either the nature of the dispute or the issues are more complex. In this sense litigation is analogous to medical treatment. Some litigation, like medical treatment, is relatively simple and risk free. Some litigation, on the other hand, like some medical treatment, is highly complex and more or less risky . . . someone may have the capacity to litigate in a sim-ple case whilst lacking the capacity to litigate in a highly complex case . . . .
>
> (paragraph 39)

Although this advice pre-dates the MCA (2005) it remains extant in terms of good practice. The principle is reflected in the recent ruling[3] where the inde-pendent expert gave the opinion that if the court had considered it sufficient for the person in question to understand the litigation in broad terms, then the pre-sumption of capacity was retained. However, if the person was required to have a more in-depth understanding, such as being able to understand the range of potential outcomes to proceedings, then the expert opined that litigation capac-ity was lacking. The court supported that view.

In many cases the critical questions are not so much whether the individual understood the range of potential outcomes, but whether he/she was able to do

---

2 [2004] EWHC 2808 (Fam)
3 [2017] EWCOP 5

so with assistance from legal advisers and others, and whether he/she was able to retain information for a sufficient period to understand the issues involved and to make an informed decision.

Three cases provide examples of the framework within which assessments of capacity to litigate are to be considered:

1   *Masterman-Lister v Brutton & Co*[4]
    Broadly, the question is,

> whether a party to legal proceedings is capable of understanding, with the assistance of such proper explanation (in broad terms and simple language) from legal advisers and other experts as the case may require, the matters on which their consent or decision was likely to be necessary in the course of those proceedings.

In the *Equal Treatment Benchbook*, Chapter 5, it is suggested that, the mental abilities required include the ability to:

- Recognise a problem, obtain and receive, understand and retain relevant information, including advice,
- Weigh the information (including that derived from advice) in the balance in reaching a decision; and then
- Communicate that decision (paragraph 46).

The focus is upon understanding the claim and the litigation process, rather than upon being able to conduct the claim as formulated by the lawyers (see *Dunhill v Burgin*).[5]

2   *Dunhill v Burgin*
    This case concerned a woman who had sustained a brain injury and had settled her claim on the first day of trial for a modest sum, then sought to overturn the agreement on the basis that she had lacked capacity at the time. The case went to the Supreme Court. The findings were that an individual's capacity to agree to a settlement could not be separated out from their capacity to conduct proceedings and that the woman should have been a "protected party" from the outset (Civil Procedure Rules, 1998, Part 21).

3   *Mitchell v Alasia*[6]
    Denzil Lush refers to paragraph 76 of the ruling in this case in which Mrs Justice Cox, "decided that Russell Mitchell . . . is currently a patient, but should no longer be a patient in approximately three years' time after intensive rehabilitation" (Lush, 2014, p.37).

---

4 [2003] 1 WLR 1511
5 [2014] UKSC 18
6 [2005] EWHC 11

Bearing in mind these strictures, in order to approach considerations of litigation capacity systematically, as part of a clinical assessment, it is prudent to adopt a structured interview. This ensures that all aspects of capacity to enter into proceedings are covered and that the resulting opinion is both transparent and robust. A questionnaire was developed by the author for such use and forms the basis of the cases reported below. It contains questions which may include the following, depending on context:

- Do you know what has happened to you?
- How has this affected you/changed you?
- What financial losses has this meant for you? (Responses should include references to issues such as loss of earnings; care costs; travel costs and likely future costs);
- What skills have you lost? (One would look for insight into changes to the following functions: memory; attention; ability to think quickly and clearly and communication);
- Do you know what a solicitor is?
- Who is your solicitor and what is their job?
- What do you think that you have asked your solicitor to do for you?
- What do you think is the likelihood of you succeeding?
- What are the issues?
- Who else is involved in this case?
- What are their jobs/roles?
- Who represents you?
- What can the court do? (Responses should include reference to trial/hearings; uncertainty of proceedings and outcome and potential for loss);
- Who is the court supposed to listen to?
- Who makes the decision at the end?
- Do you know what an expert is (in this case)?
- What can happen with their reports? (Responses should demonstrate an understanding of their role in agreeing to disclosure, that written questions can be put to the expert, and also an understanding of the implications of expert evidence to their case);
- If the "other side" in your claim made an offer of settlement, what would you need to consider? (There should be some understanding of the basis of the offer; different types of settlement [periodic payments or structured settlement for annual costs vs lump sum comparing the offer with the size of claim]; understanding that they cannot go back for more in the future and understanding the implications of rejecting an offer);
- What is a trial?
- What are the risks of a trial to the outcome of the case? (The person should have some understanding of the role of the Judge's view of evidence as well as the potential risks associated with the performance of experts under cross examination.)

Case 1: GA

Presenting question/problem

This is the case of a 50-year-old gentleman with a severe brain injury as a result of a car accident. He has diabetes and related health problems and was non-compliant with medical treatments including neuro-rehabilitation. He became estranged from his wife and children as a result of his violent behaviours and problem-drinking and was seeking to enter into litigation to pursue regular contact with his children. The capacity assessment is reported here.

Background to the case

Clinical issues

GA had sustained a moderately severe brain injury in an unwitnessed road traffic accident several years previously. The neuroradiology reports at the time had pointed to gliosis in the right frontal lobe, probably consistent with traumatic brain injury as well as a tiny white matter area of high signal in the left frontal lobe. The latter finding was thought to be non-specific and probably related to GA's age.

Although GA had engaged in problem-drinking prior to his injury, he appeared to lose any self-regulation in terms of intake following the accident and was drinking significant amounts of spirits, wine and beer on a daily basis. He had developed diabetes as a result and frequently appeared jaundiced and bloated. He neglected himself in terms of appearance, personal hygiene and eating habits giving such cause for concern that a full-time support worker was appointed to help to keep him safe.

Family/social context

As a result of his emotional dysregulation, partly due to brain injury and partly attributable to the effects of excess alcohol, his wife had asked him to leave the matrimonial home. GA's access to his two primary-school-aged children had subsequently become a matter for the courts as there were concerns about his ability to keep them safe and to behave appropriately around them.

There were instances of supervised contact where GA became impatient or intolerant with the children and they had begun to express a wish for no further contact with their father.

GA's elderly parents were still living and made considerable efforts to support him in terms of his health and his contact with his children. However, there were longstanding relationship complexities between GA and his father which frequently came into focus and proved counter-productive at times.

Psychological/neuropsychological matters

GA lacked insight into the effects of his behaviours on others as well as an inability to apply the concrete knowledge he had, regarding his drinking and health status, to assist him to take control of his situation. He frequently lost his temper and threatened both clinical and support staff who were part of his rehabilitation programme. He would disengage from, and verbally challenge, staff. There were a range of neurocognitive impairments noted as part of his personal injury claim, which had settled some months previously.

Assessment and rationale

The assessment comprised both structured clinical interview with specific focus on the legal test for litigation capacity, and neuropsychometric testing of brain function as well as observation of behaviours.

GA's general cognitive function was assessed (WASI-II), and he emerged in the classification of "high average" overall but with a discrepancy indicating slowed processing. This is a fairly typical clinical picture post-brain injury. A specific task of processing speed was administered (BIRT Memory and Information Processing Battery) and GA only performed at the 2nd centile, indicating that 98 per cent of the population of his age (without a brain injury) would perform better than him on that task.

On a task of visual attention and motor speed (Colour Trails Test) GA's abilities were all below what would be expected.

Measures of executive function, including problem-solving and mental flexibility (Kaplan Baycrest Problem-Solving; Brixton Spatial Anticipation Test), gave rise to a mixed picture of results. Where a task is straightforward and clear from the outset, and GA has thinking time beforehand, he can perform within normal limits. This clearly depends upon the amount of alcohol he has consumed at any given time. However, when the task requires GA to adapt his thinking style and problem-solving skills during the task, his abilities are clearly impaired.

Brief memory screening (RBANS) demonstrated the typical profile post-brain injury (also seen in those who engage in long-term problem-drinking) where GA's ability to take on new information (new learning) is compromised and that verbal memory is *relatively* better than memory for visual and spatial information.

Upon interview, GA was typically belligerent and challenging. The hypothesis was formed that some of this behaviour was organically driven, following his brain injury but, that there was also a degree of "bluster" attributable to awareness and denial of difficulty. He gave concrete and overly-simplistic answers to many of the questions but was able to give broadly appropriate responses. He knew the name of his solicitor, why he wished to enter proceedings, what might be required of him, what experts who assess him might say and what outcome was thought likely based on the evidence before the court. He was realistic yet antagonistic and presented himself as the "hard done by" victim of the process. This was in keeping with his general presentation and even with his pre-morbid personality, to a degree.

It was noted throughout that GA maintained good eye contact and had relatively fluent speech. He answered questions frankly and complied with all the testing that was required of him. He appeared to apply good strategy formulation on certain tasks and was keen to do well although it was noted that on several tasks he did confabulate to cover memory gaps.

Opinion/outcome

The matter before the court was GA's ability to instruct a solicitor in court proceedings in relation to negotiations concerning contact matters with his two children.

GA's level of cognitive functioning, even after the brain injury, is higher than average for the population of his age. It is clear that there are deficits particularly in processing speed, in some areas of memory and in mental flexibility. It is also clear that in terms of understanding the matters in hand GA has sufficient understanding of the proceedings in front of him in order to instruct a solicitor meaningfully. Although he has memory difficulties these can be surmounted by presenting GA with written information for him to take away so that he is not relying on his verbal (auditory) memory. There are difficulties with mental flexibility, as evidenced on testing, which is further compromised by slowed processing speed.

However, it appears that even within the context of excessive alcohol consumption GA retains sufficient residual cognitive reserve and capacity in order to apply his tacit knowledge to problem-solving and making decisions. Whilst it is argued that he retains capacity in that regard he will require some assistance in order to address the residual neurocognitive deficits which have been noted. For example, he may need longer to absorb information, he may need information presented in more than one format and he may need prompting to ensure that he has understood and recalled properly. GA does not experience any communication difficulties which would compromise his current level of capacity to negotiate.

Legal commentary

This example demonstrates the importance of considering whether the deficits in a person's capacity can be met by the provision of assistance in enabling understanding and the retention of information. An individual's lawyers can assist in enabling understanding by ensuring that the language and concepts used, and the time taken to explain the necessary issues, allow the individual to reach a level of understanding which is sufficient. Similarly, a person close to the individual may enable information and understanding to be retained by repetition over time at home.

Discussion/ learning points

It is important to remember in assessments of this nature that the person only has to demonstrate a "good enough" level of understanding. Care must be taken not to set the bar too high and require more of the person being assessed than would be expected of a person who seeks to litigate *in the absence of brain injury*.

Case 2: GB

Presenting question/problem

This is a young lady, of 18 years of age, who had been injured as a young infant in a car accident. A claim for damages had been pursued on her behalf throughout her childhood but on reaching her majority the question had been raised as to her capacity to enter into the litigation on her own behalf. The assessment is reported here.

Background to the case

Clinical issues

Recent neuroradiology reports indicated that there is mature left fronto-temporal and right superior frontal lobe cerebral damage. The left hippocampus is small and bright. The left mammillary body and possibly the left fornix are smaller. The left superior temporal and parahippocampal gyrus are atrophic. There is thinning of the corpus callosum and widening of the left lateral ventricle reflecting lack of white matter bulk.

Family/social context

GB lives with her mother and sister. She is engaged to a young man who has learning disabilities. They are both considered to be vulnerable adults and require daily support from their families and professionals. Both GB and her fiancé attend a local college to acquire vocational skills, in a supported learning environment, and both engage in local voluntary work projects.

GB does not manage her own finances. Her weekly welfare benefits are paid directly into an account that is managed, by agreement, by her mother. GB does receive a small amount of money each week from her mother to pay for sweets and bus fares for short, local journeys. She has a savings jar and contributes small amounts to this weekly to pay for cinema tickets and clothing purchases. She is supported in a competence-promoting way by her family.

Psychological/neuropsychological matters

GB has a limited understanding of the financial and domestic requirements of daily life. This is partly because she has only just reached her majority and has yet to be afforded the opportunities to extend her reach of independence. However, given her longstanding brain injury and neurocognitive limitations, which are extensive, caution must be exercised in terms of seeking a level of autonomy that she may never be capable of enjoying.

As a direct result of the brain injury at the age of 3 months, GB has a wide range of neurocognitive deficits which satisfy the World Health Organisation definition (1992) of a learning disability in that her level of cognitive function is two standard deviations (2×15) below the population average (100) and has been consistently at this level since she was at primary school. She experienced global developmental delay as a result of her brain injury.

Cognitive assessments undertaken as part of her personal injury claim confirmed difficulties with:

- weak attentional skills and high levels of distractibility;
- mild word-finding difficulties and verbal fluency;
- problem-solving difficulties;
- poor conceptual (abstract) reasoning;
- weak verbal comprehension; and
- motor and processing speed problems.

Assessment and rationale

The assessment comprised structured clinical interview specifically in relation to litigation capacity but also a prepared assessment of her ability to understand, use and manipulate numbers, amounts and relational operators and to apply this to finances, based upon, and adapted from, Suto, Clare and Holland (2007).

GB was aware that she had a solicitor but did not know who they were. She thought that their job was to "get money for the crash" but had no deeper understanding of the claim. Her only other awareness of the proceedings was that, "the judge gets to decide". Based on her cognitive deficits and level of understanding, it is unlikely that it would be possible to improve her grasp of the claim process.

GB was able to count and use low level numbers, recognising these in written and spoken form. She was correctly able to identify coin and paper money by sight and also able to confirm that she has a savings jar which she adds to (and withdraws from) regularly. She recognised that she relies heavily upon her mother for financial assistance but was more than happy with the arrangement and did not want any changes to be made. GB admitted to being confused by money.

Opinion/outcome

Recent neuropsychological assessment coupled with the present structured interview assessments indicate that GB experiences difficulties with understanding the specific aspects of the litigation process that is underway. She has some grasp of the most basic concepts but is unable to extrapolate and generalise from these and to weigh up information considering consequences and implications in order to arrive at decisions in relation to the litigation process. Fundamentally, she is unclear about who her solicitor is and what is their role in proceedings, which is fairly critical to her ability to conduct her own litigation. On balance of probabilities, she lacks the capacity to conduct the present litigation.

In considering GB's ability to conduct her financial affairs, reference has been made to the neuropsychological data, to the neuroradiological, neuropsychometric and educational evidence of her limited cognitive abilities as a direct result of the car accident of her early childhood. The structured interviews were able to indicate that GB has a rudimentary understanding of basic financial concepts such as number ordering, number familiarity, number value and money familiarity as well as the concept of income and savings. However, her grasp is rudimentary, commensurate with her level of cognitive functioning. GB receives significant support from her family in order to manage her limited income.

Whilst it could be argued that there is potential for GB's capacity to manage small amounts of money, which could certainly be augmented through skills based learning such as teaching her budgeting and day-to-day money management, it is unlikely that she would reach sufficient level of ability and skill in the matter of financial management in order to achieve capacity to manage her own financial affairs, particularly in consideration of the potential for a substantial settlement as a result of proceedings.

Legal commentary

There is a clear distinction between a protected party (a person who lacks capacity to conduct the proceedings) and a protected beneficiary (a person who lacks capacity to manage and control any money recovered in litigation). The different capacities should not be elided and should be kept quite separate. Whilst a person's ability (or lack of ability) to manage their own finances may provide some evidence as to their capacity to conduct proceedings, the capacities must be considered separately and, in the context solely of the capability in question.

Discussion/learning points

This is a case where the balance must be struck between the empowerment and the protection of the vulnerable. If the principle of pursuing maximum autonomy is pursued dogmatically, the person could suffer psychologically from the pressure to manage their own needs above their ability to do so, even with support. If the person's wishes are to continue to live with support, even where they may be potential for augmenting their skills so as to reduce that support, it is argued that the person's wishes should receive primacy.

Case 3: GC

Presenting question/problem

This is a case where family proceedings had been brought by the local authority which has resulted in the removal of GC's three primary-school-aged daughters into care whilst the court gathers evidence. She retains (supervised) access twice weekly. The local authority is seeking care orders on the grounds of longstanding concerns regarding "mother's vulnerability". The present assessment was requested for the purpose of ascertaining the GC's capacity to litigate. In addition to the request for the assessment, the instructing solicitor asked for advice about how best to "frame" information to mother so as to maximise her ability to participate in proceedings.

Background to the case

Clinical issues

Early GP records for GC indicated global developmental delay and a diagnosis of learning disability was made, although her family failed to comply with support and professional appointments during her childhood, largely due to a chaotic lifestyle. She attended specialist schooling until the age of 15. She was noted to experience difficulties with adaptive functioning, which is one element of the diagnostic triad for learning disability.

Family/social context

Records indicate that at the first opportunity to live apart from her birth family, GC was noted to experience difficulty with reading, medication management, household budgeting and domestic skills. The father of her children had been removed from the home on the grounds of suspected sexual abuse of the children and GC's inability to keep them safe in his presence.

In addition, the local authority expressed concerns that GC might not be able to keep herself safe as there are records of visitors to the house who are suspected of taking advantage of GC, and of dealing in drugs from her property.

Psychological/neuropsychological matters

At the time of leaving formal education, GC was unable to read or write. Despite agreeing to attend literacy classes, her engagement was so poor that she was not permitted to continue.

Assessment and rationale

The assessment plan was to establish GC's level of cognitive functioning, gauge her understanding of the present situation in terms of the legal proceedings and also to gain a measure of her ability to engage in consequential reasoning.

Cognitive assessment results indicated that GC was functioning in the "extremely low" range, in the bottom 0.1 per cent of the general population. The WHO classification (1992) would place her in the category of "mild" learning disability (IQ 50–69). The average IQ for the general population is 100. Standard units of measurement away from this average are expressed in the form of a "standard deviation". It is accepted, when discussing "normally distributed" general cognitive function, that a standard deviation is equivalent to 15 points and that two or more standard deviations away from the average (i.e., 100) is considered to be "abnormal". Therefore, the *maximum* IQ that a person can have and still be eligible for the diagnosis of learning disability is 70. An IQ of 70 is equivalent to functioning in the bottom 2 per cent of the adult general population.

GC's ability to attend to (and understand) new information, to process it into memory and recall it when needed is severely compromised. She struggles to process information and needs significant repetition in order to take on board what she is being told. She was unable to problem-solve and her level of reasoning demonstrated that she could not associate "knowing" with "doing". Put another way, she was unable to draw upon her concrete knowledge in order to develop strategies or actions that would serve her interests.

GC knew the name of her solicitor and that she could, "ask her anything" but was unable to substantiate this further. She appeared to have adopted a passive role in proceedings and did not consider the possibility that she could challenge any views or findings. She did not understand why the children had been taken into care, expressing the view that she had been told that she mixed with people who, "do drugs".

Throughout the assessment GC answered all questions that were put to her and complied with all requests to undertake psychometric tests. She gave brief but open answers and at no time gave the impression that she was attempting to influence the outcome of the assessment. She maintained good eye-contact and frequently smiled when responding, giving the impression that she was eager to please.

GC frequently needed to have instructions and questions repeated and reframed in order to prompt her to stay on task or to understand what was required of her in relation to the task.

On occasion, GC was observed to vocalise whilst on task. It is hypothesised that this was a strategy used in order to assist her to stay on task and to assist her concentration. It was noted that she experienced difficulty pronouncing many words of common usage although it is not possible to say that this represents a specific communication disorder.

Opinion/outcome

GC has been assessed as having an IQ between 52 and 60. This is incompatible with the complex cognitive skills required to litigate in complex child care proceedings. However, in and of itself, an IQ figure is insufficient to suggest that an individual does not retain the capacity to litigate. There is a clear absence of her being able to tie facts and assertions together with the evidence that has been collected over a lengthy period of time by the local authority. This is less likely to represent denial of her difficulties and is more likely to be as a result of her impaired ability to comprehend due to her extremely low level of cognitive functioning.

This assessment has clearly indicated that GC experiences marked comprehension difficulties as well as problems with conceptual or abstract reasoning such as would be required in the earliest stages of decision-making. Once key information is understood, the individual needs to draw on sufficient mental flexibility, perspective-taking and consequential reasoning in order to formulate possible solutions to the matter under consideration and to keep the information under review as circumstances change and develop. GC experiences marked difficulties with each of these neurocognitive skills, predominantly as a result of her low level of cognitive functioning but also because of her inability to judge the motives of others and to protect herself from exploitation. She is easily influenced and, as a result of this suggestibility, is extremely vulnerable.

Given that GC experiences difficulties with understanding, concentrating and with recalling information presented orally, parties in proceedings could best assist her as follows:

- Provide her with written copies of conversations (produced with brief words and sentences and possibly accompanied by the use of visual icons);
- Provide her with a diary or calendar (to be displayed prominently in her house) so that she can record dates of appointments, key dates for court, deadlines for bills and the like;
- Go through relevant papers and documents with her to ensure that she has understood *and* recalled key information. It is probably the case that she will need such information presented to her more than once before she is able to retain it in memory and use it as a basis for decision-making;
- Ensure that verbal communication with her consists exclusively of short sentences and avoids the use of complex terminology. If the latter is unavoidable then all efforts should be made to explain, using straightforward language;
- Ensure that the pace of communication and verbal interchanges during proceedings is commensurate with GC's abilities; and
- Do not assume that just because GC tells you she understands that she *actually* does. The safest way to avoid this situation would be to ask her to repeat back what has been said to ensure that she has grasped the key points rather than to rely on an affirmative answer to the question "do you understand?"

Legal commentary

This case highlights the importance of differentiating a parent's ability as a parent to care for their children from their ability to conduct proceedings. The detailed assessment of the support which would enable GC to have capacity to conduct the litigation demonstrates the importance of not simply assessing capacity relative to the individual's standalone cognitive skills. With assistance many people can demonstrate capacity when otherwise they might not be able to do so.

Discussion/learning points

It is encouraging that in the context of requesting an assessment of a person's capacity to litigate, the instructing solicitors were able to recognise the importance of acknowledging and working positively with an adult who is clearly vulnerable. The MCA (2005) is not about disempowering or excluding adults from the support and authority of the courts but ensuring that their rights and freedoms as protected as far as possible and practicable.

Case 4: GD

Presenting question/problem

This is the case of a 20-year-old mother whose two children had been removed from her care. An assessment was sought as to the level of functioning of GD, the degree of any learning disability that may be present and GD's capability to provide instructions direct to a solicitor in connection with proceedings.

Background to the case

Clinical issues

GD has a physical disability as a result of a childhood cancer. GD reports no history of alcohol or drug misuse, no history of head injury or epilepsy nor any other significant medical events in her past. There are no other pertinent clinical issues in the available records.

Family/social context

GD was brought up in the family home. Her upbringing was somewhat chaotic as the family moved home frequently, often over long distances. She attended primary school on the south coast of England, secondary school in England and Wales, finally settling in Wales just before reaching adulthood. It is not known why the family moved around the country in this way.

GD left school at 16 and attended a local college for a few months, studying IT, Business Studies and Art before becoming unexpectedly pregnant with her son who is the focus of the present proceedings. Her partner, and the child's father, was said to have been physically and emotionally abusive. GD is no longer with him. She has admitted that she used to lie to the local authority to cover up for his behaviours because she was afraid of potential consequences for herself.

Psychological/neuropsychological matters

There was no information provided in the instruction which gave background in terms of cognitive or psychological functioning. However, the reportedly abusive relationship with the father of her child certainly needs to be taken into account in the present assessment as it suggests a degree of vulnerability and susceptibility to coercion which may not serve the interests of either GD or her child.

Assessment and rationale

The assessment comprised a structured interview in relation to capacity to litigate as well as cognitive assessment to establish GD's level of functioning. Tests of executive function, including skills of problem-solving, estimating, organising and exercising judgement as well as mental flexibility were also included in the battery.

In terms of structured interview, GD was able to answer most of the administered questions to a reasonable standard, knowing her solicitor, their role, her role in proceedings, the other parties in proceedings and what their concerns might be, what is expected of her in the context of the case and what the potential outcomes could be.

In terms of cognitive functioning, GD emerged as operating at a level commensurate with borderline learning disability (IQ 67–75). However, the profile of scores did not conform to the typical pattern seen in developmental disability. There was a clinically and statistically significant difference between her verbal and performance scores, in favour of performance. This is unexpected and, along with her uninterpretable performance on a pre-morbid test of reading, points to GD probably experiencing a specific reading or language-based disorder which may not have been diagnosed during her educational career.

Executive test results indicate that GD experiences difficulties with formulating and implementing a plan of action in order to solve a problem (Key Search test), problems with estimating time (Temporal Judgement test) and estimating plausible answers to everyday questions (Cognitive Estimations test). There was also evidence of slowed processing and problems with being easily distracted whilst performing a task (Trail Making test). It is not unsurprising for a person with a relatively low level of cognitive functioning to struggle on executive-based tasks as these are heavily loaded on to frontal lobe functions which are compromised relative to IQ. However, the results are illustrative in the context of the present assessment question.

During the assessment, it was observed that GD was attentive and socially appropriate to the situation. She appeared to give a frank account of herself and her situation. GD was heavy with cold during the assessment but remained able to concentrate well on the tasks set for her. She appeared to have good insight and self-monitoring skills and was able to detect when making an error on tasks.

Opinion/outcome

GD's level of intellectual/cognitive functioning is at the "borderline" level of learning disabilities. However, there is a clinically and statistically significant degree of difference between her verbal and non-verbal (performance) scores in favour of non-verbal skills. Whilst this might be an artefact of testing, it is more likely that this is due to a combination of specific problems with literacy and interruptions to schooling either through serial absence (for which there is no evidence available) or as a result of serial family relocations resulting in changes of school at critical periods in her education.

It is clear from the profile of test results reported above that GD is functioning at the level of borderline learning disability and as a result, experiences significant difficulties with the following "executive" functions:

- planning;
- judgement;
- decision-making;
- problem-solving;
- acquiring new information presented orally;
- deterioration of ability as task difficulty increases; and
- mental flexibility.

Clearly, this may have implications for the level of support she may need in her parenting responsibilities.

It is argued that GD does retain sufficient capacity to instruct a solicitor. That said, she may need additional support to do so based on her profile of neuropsychological weaknesses reported above.

Legal commentary

The conclusion is a reasonable one. It reiterates the need to consider the test for capacity for the particular task under consideration; namely, conducting the proceedings. The fact that the individual may be vulnerable is not directly relevant to the issue of capacity. In *Masterman-Lister v Brutton & Co*[7] the court recognised that there were many means by which a court could protect against vulnerability, and that concentration should be focused on the task in question; namely, the conduct of the proceedings. Chadwick LJ said that "The question of difficulty in any particular case is likely to be whether the party does have the mental capacity with the assistance of such explanation as he may be given, to understand that nature and effect of the particular transaction" (paragraph 60).

At paragraph 75 he described the test as being

> whether the party to legal proceedings is capable of understanding, with the assistance of such proper explanation from legal advisers and experts in other disciplines as the case may require, the issues on which his consent or decision is likely to be necessary in the course of those proceedings.

It is also important to highlight Chadwick LJ's reiteration of the fact that it is not for the courts "to prevent those who have the mental capacity to make rational decisions from making decisions which others may regard as rash or irresponsible." This comment simply serves to emphasise the need to focus on the capacity to conduct proceedings, rather than on the perceived quality of the decision making.

---

7 [2003] 1 WLR 1511

Discussion/learning points

This is an exemplar of the different approaches of the law before the MCA (2005) and since. Previously, capacity would be assessed in diagnostic terms, in which circumstances, GD would certainly have been considered to lack capacity in the present context. However, the MCA (2005) dictates a functional approach where the presumption of capacity stands until it is robustly overturned, an outcome which must be based on evidence of a person's inability to do something rather than a general diagnosis.

References

Civil Procedure Rules. (1998). Retrieved from www.legislation.gov.uk/uksi/1998/3132/contents/made

Judicial College. (2018). *Equal Treatment Bench Book.* Retrieved from www.judiciary.gov.uk.

Lush, D. (2014). The Mental Capacity Act and the new Court of Protection. Retrieved from http://northumbriajournals.co.uk/index.php/IJMHMCL/article/download/165/160

Ruck Keene, A. (ed.). (2015). *Assessment of Mental Capacity: A Practical Guide for Doctors and Lawyers* (4th ed.). The British Medical Association & The Law Society: Law Society Publishing.

World Health Organisation. (1992). *The ICD-10 Classification of Mental and Behavioural Disorders: clinical descriptions and diagnostic guidelines.* Geneva: World Health Organisation.

11 Capacity to plead/stand trial

Dr Tracey Ryan-Morgan

With Simon Morgan

These are issues which typically come to light at Crown Court and arise where there is a suspicion that the defendant may not be able to fully participate in the trial process due to a mental difficulty. It is understood that case law was originally established in *Pritchard*[1] but has since been updated and explained in M (*John*).[2] The test is whether the defendant can:

- understand the charges;
- decide to plead guilty or not;
- exercise the right to challenge a juror;
- instruct his solicitors and counsel (meaning that he must be able to (a) convey to his lawyers the case and matters he wishes to advance (b) understand the lawyers' questions (c) apply his mind to answering them (d) convey intelligibly to his lawyers the answers he wishes to give. It is not necessary that his instructions should be plausible, believable or reliable nor that he should be able to see that they are implausible, unbelievable or unreliable. His comments do not need to be valid or helpful either to his lawyers or his own case);
- follow the course of proceedings (meaning that he must be able (a) to understand what is said by witnesses and counsel (b) communicate intelligibly to his lawyers any comment he wishes to make on anything said by the witnesses or counsel) and;
- give evidence in his or her own defence (this means that the defendant must be able (a) to understand the questions he is asked (b) apply his mind to answering them and (c) convey intelligibly the answers he wishes to give). It does include whether he can be cross-examined.[3] The issue is now more aptly identified as "fitness to participate in the trial process". It is not necessary that his answers be plausible, believable or reliable nor that he should be able to see that they are implausible, unbelievable or unreliable. It is not necessary that he should be able to remember all or any of the matters giving rise to the charges.

1 (1836) 7 C&P 303
2 [2003] EWCA Crim 3452
3 *R v Orr* [2016] EWCA Crim 889

Failing to act in his own best interests as a consequence of a mental condition does not, of itself, render him unfit to plead/stand trial,[4] nor is a high degree of abnormality.[5]

In applying the test, the court must assess his capabilities in the context of the particular proceedings by reference to the complexity of the case and what the process will in fact demand of him.[6]

The burden of proof for a defence team that raises the question of fitness to plead is, "on the balance of probabilities". However, the burden of proof for a prosecuting team is, "beyond a reasonable doubt". The issue of fitness to plead is decided by the trial judge not the jury.

If the defendant cannot fulfil one or more of the above actions, there then follows a "trial of facts", also referred to in the literature as, "trial of issue". This is to establish if the defendant did "the act or made the omission charged" (hereafter referred to as "the act'" for convenience) which is the subject of the allegation. If the jury finds that the defendant did not do the act, the defendant is entitled to an acquittal and no penalty can follow. If the jury finds that they did the act, the court can impose a Hospital Order, a Supervision Order or an absolute discharge.

It should be pointed out that there can be technical difficulties in determining what constitutes 'the act'. A literal approach would suggest that it involves simply the physical element of the offence. However, each offence may have physical elements that are inextricably bound with other elements which import a state of mind. By way of example, "voyeurism" contrary to section 67 Sexual Offences Act (2003) is committed "if, for the purpose of sexual gratification, he observes another person doing a private act, and he knows that the other person does not consent to being observed for his sexual gratification". The relevant "act" is the actual observing of another doing a private act with the purpose of sexual gratification. In normal parlance, the purpose would be regarded as a matter relating to a state of mind. However, as the link between deliberate observation and sexual gratification is central to the statutory offence of voyeurism, the purpose must be established for the purposes of section 4A of the 1964 Act.[7] The courts have held that, although the act has two components, they are indissoluble and together form the "relevant act".

By way of contrast, in relation to an allegation of murder, it would not be permissible for the defendant to raise the issue of diminished responsibility. The act is the unlawful killing itself; diminished responsibility arises only after the act of killing and is not a constituent element of the offence. However, if there is objective evidence of it having been an accident or in self-defence, the court would need to be satisfied, beyond reasonable doubt, that those possibilities have been negatived. The point is that for the act of killing to be murder, it has to have been unlawful; proper self-defence is lawful, even where the consequences are fatal.

4   *R v Robertson* [1968] 3 All ER 557
5   *R v Berry* 66 Cr. App. R. 156
6   *R v Marcantonio* [2016] EWCA Crim 14
7   *R v B (M)* [2012] 2 Cr. App. R. 15

Accordingly, each offence must be considered in detail before a determination can be made as to the extent of the act that it is necessary to establish.

There is no provision for determination of fitness to plead at the Magistrates or Youth Courts, nor is it necessary to embark on such a course.[8] The power of this court arises by reference to the interaction between the provisions of section 37(1) and 37(3). Section 37(3) provides that

> where a person is charged before a magistrates' court with any act or omission as an offence and the court would have the power, on convicting him of that offence, to make an order under subsection (1) above in his case, then, if the court is satisfied that the accused did the act or omission charged, the court may, if it thinks fit, make such an order without convicting him.

Thus, the court can proceed to a fact-finding hearing and can deal with the accused in accordance with section 37(1), bearing in mind that section 37(1) is subject to satisfaction of section 37(2) provisions as to the necessary medical evidence etc. It also allows a court to deal with a trial and convert it to a section 37(3) hearing.[9]

However, the Law Commission consulted in 2014 on fitness to plead issues, although their recommendations have yet to be implemented. One outcome of the consultation was to separate out the issues of fitness to be tried and fitness to plead. In general terms, there was also a recommendation for the legal test to be updated to prioritise, "capacity for effective participation in trial" (but see *Orr* above), rather than the narrow focus of the Pritchard test. The Act requires that the court shall not make a determination of fitness to be tried except on the written or oral evidence of two or more registered practitioners, at least one of whom is approved under section 12 Mental Health Act (1983). It is worth remembering that, even if the experts agree, the court can still reject the evidence. Registered psychologists are named specifically as those that could assist the court with expert evidence as to the capacity of the accused.

The role of the clinician instructed to assess fitness to stand trial is, therefore, a weighty one in such proceedings.

Case 1: HA

Presenting question/problem

This is the case of a 76-year-old gentleman who was charged with numerous sexual offences against children which were alleged to have taken place when he was in his middle age. He had been investigated for subjective memory complaints and reported that he had dementia. His medical records and clinical evidence did not support this claim and an assessment was made as to his capacity to plead.

---

8 *R v Barking Youth Court* [2002] 2 Cr App R 19.
9 *R v Stratford Magistrates Court* [2007] 1 WLR 3119

Background to the case

Clinical issues

There was scant clinical information available regarding HA's clinical presentation prior to the present assessment. His wife had written to their solicitor insisting that HA had a dementing disease (vascular dementia) but clinical outpatient review letters by a consultant physician indicated that the diagnosis was not yet certain and further testing needed to be carried out on HA. There was no evidence of any co-morbidities and HA was not on any regular medication. There were, therefore, no identified cardiovascular risk factors.

A CT scan of HA's head, taken three years previously, reported a small old lacunar infarction. Other findings reported on the scan were considered to be "age-related" and, therefore, within normal limits

Lacunar strokes are a type of vascular insufficiency which result from a small branch of the cerebral arteries becoming occluded. The resulting infarcts are so minuscule that there may be no obvious clinical symptoms. Lacunar infarcts or minor strokes are mild in their effects and from which singly there may be rapid recovery. It is only when there is an increasing number of these strokes that there is a cumulative effect in a form of dementia known as a lacunar state. In lacunar state, mental deterioration lags behind the physical signs of weakness which include slowness, disturbances of gait, speech and swallowing.

An EEG conducted three years previously also failed to provide evidence for any underlying dementing process.

HA had been assessed using a battery of psychometric tests at the time of the CT scan and EEG investigation and his neurocognitive functions of attention, memory, visuospatial ability, language, executive functioning and reasoning were all measured to be within normal limits at that time. Assessment of pre-morbid functioning had, similarly, shown no evidence of decline.

Family/social context

HA has been married to his wife for 27 years and they have a 26-year-old son. Previously, he had been in a relationship with the mother of the two sisters who have brought the allegation of serial incidents of indecent assault, reporting that these occurred at a time when they were minors.

HA had spent time in borstal and approved school as an adolescent and also several periods of incarceration as an adult. He had then reformed himself, trained as a metallurgist and worked for many years in that occupation. It is not known what his previous convictions were for.

Psychological/neuropsychological matters

According to the wife, HA has difficulties in remembering the part of his life prior to his present marriage and also cannot remember having had any sexual relations with his wife. He is reported not to be able to process numbers and figures, as a result of which he gave up his local charity work where he had been an honorary treasurer. However, it emerged that he does still take full responsibility for his own banking, including processing and reconciling his bank statements, with full accuracy.

It was similarly reported that he experiences difficulties in finding the right word he wants in conversation and so will substitute a word he does not mean to use and which, often, is reported to have an opposite meaning.

The final difficulty reported by his wife is that he becomes panicky under pressure and will stammer.

Assessment and rationale

The main focus of the assessment was to comprehensively study HA's memory function, given that his reported difficulties were mnestic. It was also considered critical to interview him to assess his own subjective account of his difficulties rather than receive such information second-hand, through his wife.

HA was both anxious and also easily roused to aggression during the interview. He deferred to his wife in response to all questions. He complied with all the testing that was administered, which was substantial and somewhat time-intensive. He did appear a little fatigued towards the end of the two-hour session and a short break was offered.

The test selected was the Weschler Memory Scales, which provide a detailed assessment and comprehensive picture of memory functioning in adults. HA's results for verbal and visual recall, immediate and delayed, general and working memory were *all* within normal limits. Indeed, most results exceeded that expected for his age when compared to the performance of peers in standardised norm tables.

A widely-used test of "effort" or "performance validity" was also administered to HA and he scored full marks on both trials which were administered. This enabled the conclusion to be drawn that the results obtained were both valid and reliable and could be considered to be an accurate reflection of the functioning of his memory system. This is somewhat at odds with his subjective complaint that he is unable to recall anything of his life prior to his present marriage. Typically, autobiographical memory deficits of this nature, in the absence of underlying neuropathology, are considered to be psychogenic, whether consciously effected or otherwise (Kopelman, 2002).

Opinion/outcome

HA and his wife offer a symptom history suggestive of a dementing process. However, in the medical records there is yet to be diagnostic clarity. There is no neuroradiological, neuropsychometric or electroencephalographical evidence of any dementia. There is no psychometric evidence to support the opinion of a decline in HA's ability from a former level of functioning. It is my opinion, based on available records, comprehensive neuropsychological testing, that there is no organic basis for HA's reported memory difficulties. The most likely explanation would be psychogenic.

There is similarly no evidence that HA experiences difficulties in comprehending the evidence against him, challenging a juror or instructing a legal advisor. I would advise the court in its deliberations that, in my clinical opinion, HA is both fit to plead and to stand trial.

Legal commentary

On the face of it, the assessments support the contention that he was fit. The only real issue was his memory function. An inability to recall events does not result in his being unfit to participate in the trial process. In *R v M (John)* (above) the court specifically approved a direction to the jury which included this phrase,

> nor is it necessary that the defendant should be able to remember all or any of the matters which give rise to the charges against him. He is entitled to say that he has no recollection of those events, or indeed of anything that happened during the relevant period.

Discussion/learning points

This is a case in point to illustrate the over-riding importance of taking a robust and comprehensive clinical history when interviewing a patient. At face value, the reported symptoms would give cause for concern if not considered within the context of the *specific* elements of memory that were reported to be failing. Detailed knowledge of models of memory allow the clinician to direct their questioning at different, sequential, elements of such models in order to construct a clear understanding of the person's reported memory deficits within such a framework.

Case 2: HB

Presenting question/problem

This is the case of a 17-year-old man, remanded into care for his own protection, having been charged with several counts of theft. He had a history of a broken and dysfunctional family. The case indicates that he has a learning disability and is experiencing chronic low mood as well as being highly susceptible to influence. An assessment of his ability to plead was made and recommendations provided as to ongoing care and support.

Background to the case

Clinical issues

HB has a diagnosed learning disability, with an IQ in the region of 55, placing him in the "extremely low" category of general intellectual functioning. He also has had intermittent involvement with local Child and Adolescent Mental Health

Services (CAMHS) for periods of profound low mood and suicidal thoughts. However, records indicate that HB struggles to engage with either academic or positive social efforts to engage and guide his behaviours.

Family/social context

HB's parents separated when he was 12. He initially lived with his mother but then moved to live with his father, at which point he came to the notice of the authorities and began a career in foster care. He had a record of being caught and cautioned by police in his local area and had come to the attention of local Youth Offending Services. Records indicated that he was somewhat suggestible and under the influence of others when offending. Concerns were expressed as to his vulnerability.

Psychological/neuropsychological matters

Previous cognitive testing had identified that HB has learning difficulties. He was unable to engage in school life and had been excluded several times during his time in foster care. He expressed severely low self-confidence and profound feelings of depression when formally assessed by statutory services. He was considered to be at risk and extremely vulnerable.

Assessment and rationale

HB's cognitive function had not been assessed for some time and little of the data were available for scrutiny. To that end, it was decided to administer a comprehensive assessment of intellectual function to establish whether he is more likely to have experienced developmental delay from an early age or whether he has an atypical profile of strengths and weaknesses in his cognitive system.

Results indicated a verbal IQ of between 54 and 66 (extremely low), a non-verbal IQ of between 79 and 93 (borderline to low average) and an overall level of cognitive function of between 65 and 75 (extremely low to borderline). This is a somewhat different picture to that conjured by the widely reported "IQ of 55" in his records. The current profile indicates that he struggles with processing verbal information but that non-verbal processing is a relative strength. This profile is considered to be atypical of an individual with a developmental learning disability. It is more reflective of the profile of strengths and weaknesses of an individual who experiences difficulty in learning. This means that whilst HB might find particular tasks hard and require support he manages relatively well in other aspects of his life and can show improvements in cognitive ability when given the support that is required (and is motivated to take up this support). It is possible that he is dyslexic or has a specific language-based disorder which makes it difficult for him to engage in classroom-based learning (as evidence by his frequent truant and exclusions). This would have to be investigated further and in more detail in a separate exercise.

The Social and Moral Awareness Test (SMAT) assesses an individual's social moral rule knowledge and also their social-moral reasoning. It has been designed to assess an individual's ability to understand how to behave in common situations and to ascertain whether they understand why they should behave in that way because they know the rules and whether they have a higher level of social moral reasoning and understand the thoughts and beliefs of others. This was administered to HB whose responses indicated that he has a relatively weak knowledge of the rules of social moral reasoning but an even weaker ability to reason using these rules. The implication from this is that he finds it extremely difficult to understand the beliefs, behaviours and perspectives of others. This is a significant result in relation to his offending behaviours.

Finally, the Glasgow Depression Scale for people with a learning disability was administered to HB who scored 18. The diagnostic cut-off is at 13 and, therefore, this result indicates that he is experiencing symptoms of depression at present. When asked his mood HB was able to say that he felt low but was unable to define what this felt like or discuss it in any depth indicating that he experiences difficulties understanding, describing and accessing his emotions. This adds to his current level of vulnerability.

The Gudjonsson Suggestibility Scales represent a widely used assessment to identify interrogative suggestibility in an individual either through the means of yielding to pressure or shifting their answer in relation to pressure. It is an assessment of an individual's tendency to give in to leading questions and to cope with interrogative pressure. It is used in this instance as part of an overall assessment as to HB's vulnerability to influence. The results indicate that HB is able to recall verbally presented information rather better than many of his peers with a similar level of cognitive functioning but that he is somewhat suggestible to the influence of others in term of giving in to leading questions and considerably vulnerable in terms of shifting his responses when under pressure. He is considered, therefore, to be suggestible. In the context of his current offending and in the light of his subjective account of the offences it does appear that he is very easily influenced by others and lacks the ability to look behind the motivations of others and to reason using a moral code.

Opinion/outcome

It is my opinion based of the assessment reported above and the records which have been made available for the purposes of the present assessment that HB is an extremely vulnerable young man. It is recognised that he is at a difficult point in his life where he is entering the transition into adulthood which exacerbates the vulnerabilities identified above. He has very limited verbal skills which place him in the bottom 1 per cent of the general population for his age. His perceptual reasoning skills are still relatively low and would be considered to be low-average at best. He has limited knowledge of the moral rules around social behaviours and markedly lacks the ability to apply these in any way which would benefit him. It is also of concern that he is depressed at present and should be provided with sophisticated psychological assistance to deal with his low mood. He has limited ability to adapt his skills and is easily influenced by others by being suggestible.

My opinion is that the court could consider diverting him away from the penal system to a specialist, residential, supportive adolescent forensic service which would work in conjunction with the local LAC services to ensure that HB is protected from malign influences, provided with the psychological support and direction that he needs and given a structured, protective and nurturing environment within which he can develop the necessary life skills to live independently and safely. However, should the court wish to pursue the criminal charges against him, it is argued that he lacks the cognitive (and psychological) resources to enter a plea and stand trial.

Legal commentary

The only issue to be determined was whether his functioning prevented him from participating meaningfully in the trial process. Account would be taken of the way in which the court can control the proceedings to alleviate any unnecessary pressure, e.g., breaks in the trial, etc. As the allegations appear quite simple and the issues at trial likewise, it seems likely that he would not be found unfit. Likewise, a poor moral code is not an issue which will assist in the determination. Courts are reluctant to jump to the conclusion that a person is unfit because it has the potential affect of their being subject to sanction without conviction. Alone, suggestibility and malign influence, short of duress, are not defences and are unlikely to justify a finding that a person is unfit to stand trial. The suggestion that he should be dealt with outwith the court process is most likely to find favour. A report such as this might persuade the prosecution that it is not in the public interest to pursue the prosecution.

Discussion/learning points

There is an important lesson in this, and other similar cases, where what at face value appears to be a simple question of mental capacity, actually cannot be considered without reference to wider, psychological and social factors. In this case, HB was seen to commit the offences but was under the malign influence of others as a result of being highly suggestible and, therefore, extremely vulnerable. Just looking at his level of cognitive functioning alone would not have provided a complete picture for the court to consider in its deliberations.

Case 3: HC

Presenting question/problem

This is the case of a 65-year-old man who had a history of head injury, following a serious fall, in the recent past subsequent to which he is alleged to have sexually assaulted his young granddaughter. He has a longstanding history of alcohol abuse prior to the injury. His current clinical presentation includes chronic depression which is considered to be the mediating factor in his symptom pattern. The assessment of his fitness to plead is reported.

Background to the case

Clinical issues

In his forties, HC was physically and psychologically dependent upon alcohol. In his mid-fifties, he sustained a severe head injury when he fell from the roof of his shed. He had a GCS of 12 at scene. A CT brain scan on admission to hospital noted generalised intracranial swelling with small hemorrhagic foci on the left with a superficial haematoma over the right temporal region. A subsequent CT scan two weeks later ruled out the possibility of subsequent hydrocephalus. A more detailed brain scan (MRI) was carried out two years later which noted a slight enlargement of the lateral ventricles and no evidence of progressive hydrocephalus or focal atrophic change in relation to the left temporal lobe. The appearances overall were symmetrical without focal structural abnormality.

He was left with the typical post-brain injury symptoms of generalised fatigue, difficulties with concentrating and remembering as well as problems with emotional regulation. His wife reports that his sleep cycle has been unsettled since the injury and that he is prone to wandering and losing his way such that she has to lock the doors of the house when they are inside their home. She also notes that he will not wash unless prompted and has to have his clothes put out for him or he will select inappropriate clothing (such as wearing shorts in winter).

Family/social context

Prior to the head injury, HC had been a devoted husband, father and grandfather according to all accounts. Since the charges had been brought HC no longer has any contact with his children or grandchildren which is a source of great distress to him.

Psychological/neuropsychological matters

HC presented as tearful throughout the assessment. He was agitated when he brought up the topic of the charges against him.

As a result of the traumatic brain injury, HC has developed post-traumatic epilepsy, for which he is medicated. It has a temporal lobe focus. This is important in that there are clear and proven links between seizures in this area and their impact on memory function, due to the involvement of the hippocampus.

Assessment and rationale

It was decided to assess HC's overall neurocognitive function, his executive functioning, the validity of his reported symptoms and his mood.

Neurocognitive screening was carried out by administering the RBANS. His profile of scores was suggestive of poor attention (0.1st percentile) and memory functioning (0.5th percentile) with low scores for language ability (10th percentile). However, one of the sub-tests that feeds into the Language index is timed and can be detrimentally affected by slowed processing speed rather than impaired language.

Executive functioning was assessed by means of the Similarities and Matrix Reasoning sub-test of the WAIS-IV and the Cognitive Estimates Test. There was a mixed picture of results. HC struggled to think conceptually, as is required by the Similarities test, and only achieved a scaled score of 6 on this task. However, he achieved a scaled score of 13 on Matrix Reasoning, which is a visual reasoning (problem-solving) task. His responses on the Cognitive Estimates Test were all within normal limits.

HC was given the Hospital Anxiety & Depression Scale (HADS) to complete. His scores indicated that he was profoundly anxious and moderately depressed. The HADS is designed to measure underlying, rather than reactive, mood changes.

The validity of HC's reported symptoms was measured using a stand-alone and an embedded measure. On the Reliable Digit Span (Iverson & Tulsky, 2003) HC achieved a scaled score of 4 which is *below* the cut-off for reliable performance that is recommended by the authors. His performance on the ToMM was 49 out of 50 on Trial 1 and 50 out of 50 on Trial 2. The stand-alone measure is more robust as the authors of the Reliable Digit Span indicate that their test only achieves variable sensitivity. (Sensitivity refers to the correct identification of those who are exerting adequate effort in this instance.)

Opinion/outcome

HC's neurocognitive performance is reflective of a combination of neuropsychological, neuropathological and psychological factors where the contribution of these individual elements requires separate consideration.

Indicators would place the severity of the traumatic brain injury in the moderate category. HC has experienced fatigue, attentional and memory problems, language difficulties, some executive functioning problems (concrete thinking, problems with initiation and judgement) and sleep cycle changes. In addition, HC now has post-traumatic epilepsy, which is difficult to control with medication due to the unpredictable nature of the seizures.

The contribution of the many years of alcohol over-use cannot be underestimated in terms of neuropathology. It is commonly known that alcohol accelerates the ageing processes in the brain, leading to atrophy. A common (general) effect of atrophy is slowed processing.

Finally, there is the contribution of the mood disturbance comprising symptoms of both anxiety and depression, both of which can exert a cognitive effect.

From the point of view of assessing fitness to plead, it is clear that HC retains little decision-making capacity following his serial brain changes. He does not choose his own clothes, cannot decide to leave the house and take care of himself (safely), struggles to process information into memory (other than at the lowest level of functioning equivalent to the bottom 0.1 per cent of the population) and cannot meaningfully weigh up information from different perspectives due to an absence of abstract thought.

In the context of the legal test of fitness to plead, it is my opinion that he would struggle to understand the charges in sufficient detail, although he is aware that he is said to have committed an offence against his granddaughter. He lacks the ability to weigh up the implications of a plea or to give evidence in his own defence due to damage to his language system following his fall. I would cast significant doubt upon his ability to instruct a representative or to know when or how to challenge a juror. Finally, I do not consider that he is competent to follow proceedings. My advice to the court would be that I do not consider HC fit to plead, based on clinical assessment.

Legal commentary

In a case such as this the court would expect to be given examples of the questions that he was asked during the assessment. Significant details would be required to establish, against each of the criteria, what it was that proved that it was not met. When making the determination, the court is concerned not with the cause of the difficulties, but with the affect of it in relation to the issues the court needs to determine. Thus, if only one criterion was not met, the court could decide whether the court process could be adjusted to permit him to take an effective part in the process.

Discussion/learning points

The learning point in this case is to consider the relative and individual contributions of each of the clinical factors in the overall clinical presentation. Does one outweigh another or are they all considered to contribute with equal merit? Should one aspect of HC's presentation take precedence? For example, if the depression and anxiety were to be effectively treated, would this bring about sufficient alleviation to raise HC's level of neurocognitive capability above the threshold for capacity to enter a plea?

Case 4: HD

Presenting question/problem

This is the case of a 79-year-old gentleman, who is charged with 26 counts of sexual assault. The charges relate to alleged offences against two of his daughters. A request was received to conduct a neuropsychological assessment of reported symptoms of memory loss in the context of capacity to conduct proceedings and to enter a plea. The results indicate that his presentation did not make clinical sense and that his account of reported memory problems was contradictory.

Background to the case

Clinical issues

HD was in general good health. He alternately claimed have a head injury or be suffering from dementia. Records highlighted significant inconsistencies in his clinical presentation across different assessments undertaken within the same period of time. For example, he reported that he had experienced a head injury two years previously, when he had struck a lamppost. However, records of attending paramedics noted normal observations, including a GCS of 15 with no amnesia leading up to, or for, the event. He also reported that he felt his memory was deteriorating so rapidly, due to a dementing illness, that he could no longer remember his children's names or anything about their birth or childhoods. Medical investigations had all reported within the normal range, including a CT brain scan. It is concerning that when he was assessed by two medical colleagues one week apart, he achieved remarkably different results on basic cognitive testing, registering a much higher score (on a comparable measure) at the latter appointment. He frequently contradicted himself when being interviewed. Concerns were raised as to his mental health as an underlying explanation for this functional-type behaviour. It should be noted that throughout the period of assessment, HD was living completely independently with no support with any activities of daily living including personal care, shopping, cooking, budgeting or accessing the community.

Family/social context

HD had two daughters who had come forward (independently) to make allegations of sexual abuse, perpetrated by him on them, over a 30-year period. HD denied the allegations on the basis that he had no memories for the period.

He lives with his second wife who, since the charges were made against HD, contacts their GP almost daily to seek medical corroboration of her husband's "ill-health". The GP is on record as stating that, "says he can't remember . . . most likely to be a psych cause/depression . . . no evidence of cognitive difficulties . . . wife is a worrier."

HD's first wife had recently made a statement to the police, supporting the allegations of her two daughters, admitting that she had witnessed some of the alleged acts of abuse and had failed to act to protect her daughters.

Psychological/neuropsychological matters

There was some evidence from GP records of HD not taking as much care of his appearance since his arrest on charges of sexual abuse. This was put down to a reactive depression in the context of the situation. There was no evidence in the records of any pre-existing psychological or neuropsychological difficulties. At the outset, there were concerns that he was feigning cognitive difficulties at the present time.

Assessment and rationale

Given the apparent contradictions between clinical presentations on different days and the inconsistencies in verbal accounts given by HD, it was considered critical at the outset to assess effort (sometimes also referred to as symptom validity) by means of both stand-alone and embedded testing (BPS, 2009; Ryan-Morgan, 2012). To that end three assessments of effort were administered to HD. First, the ToMM. This is a widely-used measure of effort based on memory functioning. HD scored 49 out of 50 on both trials, indicating that he was exerting adequate effort on this test. Second, the Rey 15-item test was administered. HD scored below the cut-off score of 9, indicated less than optimum effort. Third, the Effort Index (Silverberg et al., 2007) of the RBANS assessment was calculated. He was well-above the suggested cut-off, indicating that his effort was variable. Any test results from cognitive assessments must, therefore, be treated with considerable caution. Larrabee (2005) reports that

> inconsistencies in test scores often are the result of variable effort and motivation. Variable motivation can be secondary to factors outside the patient's conscious intent or control, such as depression, anxiety or conversion disorder or may result from conscious intentional response distortion . . .
>
> (p.116)

It is my opinion that the objective evidence of HD's variable effort on the present assessment renders the profile of test results, particularly which *appear* to indicate abnormality, invalid and therefore uninterpretable.

The next phase of the assessment focused on mood. The Geriatric Depression Scale was administered to HD and, although he registered a score of 17, which is above the clinical cut-off, he did not present in any way throughout the assessment with features indicative of depression. It is recommended that his responses are treated with some caution.

At this stage, in line with HD's claims not to be able to recall large parts of his life, particularly those relating to the birth and childhoods of his two daughters who have made allegations of sexual abuse against him, it was decided to administer the Autobiographical Memory Interview. HD scored within normal limits for childhood and recent life but his scores for autobiographical data were grossly abnormal for his early adulthood. Interestingly, there was a significant difference between his ability to recall semantic memories (which was largely unaffected) and his recollection of autobiographical data. This profile of results was difficult to interpret in the absence of corroborating clinical evidence of underlying neuropathology. Kopelman (2002) discussed the possible psychogenic basis of subjectively-reported memory difficulties which conform to such a pattern.

It is noted that HD was fully oriented to time, place and person at the time of assessment. A neurocognitive screening assessment (RBANS) was administered. The results did not make neuropsychological sense, when interpreted in the context of an absence of medical evidence of cognitive difficulty and with the range of inconsistencies elicited during interview. In addition, the Effort Index (referred to above) indicated that the results were invalid and unreliable. No further comment is made in relation to these data.

In terms of clinical observations, there was no hesitation in any of HD's responses and he undertook testing with a systematic approach. He readily grasped all instructions given to him and completed all written materials with a steady hand. Although he and his wife were keen to point out the implications of the apparent head injury and subsequent arrest of HD's cognitive functioning and clinical presentation, neither offered specific, detailed or consistent responses for this to be explored meaningfully. He participated in the assessment for two and half hours and concentrated well throughout. He declined several offers of a break.

Opinion/outcome

The procedure for determining whether an accused is "under a disability" is governed by the Criminal Procedure (Insanity) Act (1964) as amended by the Criminal Procedure (Insanity and Unfitness to Plead) Act (1991) and the Domestic Violence, Crime and Victim's Act (2004). The position is that it has to be established that the accused is under a disability on balance of probability if raised by the defence. It is understood that if the question of disability is raised by the prosecution or judge it has to be proved beyond reasonable doubt.

There are several issues to consider in relation to HD's presentation.

First, the range and extent of inconsistencies at play. There are numerous inconsistencies between information presented at interview in relation to what HD can do on a day-to-day basis in terms of independent living (washing, shopping, reading newspaper and watching films) to information provided by his wife in particular, that he is largely unable to function without her assistance. In addition, there are inconsistencies across test results which cannot be interpreted within known models of neuropsychological functioning, and which are considered to reflect variable effort during testing on the part of HD and which are, in themselves, contradictory. There are also inconsistencies in the psychological test data where these appear to indicate the presence of mild depression, but which is not borne out by self-report, interview, observation or clinical presentation.

Second, there is no objective evidence that HD's collision with a lamp-post, two years earlier, was anything other than a non-significant bump on the head. Classification of head injury is by consideration of key indicators such as scores on the Glasgow Coma Scale, length of loss of consciousness and length of post-traumatic amnesia. There is also expected to be corroborative neuroradiological evidence, although this is less likely in milder head injuries. According to records, HD's GCS score at the scene of the incident was recorded at the maximum possible (15/15) indicating that even if there was a period of change in consciousness, this was likely to have been transient. There is no evidence of loss of consciousness. Equally importantly, there is no evidence of any post-traumatic amnesia as HD was clearly able to recall the minutes leading up to the incident with no apparent gaps in memory. Even if HD could be considered to have been concussed as a result of the incident, research evidence would lead to the expectation that this would have completely resolved within three to six months of the incident. Most concussions resolve within days. Of greatest concern is the apparent claim by both HD and his wife that his memory has significantly deteriorated since the incident with the lamp-post. This is not borne out by medical records and runs "contrary to the natural history of traumatic brain injury" (Margulies, 2000, p.402).

Third, there is no clinical or objective evidence of a dementia in HD's current presentation. The cluster, pattern and progression of symptoms as described by HD and his wife does not conform to any known model of dementia.

An appropriately completed Certificate as to Capacity to Conduct Proceedings was completed and submitted to the instructing solicitor in this case.

Legal commentary

This assessment is likely to cause a judge to raise eyebrows at the suggestion that the defendant is unfit. Most, if not all, is self-reporting and that is not supported in areas where support might be expected (lamp-post incident). Inconsistent results make his position virtually untenable. His wife's evidence is likely to be viewed with significant scepticism, although she may recount what she genuinely perceives to be the position. The defendant's assertion is unlikely to succeed.

Discussion/learning

From a clinical point of view, there are two lessons to learn from this case. The first relates to the importance of pursuing a rigorous approach to assessments, particularly in a context where there is considerable secondary gain to the subjective reporting of cognitive symptoms. Second, it is critically important to manage the tension in such assessments between accepting the description of symptoms at face value, which underlies training in clinical psychology and psychiatry and needing to critically appraise such information in the context of known models of brain dysfunction (scientist-practitioner approach within clinical neuropsychology). When combining these two imperatives, the advice is to adopt a position of *clinical scepticism*, "it is an attitude that insists on evidence and acknowledges uncertainty. It demands that you critically evaluate everything you are told, not in a spirit of cynicism, but in the recognition that human beings get things wrong" (Poole & Higgo, 2017, p.94).

Case 5: HE

Presenting question/problem

This is a case of an 18-year-old man, charged with murder, on remand in prison. He had a history of having been physically abused and neglected as a child and also of binge drinking. He had frequently truanted from school. An assessment of his level of cognitive functioning (IQ) was requested in the context of his capacity to plead in the case.

Background to the case

Clinical issues

Medical records indicated that HE presented at the local Emergency Department no fewer than 20 times between the ages of 9 and 17 with non-accidental injuries and was placed in foster care on several occasions.

HE was noted to be a frequent binge drinker, typically engaging in such behaviour three or more times per week. He reported that he would mix beer and spirits and felt no need to impose limits upon himself.

Family/social context

HE confirmed that he had attended mainstream schooling and, although he had failed all public examinations and left school early, he had not been formally identified as needing support and assistance to learn. His view was that he just, "didn't try hard enough" and frequently truanted from school.

Psychological/neuropsychological matters

There was nothing in available records to indicate any previous psychological or neuropsychological issues.

Assessment and rationale

The case was straightforward in that the instructing party had requested a clear picture of HE's current level of cognitive functioning. To that end, three tests were selected that were in common usage at the time of the assessment:

- The National Adult Reading Test (version 2) – this has since been replaced by the Test of Premorbid Function. It was selected to provide an accurate indicator of premorbid general intelligence against which a concurrent cognitive assessment can be compared. It was administered to HE who achieved an Error Score of 31. This yields a predicted Full-Scale IQ of approximately 102, which is in the average range. It also predicts a Verbal IQ of around 101 and a Performance IQ of around 104. These predictions are used as a basis for comparison with the results of the Wechsler Abbreviated Scale of Intelligence reported below.
- The Weschler Abbreviated Scales of Intelligence – there is now a second, updated, version of this test. This is a short and reliable measure of cognitive function which is individually administered and designed for use with individuals aged from 6 to 89 years. It is nationally standardised and yields

the traditional Verbal, Performance and Full-Scale IQ scores. It comprises four sub-tests namely, Vocabulary, Block Design, Similarities and Matrix Reasoning. These sub-tests have the highest loadings on General Intellectual Functioning. This was administered to HE who yielded the following scores: Verbal IQ 82–93; Performance IQ 94–106 and Full-Scale IQ 88–96. This places his level of functioning in the low-average to average range and identifies a clinically and statistically significant difference between his verbal and performance skills in favour of non-verbal functioning.

On the face of it, there appears to have been, a decline in cognitive functioning from that predicted by the NART-2. However, this is considered unlikely for several reasons:

i)   HE's full scale IQ still lies within the average range, as predicted by the NART-2.
ii) His lowest score is on the Verbal IQ dimension and this is one which is heavily loaded on educational attainment. By HE's subjective account he reported that he made little effort at school and didn't engage optimally with formal education. It is considered that his relatively low score on the verbal sub-tests is a reflection of this and not of underlying cognitive decline.
iii) The way scores are calculated in terms of IQ means that the Full Scale IQ obtained on the WASI, which is between 88 and 96 (92) has been lowered by HE's relatively poor score on the verbal sub-tests.
iv) It should be noted with reference to Scaled Scores that HE's scores are largely in the average range with the exception of his Similarities scaled score of 7, which is considered to be low average.

•   The ToMM (a stand-alone test of effort/symptom validity). HE achieved 49 out of 50 on Trial One and 50 out of 50 on Trial 2. Based on this performance on the ToMM, it can be reliably established that HE was exerting an appropriate amount of effort throughout testing on the present occasion and that the above profile of test scores is a valid indicator of his current level of cognitive functioning.

HE was interviewed in prison. He presented with flat affect. Although he exerted good effort and was socially appropriate during the assessment, it was clear that his mood was somewhat lowered. Throughout the assessment HE sought feedback and was keen to perform well on the tests that were administered. It was noted that he applied systematic strategies in his approach to testing. He confirmed that he can read and write and is, effectively, literate and numerate. He reported that he occasionally reads but this is not an activity that he routinely engages in.

Opinion/outcome

From HE's subjective account, which it has not been possible to independently verify for the purposes of this assessment, it appears that he exerted little effort at school.

He appeared not to be motivated to do so and left school at approximately age 15 with no formal public examinations to his name. It is understood from his self-report that he did indeed sit at least three public examinations (these are assumed to have been GCSEs) although he did not pass any. It has been noted from his medical records that between the ages of 9 and 17 he attended the local hospital Emergency Department on 20 occasions with non-accidental injury to his body. During this time, it was noted that the local authority had expressed concerns over his care and had found a series of foster placements for him. Although this particular aspect of his background is not directly relevant to his level of cognitive functioning, there is a significant body of research evidence which confirms that early experiences of this nature can exert a negative effect on cognitive development and, if there were difficulties in HE's home, that this may offer a part-explanation for his de-motivation and lack of engagement in formal education, at the very least.

Based on the assessment reported here, it is clear that HE is of approximately average intelligence and that his level of functioning should not present any particular difficulties to the current legal processes under way in terms of criminal proceedings against him. There is no evidence presented to date of developmental delay or to suggest that he has specific intellectual or learning difficulties. During the present assessment it was noted that he was clearly able to follow instructions and was fully able to participate in the assessment process.

Legal commentary

There is no difficulty in this case. He does not show any signs which suggest he could not participate in the proceedings.

Discussion/learning points

This is a case where the instruction is simple, and the assessment is straightforward. It is not the place of the assessor to over-complicate the matter before the court by musing over possible contributions to HE's behaviour patterns or, indeed, to attempt to rescue him from his poor early life experiences and later ill-advised choices. It is not the place of the assessor to hypothesise over the possible motivations for the actions which lead to HE having been arrested on a charge of murder, however compelling.

Case 6: HF

Presenting question/problem

This is the case of a 52-year-old man, charged with having a blade in a public place. The police case is that he challenged a female in the pub where he was drinking and drew a "knife-like" object with which he threatened her.

His clinical history is significant as he had a sub arachnoid haemorrhage (SAH) at the age of 40 for which he was treated neuro-surgically. Following this,

his behaviours became bizarre and unpredictable and his medical notes are peppered with entries where the attending doctor was unsure of how to interpret or respond to his unusual behaviours. An assessment was requested in the context of his fitness to enter a plea to the charge.

Background to the case

Clinical issues

Prior to his SAH, HF had no significant clinical history. He had two aneurysms (one in the region of the left middle cerebral artery or MCA and one anterior communicating artery or ACoA) which gave rise to the SAHand which were surgically clipped via a craniotomy procedure. He then developed hydrocephalus for which a VP shunt was inserted in the right frontal brain region. Neuroradiology reported an infarct in the right frontal lobe area as well as shallow bilateral subdural collections which were not causing any significant mass effect. The one on the right was slightly dense superiorly which reflected the haemorrhage.

Family/social context

HF lived with his wife who reported that she was struggling with his behaviours since the SAH. She frequently rang the GP to seek assistance and was, on occasion, concerned for her own safety. HF had not returned to his former job since the brain injury.

Psychological/neuropsychological matters

As a result of the SAH and subsequent symptoms and behaviours, HF was diagnosed by a consultant neuropsychiatrist with organic personality disorder, secondary to SAH. He would become aggressive, with little or no provocation and had bouts of "black moods". In addition, HF began drinking heavily and this increased his somewhat disinhibited behaviours, effectively lowering the threshold for their occurrence.

There was evidence of a previous neuropsychological assessment, as part of his NHS treatment following the SAH.

Assessment and rationale

The assessment was planned to comprise both clinical interview, observations and psychometric assessment of HF's current level of functioning. It was requested that his wife also be present as collateral informant on the basis that HF may not retain full insight into his difficulties due to the nature and location of his brain injury.

At the outset, HF refused to engage in testing and became agitated at the thought of participating. It was decided to abandon this element of the planned assessment so as not to escalate his anxiety and agitation and, instead, to draw upon records of previous (post-brain injury) neuropsychometric testing.

Clinical interview comprised a structured element, designed specifically to gauge HF's understanding of the charges and his role in proceedings. A further, unstructured, clinical interview was undertaken with HF and his wife.

HF reported a series of symptoms including needing the light switched off as lights cause him to "close down". He was socially inappropriate at the outset of the assessment, behaving in an aggressive and somewhat agitated manner. This was explained by his wife as him having a "strange" sense of humour since the SAH. He also reported a "loss of physical balance", "loss of cognitive skills" and described a range of somatic symptoms which are not recorded elsewhere in his medical notes.

HF described the deterioration in his memory in terms of losing the ability to cascade remembered material from a single stimulus. He used the analogy of the information he wished to retrieve as being located in a file space in his brain but that the adjacent drawers in the filing cabinet will not open for him. HF claims that his short-term memory is particularly hopeless and upon detailed questioning it appears that this largely relates to new learning and working memory. His wife confirms that he does write things down in order to assist his prospective memory (the ability to recall the need to carry out an action) deficits, although HF claimed during the assessment that he could no longer write.

HF's sleep cycle appears to be largely irregular with him being asleep for no more than three to four hours at a time followed by a period of wakefulness of a similar length of time. He does experience high levels of fatigue since his SAH which is confirmed by his wife. He reports a recent loss of interest and drive which is hypothesised to be neurogenic given the location of his acquired brain injury.

HF's wife reports that since his SAH, and subsequent neurosurgery, she has noticed that his personality is qualitatively different in that he can be quite socially inappropriate and disinhibited and that his sense of humour can often be inappropriate.

In terms of work, HF did want to go back to work and reports that he under-took a few adult learning courses including the European Computer Driving Licence. It is understood that he got as far as Part 2 and then started to notice difficulties with his cognitive functioning which meant that he was unable to complete this. According to his wife, HF did see a disability employment advisor at the local Job Centre following his recovery, but he was sent on a retail work placement to PC World which did not work out for him. HF is an electrical engineer by background and he wished to work with computers rather than to be on a work placement where he was expected to sell them. Given the reported behaviour changes, it is not unsurprising that he would struggle to succeed in a customer-facing role.

At this point HF was asked about the index offence with which he has been charged and he was adamant at the outset that he would not talk about the inci-dent in front of his wife in case she would be called to testify against him at which point he started citing what he believed to be sections of the Terrorism Act as to why his wife could not hear his account. However, with no persuasion whatsoever he then recounted, in considerable detail, his recollection of events leading up to and during the index offence. His account contradicts the available statements.

HF's belief is that this was an unprovoked assault to disguise an attempted robbery of himself. The alleged weapon was described by HF to be a penknife belonging to his father which he used as a tool for sharpening pencils and "fixing things".

The following was observed during the assessment:

- HF's conversation was tangential, and it was difficult to keep him on topic. When asked open questions he gave long, meandering and largely disconnected replies and this extended the allotted assessment appointment considerably;
- It was clear throughout that there was evidence of both spontaneous and provoked confabulation which he believed absolutely and which his wife was able to refute (drawing on factual knowledge) on several occasions.

Brief records of a previous neuropsychological assessment indicated that HF is functioning in the high-average range of cognitive function but that he has explicit frontal lobe dysfunction including behavioural perseveration and mental inflexibility, difficulties with problem-solving and applying judgement, and social disinhibition. This is a typical picture of what is sometimes referred to as "frontal-lobe syndrome" where the person loses the ability to apply concrete knowledge in the relevant situation such that their behaviours are frequently inappropriate to the circumstance and they fail to adapt in the light of personal experience. This occurs in the absence of insight or self-awareness.

Opinion/outcome

There is a clear literature on the presentation of patients with a subarachnoid haemorrhage due to ruptured aneurysms of the anterior communicating artery (or ACoA) who have historically been observed to suffer from a poor neuropsychological outcome. The ACoA syndrome consists of memory loss, confabulation and altered personality. Such patients also report memory problems of varying severity and continue to exhibit the described personality alterations such as impulsivity, disinhibited behaviour, apathy, emotional lability, depression, problems in decision-making, organisational difficulties and poor judgement in social situations. The changes in memory, emotionality and judgement which appear to be chronic and resistant to change, typically have unfortunate consequences for such patients and their families.

There is a literature which suggests that these particular patients also exhibit increased risk-taking behaviour as opposed to simple behavioural disinhibition or impulsivity. Typically, patients with ruptures to the anterior communication artery suffer symptoms secondary to lesions to the ventromedial or orbito-frontal cortex. In addition, there is confabulation, which has been described as both spontaneous and provoked, typically associated with frontal lobe damage in the ventromedial regions. Spontaneous confabulation is where there is a persistent unprovoked outpouring of erroneous memories often held with firm conviction which can be preoccupying. There is also momentary or provoked confabulation which refers to fleeting intrusion errors or distortions made in response to a challenge to recall a specific memory. HF's presentation is highly suggestive of spontaneous confabulation and this is consistent with his area of brain injury.

This is a difficult case in terms of assessing fitness to plead as, on the one hand, HF presents with preserved cognitive function and can, on the face of it, appear to be neurocognitively intact. However, the extent and location of his organic brain damage means that he presents with personality difficulties which have a basis in his injury but appear to be HF just "being difficult". He struggles with fatigue and poor sleep, attention and memory problems, poor insight and awareness of others, difficulties understanding issues from more than his own perspective, an inability to weigh up information and make decisions based on a combination of stored knowledge and a "reading" of the situation. He is easily provoked to agitation and aggression, referred to commonly as episodic dyscontrol or a lack of a "cerebral brake". It is difficult to see how, with this litany of post-brain-injury deficits, HF could meaningfully and equitably enter a plea and fully participate in proceedings without being at a significant disadvantage.

Legal commentary

The defendant clearly has significant problems which might explain the commission of the offence. However, to establish fitness, it would be necessary to direct questions specifically geared to deal with the relevant issues. On the face of it, he knows what he is alleged to have done and is able to deny and explain it. Although his observations may seem bizarre, he knows what he wants to say and what his case is. As he could explain his position during the assessments, he could, presumably, do likewise to his lawyers. Plausibility, credibility and reliability are not necessarily inconsistent with an ability to participate in the process. However, the court is required and would be expected to monitor the position throughout the trial. In those circumstances, it may become apparent, for example, during cross-examination, that he is not fit (see *Orr* above). Although specifically asked to do the assessment tests in the presence of his wife, she was, potentially, the only "independent" support of his position. The "Learning points" refer to collateral informants and the need for close interrogation of them. Having the spouse present at assessments potentially dilutes the value of her independent account.

Discussion/learning points

This is a typical case of the dissociation between knowing and doing that is referred to by Teuber (1964) which is commonly seen following pre-frontal cortex injury in adults and has, more recently, been discussed with specific reference to the MCA (2005) by George and Gilbert (2018). Many such patients can "pass" neuropsychological tests but struggle to function in day-to-day life, a feature frequently referred to as the "frontal lobe paradox" (Walsh, 1985). In such cases, it is critically important to either observe the person at first hand in the real-life situation where the skills in question are needed or, to closely interview collateral informants who have extensive knowledge of the person's behaviour in different contexts.

Case 7: HG

Presenting question/problem

This is a case of a 25-year-old gentleman who had a significant forensic history where he had frequently attended Magistrates' Court for "petty" offences. However, since being charged with his most recent offences, and prior to being before the local Magistrates to answer the charges, HG had sustained a severe head injury as a result of an RTC. The letter of instruction contained three elements:

- fitness to plead;
- ability to effectively participate in a trial; and
- suggestibility and compliance.

Background to the case

Clinical issues

In the accident in question, HG was found 50 metres from his motorbike. His helmet was not on his head but was found a short distance away. He was agitated and combative at scene, moving all limbs with GCS 11/15. He was intubated and ventilated for neuroprotection. Neuroradiology confirmed the presence of a SAH in addition to a small extradural haematoma in his left frontal lobe. He continued to be agitated and combative. His head injury was conservatively managed, but his severe agitation required management by a range of psychotropic medications quetiapine, lorazepam, carbamazepine and clonidine and he was sectioned under the Mental Health Act for his own safety

Family/social context

HG lives at home with his mother since the injury. Previously, he had lived with his girlfriend of two years. He is cared for 24 hours a day as none of those close to him believe that he is safe to be left unattended. His mother works part-time so HG's partner makes sure that she is with him whenever his mum is out.

Psychological/neuropsychological matters

Since his injury, HG has presented with agitation, aggression, paranoia, behavioural disinhibition and communication difficulties. He has proved so difficult to manage within a neurorehabilitation ward environment that he had to be detained under Section 2 of the Mental Health Act and was prescribed a range of psychotropic medications, primarily designed to manage his agitation and behavioural outbursts in order to keep himself, and others, safe. Since discharge home, the medication regime has been continued and he is subdued to the point of non-engagement in his environment. He initially experienced seizures, which were post-traumatic in origin, causing him to fall out of bed on more than one occasion, but these seem to have abated since he was started on medication.

Assessment and rationale

The *planned* assessment comprised:

- structured interview;
- ToMM (a test of symptom validity that it is standard practice to administer during neuropsychological assessments);
- WASI-2 (a brief standardised assessment of general cognitive function);
- SMAT (a test of social and moral reasoning to assess consequential thinking);
- GSS-1 (a test of interrogative suggestibility);
- RBANS (a brief standardised test assessing functioning in five key neuropsychological domains); and
- CET (a test of cognitive estimation ability).

However, on arriving at his home and meeting him, it was clear that HG would be unable to participate in anything other than the most basic of verbal interviews, and he only effectively managed to do so with the prompting and direct support of his mother who remained present throughout at his request.

He was still in bed at the appointed time and his mother was requested to bring him downstairs for the assessment to take place in their living room.

HG was observed to struggle to descend the stairs without physical assistance and verbal prompting from his mother. It was confirmed that she never leaves HG alone as she is concerned that he is unable to keep himself safe without support.

HG was asked about his head injury and he was unable to say anything other than, "I had an accident . . . why is she saying this to me?" (The latter question was directed to his mother about me.) He appeared unable to take on board information about who I was or why I was there to meet him. He was noticeably over-medicated.

HG was then asked about the present proceedings using the structured interview developed to assess fitness to plead. The questions contained within the structured interview are listed below, with HG's responses included:

- Do you know what the police say you have done?

    I don't know what that means.

- Do you know the difference between saying "guilty" and "not guilty"?

  I don't know what you are saying.

- Can your solicitor tell your side of things? Do you know who your solicitor is?

  Unable to answer

- If you think that a witness in court is not right in what they say, who could you tell?

  Unable to answer

- Do you know what it means if they say that you can object to someone on the jury in your court case?

  Unable to answer

- Do you understand what happens in court and what you have to do in court?

  Unable to answer

HG was unable to answer many of these questions. He gave the impression that he did not understand the questions and appeared disorientated. At this stage, questions were posed to HG to assess his level of orientation. He was disorientated as to day, date and year but was able to recall his date of birth. When asked his address, he spontaneously gave a previous address. He appeared to struggle to focus visually on his surroundings and was unsteady on his feet.

His mother reported that HG's behaviour at time of assessment was consistent with his day-to-day presentation. She confirmed that his partner will attend the house to help him with washing and dressing but that he is unable to undertake any activities of daily living (ADLs) without support and direction. His mother also confirmed that HG is generally unable to recall information regarding his daily life and has a reduced awareness. He was certainly noted to be disorientated and it is possible that an element of this is iatrogenic. Table 11.1 is taken from a print out on his medication box from the pharmacy.

HG was noted to be somewhat irritable and paranoid throughout the appointment. He deferred all questions to his mother and frequently, and repetitively, sought reassurance from her that they weren't planning to leave the house that day. He displayed reduced awareness of his surroundings.

Table 11.1

Medication	Strength	Dose
Quetiapine	300mg	Once a day
Sertraline	50mg	Once a day
Tegretol	100mg	150mg twice a day
Tegretol	400mg	Once a day
Tegretol	200mg	200mg twice a day

Opinion/outcome

The following is the detailed framework provided by the instructing solicitor in terms of what they required the assessment of capacity to consider:

Fitness to plead

- whether he can plead to the indictment or not; and
- whether he is of sufficient intellect to comprehend the course of the proceedings, so as to be able to make a proper defence
  - understanding of the charges
  - deciding whether to plead guilty or not
  - exercising his right to challenge jurors
  - instructing solicitors and counsel
  - following the course of the proceedings
  - give evidence in his own defence.

Effective participation

The fundamental test is that, in order to be able to effectively participate, he must be found to be able to:

- understand the charges and potential consequences
- understand, in general terms the difference between right and wrong
- understand the court process
- understand the defences available to him
- participate with his legal team in the preparation of his defence; and
- participate in the court process (including giving evidence on his own behalf and being cross-examined).

Suggestibility and compliance

- suggestibility and compliance in relation to giving evidence on his own behalf during the court proceedings;
- in being cross-examined by the prosecution; and
- in being able to participate by giving instructions on the evidence to his solicitor.

HG sustained a significant head injury which resulted in bleeding within the brain. He was sufficiently disorientated and combative at the scene of the accident to have been intubated and ventilated. A Glasgow Coma Scale score of 11 at scene is indicative of a "moderate" brain injury. The location of the bleeding in the left frontal lobe is informative in that damage to this area can often give rise to neuropsychiatric complications such as reduced empathy, behavioural disinhibition and impaired self-regulation as well as marked irritability and aggression. All of these signs and symptoms are evident in HG's clinical presentation.

It is understood that a local neuropsychiatry unit had attempted to admit HG on a voluntary basis some months previously but that he self-discharged the same day and was not considered unwell enough to be detained under the Mental Health Act at that point. Going forward, he would benefit from a detailed neuropsychiatric assessment and a review of his current medication regime. Once assessed, HG may well be amenable to treatment to improve his current level of awareness and orientation in addition to addressing his post-injury levels of disability. This may have an impact on his fitness to plead but the timescale of any potential improvements may not be one which suits the court to wait.

In my opinion, there is no doubt that HG is presently unable to understand much of his surroundings. He is disorientated to time (day, date, year) and presents as having no awareness of present proceedings. He does not know the name of his solicitor or the charges made against him. He struggles to follow conversation, showing difficulties with both expressive and receptive (received) language. He displays a degree of paranoia which is contrary to effective understanding of the roles of others in proceedings. He is neither fit to plead nor to participate in present proceedings.

Legal commentary

The issue-specific questions assist considerably in making a determination. Such questions are vital. The assessment must be in-depth in relation to the issues that the court has to determine. The court would expect questions going to the same issue to be asked in different ways, using different levels of language and different scenarios; this allows the court to know that, for example, using simpler language or concepts might produce a different response. Such a change might allow the court to change its procedures to allow a proper trial to proceed or affirm a report that he is unfit.

Discussion/learning points

When assessing a person who is subject to an extensive medication regime, it is critically important to do all that is possible to extrapolate the individual effects of medication from the brain injury sequelae as the former is transient and the latter is permanent. Assessments of capacity relate to a specific point in time, but it may, on occasion, be appropriate to advise the court as to the benefits of postponing the timetable for entering a plea in order to maximise a person's capacity to enter one and to participate in subsequent proceedings without being placed at a disadvantage.

References

BPS. (2009). Assessment of effort in clinical testing of cognitive functioning for adults. Professional Practice Board. Retrieved from http://shop.bps.org.uk/assessment-of-effort-in-clinical-testing-of-cognitive-functioning-for-adults.html.

George, M. & Gilbert, S. (2018). Mental Capacity Act (2005) assessments: Why everyone needs to know about the frontal lobe paradox. *The Neuropsychologist*, 5, 59–66.

Iverson, G. L. & Tulsky, D. S. (2003). Detecting malingering on the WAIS-III: Unusual Digit Span performance patterns in the normal population and in clinical groups. *Archives of Clinical Neuropsychology*, *18*, 1–9.

Kopelman, M. (2002). Disorders of memory. *Brain*, *125*, 2152–2190.

Larrabee, G. J. (2005). *Forensic neuropsychology: A scientific approach.* Oxford: Oxford University Press.

Margulies, S. (2000). The postconcussion syndrome after mild head trauma: Is brain damage overdiagnosed? Part 1. *Journal of Clinical Neuroscience*, *7*(5), 400–408.

Poole, R. & Higgo, R. (2017). *Psychiatric interviewing and assessment* (2nd Ed.). Cambridge: Cambridge University Press.

Ryan-Morgan, T. (2012). Symptom validity (effort) testing in clinical neuropsychology, *PI Brief Update Law Journal*, September.

Silverberg, N. D., Wertheimer, J. C. & Fichtenberg, N. L. (2007). An effort index for the Repeatable Battery for the Assessment of Neuropsychological Status (RBANS). *The Clinical Neuropsychologist*, *21*(5), 841–854.

Teuber, H. L. (1964). The riddle of the frontal lobe function in man. In J. M. Warren & K. Akert (Eds) *The frontal granular cortex and behaviour* (pp.410–458). New York: McGraw-Hill.

Walsh, K. W. (1985). *Understanding brain damage: A primer of neuropsychological evaluation.* London: Churchill Livingstone.

12 Deprivation of Liberty Safeguards (DoLS), Cheshire West and positive risk management

Dr Tracey Ryan-Morgan

With Katherine Barnes

The Law Commission's report on the Mental Capacity and Deprivation of Liberty was published on 13 March 2017. The Supreme Court judgement referred to commonly as "Cheshire West" had led to a significant increase in applications for DoLS resulting in significant backlogs, delays in authorisation and, as a result, breaches of agreed timescales for processing applications and reviews. One positive aspect of "Cheshire West" that has been welcomed by clinicians is that the test for DoLS is now brief, clear and unequivocal. If a person is under continuous supervision and not free to leave then they are, effectively, being deprived of their liberty and the relevant wapplication for authorisation needs to be completed and submitted to the local authority.

The proposed Liberty Protection Safeguards, put forward by the Law Commission, would put in place consideration of the justification for depriving a person of their liberty before it takes place, unlike under the present DoLS arrangements. It would also roll out the safeguards to include non-hospital or residential care facilities, such as shared living or private domestic accommodation, respite care and transport between facilities. The present arrangements require a direct application to the court for the latter such eventualities which is time-consuming, insufficiently flexible for the day-to-day life of individuals subject to DoLS and an inefficient use of judicial resources. As stated by Ruck-Keene (2017), ". . .we need to do something about DoLS. That much is obvious, and I would venture to commend to your approval the solution proposed by the Law Commission."

The government has responded with the Mental Capacity Amendment Bill which is currently making its way through the various stages of parliamentary process. However, the Bill appears to have missed many opportunities for reviewing the more contentious aspects of the current legislation, such as giving greater weight to the notion of Best Interests, and has, it seems, focused almost exclusively on revising the current systems and processes inherent in the deprivation of an individual's liberty. The existing DoLS are proposed to be replaced with the Liberty Protection Safeguards (LPS), although in its current form, the Bill does not actually refer to them in this way. The major changes appear to be:

- LPS applies to all settings, including a person's home;
- The "Responsible Body" will no longer automatically be the local authority but will be determined by where the person is residing and who is funding/overseeing their care. If in hospital, the NHS manager will be responsible. If in the community but in receipt of continuing health care, it will be the Clinical Commissioning Group (England) or Local Health Board (Wales). If in the community receiving other care, such as in a care home, it will be the local authority.
- Although the initial period for authorising a deprivation of liberty will be capped at twelve months, it can be extended to three years if agreed.
- The conditions for authorisation are clearly described in terms of:
  - demonstration that the individual is of "unsound mind"
  - evidence that the individual lacks capacity
  - clear evidence that the deprivation is both necessary and proportionate.

  All of this evidence is to be scrutinised via a pre-authorisation review process undertaken by a person not involved in the individual's care.
- The Responsible Body has to demonstrate that it has consulted both the individual in question, either personally or through an Independent Mental Capacity Advocate or "appropriate person" or both, as well as all relevant and interested parties.
- Two independent (of each other) assessors have to undertake the necessary assessments of the individual. Their requisite skills and qualifications are to be specified in a new Code of Practice to accompany the revised Act.
- If the person is objecting to the deprivation, then an Approved Mental Capacity Professional would be appointed to scrutinise the process and outcome.

Baker, J cited Munby, J in *Re MM*[1]

> the fact is that all life involves risk, and the young, the elderly and the vulnerable, are exposed to additional risks and to risks they are less well equipped than others to cope with . . . Physical health and safety can sometimes be bought at too high a price in happiness and emotional welfare. The emphasis must be on sensible risk appraisal, not striving to avoid all risk, whatever the price, but instead seeking a proper balance and being willing to tolerate manageable or acceptable risks as the price appropriately to be paid in order to achieve some other good . . . what good is it making someone safer if it merely makes them miserable?

Or, as Lady Hale succinctly stated,[2] "a gilded cage is still a cage".

---

1 [2007] EWHC2003 (Fam)
2 [2014] UKSC 19, [2014] MHLO 16

Case 1: GA

Presenting question/problem

GA received a severe traumatic brain injury as a result of a vicious assault, where the attacker left her for dead. She was both drunk and under the influence of illicit drugs at the time. She had a lengthy history of substance misuse and, despite the severity of the brain injury, had relatively well-preserved cognitive function, as assessed during neurorehabilitation. This allowed her to present to DoLS assessors with a veneer of competence. Initially, she had not been considered to be subject to DoLS but gradually, over time, her decision-making led to behaviours which consistently placed her at risk. Once subject to DoLS, she immediately instructed her IMCA to seek to appeal against it and clinicians worked hard to strike a balance between keeping her safe and working with her to positively manage the risks she presented to herself and others. This approach led to mixed results.

Background to the case

Clinical issues

GA was found unconscious on her bathroom floor with, multiple head wounds following an alleged assault. Her GCS was 5 on arrival at hospital. Neuroradiological investigation revealed focal contusions to the right frontal lobe and an acute subarachnoid haemorrhage. She was intubated and sedated, remaining in ITU for over three weeks. Her traumatic brain injury was treated conservatively with intracranial pressure (ICP) bolt and monitoring. Within a few weeks, she was found to have a small subdural haematoma which was subsequently surgically evacuated. Whilst in ITU, GA suffered a hospital acquired pneumonia which was treated with antibiotics. GA had a tracheostomy inserted and experiences persistent headaches following her head injury.

GA has an ataxic gait and some gross motor issues including decreased co-ordination and balance, but she is fully mobile. Improving her physical ability is one of her primary goals as she has had a series of (relatively minor) falls since her injury.

GA's sleep hygiene routine is poor as she goes to bed very late and then sleeps in late, requiring significant prompting to get up and engage with rehabilitation. As a result, GA experiences significant fatigue but cannot always recognise or communicate this.

GA has been assessed as having mild dysarthria as well as a slow rate of speech but can make her needs known verbally. She also sustained a loss of vision following her head injury but is experiencing steady improvement in this which is helped with the use of prescribed glasses.

GA is noted to be physically able and is independent in activities of daily living but requires strict daily structure, external motivation and significant prompting in order to function.

Family/social context

GA has a complicated social and family history, having been placed in foster care at the age of 13 with only limited contact with her parents from that point. However, since her brain injury GA has had daily contact with her parents although this has been conditional upon her engaging in neurorehabilitation, avoiding all former acquaintances, agreeing not to frequent former "haunts" and, essentially, agreeing to all boundaries and rules her parents wish to put in place for her. Needless to say, this arrangement rapidly broke down and within a few weeks, GA was once again estranged from her parents.

Psychological/neuropsychological matters

Prior to her traumatic brain injury, GA had several voluntary admissions to a local psychiatric unit due to self-harm and deliberate overdose by ingestion of poison. She remains on the active caseload of a local consultant psychiatrist within the community services. GA also has had a long history of alcohol and intravenous drug use from a young age, which has led to a diagnosis of hepatitis C $^+$.

She has a good level of attention and her memory skills appear relatively intact, but she engages more readily in things she likes, and she will create reasons for not completing tasks she doesn't enjoy or see as beneficial to her.

Assessment and rationale

There were several aspects to the assessment of GA. First, her general cognitive functioning was assessed. Second, her insight and ability to engage in neurore-habilitation was assessed. Third, GA's perception of risk and ability to engage in therapeutic contracts was assessed. The whole purpose of the assessment was to gather robust information which would assist with her rehabilitation, a key element of which related to whether or not she should continue to be detained under a DoLS.

The rationale of this approach was to build up a clear picture of whether any difficulties are neuropsychological or psychological as this would dictate different therapeutic approaches to augmenting her capacity to access the community safely and increase her independence.

GA's cognitive functioning emerged slightly above average (Full Scale IQ = 111) and there was a discrepancy between verbal and performance skills, in favour of verbal, as would be expected in a case of traumatic brain injury. Non-verbal skills are measured by means of timed tests and, typically, traumatic brain injury leads to reduced processing speeds which leads to the individual achieving relatively lower scores on non-verbal tasks. GA, therefore, gave the superficial impression that there had been no appreciable neurocognitive effects of the traumatic brain injury, despite clinical evidence to the contrary. Where she struggled, and this is typical of the "frontal lobe paradox" first described by Walsh (1985) and more recently explored in relation to mental capacity by George and Gilbert (2018), was on applying her concrete knowledge in a "real-life" setting. To the untrained eye, GA presented as an individual who was competent.

Second, GA's insight and ability to engage in neurorehabilitation was assessed. She displayed a superficial understanding of the extent and impact of her brain injury in conversation, but her behaviours indicated that she was actually more aware than she was prepared to admit. Essentially, if she was asked to undertake a task she would refuse support and find a reason not to perform the task (for example, removing her bedclothes and organising her laundry) as she was sufficiently aware to realise that she would struggle without prompting and support. She exerted significant effort to avoid what she saw as "failure" and repeated the pre-injury patterns of destructive behaviours when faced with a challenge.

Finally, the notion of positive risk management was put to her as a way forward which would satisfy all. She would be able to "earn" increased (safe) independence and the clinicians supporting her would be able to work with her to achieve rehabilitation goals necessary for discharge. Ultimately, it would result in the removal of the DoLS, if successful.

Positive risk management is a process where all possible risks to the person are identified in terms of increasing their community access and decreasing the support provided. These are mutually agreed between the brain-injured person and the clinician responsible. A plan is then drawn up for gradual and safe exposure to the risks whilst incrementally increasing independence. A contract was drawn up with GA where mutual expectations were clarified and written down so that there was no room for renegotiation or misinterpretation.

- GA would agree to ensure that each time she left the unit as part of the programme, she had a charged mobile phone which was in credit, she had sufficient money for the purpose of the outing, she agreed to pre-arranged "safe-and-well" calls, she would remain abstinent of alcohol or drugs, she would avoid former "haunts" and associates.
- Staff would work with GA to put together a community access programme which allowed her to engage in enjoyed activities (surfing, skiing, music) with increasing freedoms in exchange for successful outings. It would also promote progress towards agreed neurorehabilitation goals:

  o **Physiotherapy** goals regarding mobility and graded pacing to increase distance walked safely;
  o **Occupational therapy** goals regarding independent travel, budgeting and purchasing items from different places;
  o **Neuropsychology** goals regarding management of fatigue and executive functions (multi-tasking, organising, planning and foreseeing consequences).

- A plan was drawn up with the following two factors to be varied as progress was made:

  Time away from unit – starting with local community where no transport would be required and tapering up to longer time away from the unit;

Distance away from unit – starting with half hour purposeful visits to local community and tapering up to travelling by public transport further afield;

- DoLS assessors were kept informed of the programme and progress made and were fully supportive of the approach as it presented a clear plan for removing the DoLS, if successful.

Opinion/outcome

The first two weeks were successful in that she followed the programme and expressed satisfaction at her successes. However, GA quickly expressed frustration at what she perceived as the slow pace of the programme – she wanted to leave the unit for a whole day to do Christmas shopping in a different city – ignoring her high levels of fatigue, mobility problems and difficulty with crowded places (which she could not cope with). She remained adamant that she should be allowed to go. The relationship between GA and clinical staff became somewhat tense but the decision was made to persevere with the plan.

GA then absconded from a planned trip and was found unconscious (under the influence of drugs) in a hedge, partially dressed, by police after they were alerted to her absconsion.

The "failed" community visit was discussed with GA who remained defiant at first and denied that there was had been any problem. It was decided to restart the planned programme from the beginning again, with the contract being reaffirmed. GA eventually engaged again and began to make progress, but a crisis occurred which changed everything.

GA returned to the unit as agreed and took her meal to her room. At this stage, GA was on 15-minute observational checks as staff were strongly suspicious that she may have been accessing drugs in the community although this was denied by GA. At one observation point in the early hours of the morning, GA was found cyanose and not breathing. The staff followed procedure, attempting CPR whilst also calling for an emergency ambulance crew, who arrived and administered naloxone and continued CPR until return of spontaneous circulation was established.

A subsequent room search uncovered class A drugs hidden in a drawer, in contravention of both the tenancy agreement and the therapeutic contract underpinning the positive risk management plan. When discharged back from hospital, GA was extremely remorseful, but the unit was no longer able to safely manage the risks posed by her (longstanding) behaviours and she was removed to an alternative environment.

Legal commentary

The test for subjecting P to a deprivation of liberty is often referred to "Best Interests plus". This is because the deprivation must not only be P's best interests but must also be a proportionate response to the likelihood of P suffering harm and the seriousness of that harm.[3] In other words, the deprivation must be the least restrictive option available.

From a legal perspective, a positive risk management approach is to be encouraged because it reflects the need for proportionality in the statutory framework – restrictions are kept to the minimum necessary and the emphasis is on increasing freedom in an appropriately supported and supervised manner. As such, it is likely that this is one of the reasons that the Court of Protection endorsed the standard authorisation in place for GA when she appealed.

It is also worth noting that the DoLS procedure is only available for those deprived of their liberty in hospitals or care homes. The "unit" in which GA was accommodated and cared for *was* a care home. If this were not the case, however, then it would have been necessary to make an application to the Court of Protection. It is hoped that this inconsistency is removed, as recommended by the Law Commission and as, at the time of writing, the Mental Capacity Amendment Bill proposes.

Discussion/learning points

The fact that this particular positive risk management approach was unsuccessful is not sufficient to deny its use with others with an acquired brain injury. The alternative to positive risk management is risk aversion and this is not a successful rehabilitation approach. This latter approach is paternalistic, controlling and competence-inhibiting and is in contravention of the very principles of the MCA (2005). It is considered good clinical practice to constantly review the rationale for a person being detained on a DoLS and whether or not it continues to be the most appropriate vehicle for their protection. A risk-averse approach can not achieve this as it does not place the individual's autonomy at the centre of their treatment or management programme, "mental capacity, then, is not the gatekeeper to autonomy, but it is an important part of the legal threshold for autonomy as a right" (Skowron, 2018, p.23)

For example, a patient with (very occasional) absence seizures and a love of swimming was being prevented by a risk-averse case manager from attending aquafit classes (with a qualified instructor) in the shallow end of a public pool, whilst being supported by a support worker with life-saving qualifications. This led to the patient/case manager relationship breaking down and the rehabilitation programme being put at risk. In the words of a well-regarded consultant neuropsychiatrist, Dr Seth Mensah, the principle should always be: "start low, go slow, *but go!*" In other words, establish a gentle start, take your time, but move forward.

---

3   Para. 16 of Schedule A1 to the MCA (2005)

Case 2: GB

Presenting question/problem

GB is a 38-year-old woman with a long history of alcohol misuse which has resulted in permanent brain damage (Korsakoff's syndrome). When admitted to hospital she was severely malnourished and was living in squalor. She had previously been married with a young baby and held down a full-time administrative post until weeks before her admission. Her deterioration was attributed to her husband leaving her and taking the child with him.

As a result of her brain injury, she is unable to form new memories with any reliability and completely lacks insight into why she is in hospital. She has significant gaps in her autobiographical memory which render her extremely vulnerable.

Background to the case

Clinical issues

GB has a long-standing documented history of alcoholism and alcohol-related admissions to hospital with a number of failed medically-managed detoxifications from alcohol. GB lived alone, and the most recent hospital admission was a result of her being found by her family at home in an extremely poor state of self-neglect. GB presented in hospital in a confused and disorientated state and has been diagnosed with an advanced frontal lobe impairment secondary to alcohol-induced encephalopathy and Korsakoff's disease. At the time of assessment, she was on a medical ward in a district general hospital, being cared for on a one-to-one nursing basis, and was considered so cognitively impaired and disorientated as to be unsafe for discharge. She had been placed on a DoLS for her own safety, even though she was not trying to leave the ward or go home.

GB requires significant prompting with all aspects of her care as she frequently forgets whether she has washed or eaten. GB has a normal level of physical function however her severe cognitive impairment affects her ability to initiate any tasks. GB has previously lost weight due to poor dietary habits and was under the care of a dietician such that she began to gain sufficient weight and is eating better. Her medical treatments include vitamin replacement therapy and a range of mild sedatives.

Family/social context

GB had previously been married and has a son who was born with foetal alcohol syndrome. Her husband had left her prior to her most recent deterioration and had taken their son with him. GB's parents have access to their grandson courtesy of an informal arrangement with their son-in-law. GB has a much younger sister who is still in full-time education and lives at home.

Prior to admission, GB had just been sacked from a longstanding clerical job at a national hotel chain. It was assumed, from available information, that her continued reliance on alcohol may have affected her punctuality, attendance and/or job performance.

Psychological/neuropsychological matters

GB's total lack of awareness of her surroundings and lack of insight into her injury or its impact on her future meant that her mood was largely buoyant. She was mostly affable and obliging to others on the ward, making herself useful to the staff by undertaking tasks in support of the more physically unwell patients, such as refilling their water jugs.

However, she frequently experienced spikes in anxiety and would seek almost constant reassurance from staff. This had an impact on her sleep cycle as she would take a considerable time to settle at night and then be fatigued for much of the following day.

GB was unable to form any new memories which resulted in her being largely oblivious to how long she had been in hospital, why she was there or when she might leave. She did express an expectation that she would go home from hospital as she had no recollection that her home had been in absolute squalor prior to her admission. For example, when she was found, minimally conscious at home, her toilets were blocked, and she had been evacuating her bowels in her bath and sink and was caked in excrement.

Assessment and rationale

It emerged that GB began drinking when in the lower years of senior school by saving up her dinner money and buying alcohol from a local shopkeeper. It is understood that she had been unhappy at home and began using alcohol as a coping strategy from an early age.

The main focus of the assessment was to assess both the extent of GB's cognitive impairments as well as to form an understanding as to her level of self-awareness as this directly impacts on her vulnerability.

It was clear on interview that GB lacks insight into why she was in hospital and often referred to herself as being on a train back from university in Derby to visit her family. She held on to this view despite the fact that she was sat down on her own hospital bed, clearly on a ward with nursing staff in uniform in attendance. This indicated that she was unable to use visual or environmental cues to modify her beliefs.

GB talked about her "daughter" Maisy, who she believed to be 2 years old, but GB has a son who is 2 years old and it is her sister who is called Maisy. This demonstrated significant impairments in autobiographical memory. When given information to enable her to orientate to being in hospital, GB did not get upset or agitated by that fact and could only fleetingly remember this information to inform her orientation.

GB often wandered off topic when talking and although there was only limited information about her pre-morbid life it was clear that there was a significant level of confabulation present in her account. During interview, GB thought she had only been in hospital for 3–7 days. She did not know the day, date, year, season or her own age (GB stated she was nearly 30 whereas she was nearer to 40). When asked about who was in her family, she referred to her husband as though they were still together and became upset about missing her "daughter".

Based on the above bedside assessment, a range of risks was identified in terms of the need to protect her vulnerabilities:

- further alcohol intake is likely to have catastrophic effects on her health;
- potential for wandering due to disorientation;
- potential for abuse/exploitation by others if not protected;
- risks related to further deteriorations in cognitive function;
- risk associated with sexual vulnerability; and
- risk of self-neglect.

Due to GB's inability to lay down new memories, she would frequently eat one meal after the other, having forgotten that she had recently eaten. This led, over time, to substantial weight gain and associated health risks. From admission to the time of assessment she had gained over 20 kg.

Cognitive assessment using an abbreviated scale of intelligence yielded an interesting profile of results. Her verbal skills were relatively well preserved, and she could engage freely and animatedly in conversation. However, she was unable to use her verbal or non-verbal skills to problem-solve. Her overall functioning was in the "borderline" range of 70–79, confirming her level of vulnerability if a certain level of protection was not put in place.

Visual and verbal memory was assessed and, overall, she was functioning below the bottom 2 per cent of her age peers for both areas of mnestic ability. This held for both free recall and recognition memory. Her overall speed of processing was between the 2nd and 5th centile, meaning that 95–98 per cent of her age peers would perform better than her on the same task.

As the assessment period progressed, GB developed paranoid ideas about staff and had several outbursts about her coffee having been "spiked" and that staff were holding her against her will, that she was in prison and had not done anything wrong. Her level of distress escalated over several days and an urgent medication review was undertaken.

Opinion/outcome

GB lacked capacity to consent to admission. She remained disorientated and she demonstrated a consistent and alarming lack of insight both into the impact of her drinking on her brain function and in terms of her continued vulnerabilities. In addition, she demonstrated an extremely impaired memory and there was objective evidence of her experiencing difficulty in weighing up information over time and considering potential consequences in order to make an informed decision. A Standard Deprivation of Liberty Safeguard was applied for in order to ensure an adequate level of protection for GB. Unfortunately, her brain injury is permanent and although she may make some functional gains such as low-level budgeting (money for a daily paper or toiletries), or simple meal preparation through a neurobehavioural learning model, her cognitive function will not improve over time. She is likely to remain vulnerable.

Legal commentary

The case of GB is a useful reminder of the broad approach taken by the courts in understanding that which constitutes a "deprivation of liberty". It seems that GB has never made any attempt to leave the ward or to go home. Indeed, there are even signs that she enjoys the hospital, involving herself in simple nursing tasks for less physically able patients. However, it is very clear that despite these considerations the "acid test" for judging a deprivation of liberty is met here. The first question is whether GB is subject to continuous supervision and control. GB may not be aware that this is the case, but the reality is that she is under the constant watch of health care professionals. The second question is whether GB is free to leave. It is irrelevant in this regard that GB has never expressed a desire to leave. Rather, one must consider the position if she tried to leave the hospital. In practice she would be stopped and returned to the ward. As a result, the necessary steps must be taken under the MCA (2005) to ensure to the deprivation of liberty is lawful.

Discussion/learning points

One of the difficulties in gathering evidence in support of an application for DoLS comes when an individual with substantial cognitive impairment but preserved verbal and social communication skills meets a non-clinical DoLS assessor and can, at first blush, appear quite plausibly competent. This is probably more true of GA than GB but it is interesting that GB was able to hold down a clerical job almost until the point of emergency admission whilst clearly engaging in problem drinking as this illustrates the exact point. Despite being emaciated through self-neglect and with deteriorating cognitive function, her vulnerabilities were not immediately evident behind the façade of articulate communication. She had been, to all intents and purposes, a functioning alcoholic for some time and did not come to the attention of the appropriate services until it was almost too late. It is not too great a stretch of credulity to allow that there may be many more in the same vulnerable position.

Case 3: GC

Presenting question/problem

GC is a 60-year-old man with a complex clinical history including learning disabilities, serial head injury (as a result of assaults), strokes and poorly controlled epilepsy. He also has a history of alcohol misuse. Prior to admission he had been on an acute medical ward with severe malnourishment and haematemesis (vomiting of blood). He lacked insight into his vulnerabilities and also lacked the ability to self-manage his intake of alcohol within safe levels. When, in the past, he has been left to his own devices he would drink too much, not eat, stop self-caring, forget to take his medication, experience an increase in seizures and also place himself at risk of further assault due to lack of awareness of his vulnerabilities. He experiences profound communication difficulties and is limited to single word responses, hand gestures and tone and volume of voice to make his needs known.

Background to the case

Clinical issues

GC has a history of long-standing brain injury with cerebrovascular accident in the early 2000s. There is scant detail regarding the original injuries, but a CT scan reports prominent ventricles, sulci, fissure and basal cisterns consistent with involutional changes. There is also evidence of marked dilatation of the left lateral ventricle consistent with previous infarcts and loss of volume. Low attenuation has been noted in left anterior parietal and posterior parietal regions due to infarcts. Periventricular low attenuation has been noted and is attributed to small vessel disease.

He has a longstanding history of alcohol misuse (consuming approximately 28 units of alcohol per week) and poorly controlled seizures as well as profound communication difficulties. GC was seizure-free on admission but experienced a cluster of five seizures over two days. These were complex partial seizures with secondary generalization. GC was rendered unconscious during each seizure but had a spontaneous recovery. The seizures did not warrant emergency treatment. However, GC did require an increase in medication.

He has a history suggestive of learning difficulties, but no official documentation or diagnosis could be found in his extensive medical notes. GC has had a duodenal ulcer in the past and has also been treated for anaemia.

Family/social context

GC was previously living at home with the support of home care services but has had frequent admissions to hospital due to falls and episodes of haematemesis. He has two sisters which visit him but cannot support him in terms of living with him because of his high level of health needs and challenging behaviours.

GC is also a vulnerable adult with a previous history of local teenagers taking money from him. The staff currently looking after him feel he needs more specialist input to meet his needs. An urgent and standard application for DOLS was made by the acute medical ward staff as GC was self-propelling in a wheelchair away from the ward and was found on a different ward on one occasion. He was not considered by ward staff to be able to keep himself safe if discharged home.

However, his social worker did not agree that he needed to be on a DoLS and requested a detailed capacity assessment. She felt that GC had longstanding issues that were primarily "social" in nature and that a DoLS was too restrictive. She cited evidence that GC has been reported to have got himself into some risky social situations when out in the community particularly when accessing local pubs. He has a record of aggravating people who then start fighting with him, which has placed him at significant risk. It is as a result of this behaviour that he was previously assaulted by a gang of local youths.

Psychological/neuropsychological matters

GC has been observed to enjoy social interaction with both staff and service users. He actively seeks the company of others and spends much of his time in the communal areas. He has displayed several relatively short bursts of verbal and low-level physical aggression since admission, but these were in response to frustration at having run out of cigarettes and also following minor misunderstandings with fellow patients.

Assessment and rationale

GC has under gone a medicated detox whilst on the ward and has not accessed alcohol since being there. The fact that he is presently clean of alcohol means that cognitive assessment results will be reliable and valid. However, the staff team are struggling to manage his challenging behaviour which manifests as verbal abuse, swearing and some violence towards others. There have been some incidents of challenging behaviour on the ward usually caused by GC not being able to communicate his needs or not being able to go for a cigarette on demand.

On assessment, GC was generally orientated on a daily level in that he could tell morning from afternoon but would not know the month or the year. GC was not able to read but could reliably use picture recognition to aid communication.

Neuropsychological assessment was limited owing to his communication impairments and right-side weakness, as GC is right-handed.

GC's attentional abilities, as measured on a selective and sustained attention task (the Symbol Cancellation of the KBNA) places him in the <2nd centile. This means that 98 per cent of his age peers would perform better on this task. His performance on this test is also indicative of significant impairment of processing speed.

With regard to memory abilities, GC's performance on a spatial memory task (the Spatial Location of the KBNA) places him in the <2nd centile. GC's performance on identifying line drawings of objects presented to him just over 10 minutes earlier places him in the 16th centile regarding abilities of episodic memory-consolidation and visuo-perceptual memory. GC was able to correctly identify items (everyday objects and geometrical blocks) that he had been asked to remember, from amongst others, after a delay of a few minutes.

GC's performance on the Clocks subtest of the KBNA places him in the <2nd centile, suggesting significant impairments in visuo-perceptual and visuo-constructional abilities, as well as visuo-perceptual memory. These may also be due to some extent to more basic visual problems such as shape and size discrimination, which may have an underlying visual acuity impairment. GC's primary neurocognitive deficits are in relation to:

- verbal communication;
- cerebral processing speed;
- visuospatial skills and space perception; and
- recall of previously seen visual information.

When interviewed, GC kept asking to leave the ward and be taken to the local pub (where he had previously been assaulted and subsequently banned). He would seek out alcohol whenever he was away from the ward and would verbally agree to limit his drinking but be able to implement this without considerable support.

Opinion/outcome

The results of the assessment are indicative of global cognitive impairment. GC is unable to identify risks to himself or even to put in place measures to keep himself safe when those risks are identified to him. Areas of risk include:

- self-neglect;
- alcohol misuse;
- misreading social cues and situations;
- verbal and physical aggression towards others which could result in provoked violence towards himself;
- non-compliance with seizure medication;
- inability to keep his money safe.

The overall impression is of an extremely vulnerable man with permanent, global, brain injury, mobility, communication and health problems, challenging behaviour towards others, non-compliance with medication and a history of being abused by others. The only means of keeping him safe whilst engaging him in neurorehabilitation is to request an Urgent DoLS, which was done.

Legal commentary

The case is GC is of interest given the range in professionals' views. This, therefore, reinforces the need to follow carefully the steps for justifying a deprivation of liberty under the MCA (2005). The first step – having established that the situation amounts to a deprivation of liberty (see the legal commentary in respect of GB) is to determine by way of a comprehensive assessment whether GC has capacity to consent to the regime in question. If GC had been found to have capacity, then that would have been the end of the matter under the MCA (2005) (consideration of the Mental Health Act [1983] would also have to be given).

It is only once that preliminary issue is clear that best interests (and the proportionality of the deprivation) can be addressed. Here, too, there may well be disagreement between professionals and/or family members. If a dispute remains, ultimately this will be a matter for determination by the Court of Protection.

Discussion/learning points

The main learning point here is to ensure clear and consistent communication between professionals working with a physically, psychologically and neurologically vulnerable adult so that a consensus develops about their needs and how they can be protected in a competence-promoting way. Although there is space for professionals to respectfully question each other's opinions, divergence on the basis of whether a need is "social" or "health" is helpful to no one and can result in delaying access to the necessary support.

References

George, M. & Gilbert, S. (2018). Mental Capacity Act (2005) assessments: Why everyone needs to know about the frontal lobe paradox. *The Neuropsychologist*, 5, 59–66.

Law Commission. (2017). Mental capacity and deprivation of liberty. Retrieved from www.lawcom.gov.uk/project/mental-capacity-and-deprivation-of-liberty/

Ruck-Keene, A. (2017). The MCA – big issues for the next 10 years. Retrieved from www.mentalcapacitylawandpolicy.org.uk/the-mca-big-issues-for-the-next-10-years/

Skowron, P. (2018). The relationship between autonomy and adult mental capacity in the law of England and Wales. *Medical Law Review*, doi:10.1093/medlaw/fwy016

Walsh, K. (1985). *Understanding brain damage: A primer of neuropsychological evaluation*. London: Churchill Livingstone.

Part III

13 Summary of key learning points and guidance on the application of transferable knowledge

Dr Tracey Ryan-Morgan

This final chapter of the book provides a useful opportunity for review, analysis and future-thinking. From a clinician's perspective there are many benefits to the MCA (2005). First, the question of mental capacity and the rights of the individual are now one of the first considerations with any clinical assessment or treatment. This represents a significant shift in practice as a direct result of the legislation and contributes to the changing view of patients from passive recipients of health interventions by journeying towards them being active participants in their health and social care experiences. Clearly, there is a long way to go, and some progress will only be made by identification of deficits in practice and deficiencies in approach, hence the safeguard of the crimes of neglect and wilful mistreatment within the Act (section 44) and the further clarification of how to conduct best interests' assessments that is contained with the NICE guidance (2018).

As it stands, however, there are a number of questions which the MCA (2005) and Code of Practice do not usefully answer for clinicians, and which make their position and perspective somewhat fragile. For example, for how long does an assessment of capacity have currency? It appears straightforward to consider that a re-assessment would only be required if there was a change in the health status or personal circumstances of the individual, depending on the issue at question. What about cases where capacity can fluctuate across a day, for example, in cases of severe traumatic brain injury where fatigue becomes cognitively disabling as the day progresses and directly impacts on an individual's ability to engage in the assessment process?

In clinical practice, it is fair to say that matters are rarely clear cut. For example, it can often be the case that an experienced clinician will conduct a capacity assessment of a patient on a ward but then the appointed social worker will request a further capacity assessment to satisfy their own procedures or paperwork, leading to delays in implementing the appropriate treatment or discharge response for the patient and leading to duplication of effort. This process- rather than person-centred approach can be, sadly, typical.

A further question relates to how to resolve deadlocked best interests' discussions. Who holds the "trump card" when an *impasse* is reached? Such circumstances are not as rare as would be expected. How to implement a difficult best interests' decision and continue to maintain positive and reciprocal relationships with those diametrically opposed to the same remains a challenge for which there is little practical guidance. A recent case explored the jurisdiction of the courts when such issues are unable to be resolved by the parties involved.[1]

In the early years of implementation of the MCA (2005), reviews uncovered discrepancies of approach between different professionals and pointed to a failure by many to grasp the underpinning principles of the MCA (2005). Community Care (Pitt, 2010) reported that:

> More than half of health and social care professionals are failing to comply with the Mental Capacity Act 2005's requirements when conducting assessments of capacity.

> A study by the Mental Health Foundation revealed 52% of professionals were assuming that service users did not have capacity before conducting an assessment . . . 38% of respondents said they conducted an assessment because of a service user's disability or illness and not because of any problems the person had making a decision. A further 25% said they conducted an assessment simply because they felt the service user's decision was unwise . . ."

In this survey, 1500 professionals had responded to the Mental Health Foundation's online Assessment of Mental Capacity Audit Tool. The purpose of the research was to provide a place for health and social care staff to self-assess their implementation of the MCA (2005). The results made disturbing reading at the time.

In 2012, the Mental Health Foundation produced a review which highlighted trends and themes of confusion and misunderstanding in relation to implementation of the MCA (2005). The following were referred to in particular:

- Standardised capacity assessments were too restrictive in that there was no room for consideration of the person's emotional state or of the impact of physical functioning on decision-making ability;
- Substitute decision-makers were often unable to speak for the wishes of the service user;
- Advanced directives were often too limited by their over-specificity;
- Families were often under-involved in the processes of assessing decision-making capacity and pursuing a best interests' approach.

The overwhelming conclusion was that health and social care staff required further training on communication with patients and families on topics which can be emotive and challenging, best interests' decision-making and advanced directives.

1 [2017] UKSC 22 on appeal from [2015] EWCA Civ 411

The National Institute for Health and Care Excellence also identified gaps in both the skills and practices of health and social care professionals and was asked by the Department of Health to draw up specific guidance to address such deficits, for the benefits of both staff and patients alike. Draft guidance was consulted upon from December 2017 and the definitive guidance was published in October 2018. The consultation document was clear to point out that the guidance would not have the status of a "comprehensive manual for frontline practice, rather it focuses on areas where practice need to improve, and where there is a paucity of guidance in existence" (p.5). Alex Ruck Keene of Essex Street Chambers provides a brief commentary of the perceived limitations of the guidance (2018).

From a legal perspective, there are a number of planned changes afoot to the legislation through both statutory revision and developments in case law. The two most notable recent progressions relate to the Mental Capacity (Amendment) Bill. At time of writing this is going through the parliamentary processes (the final revised Act is not realistically expected until 2020) and the Supreme Court Ruling on case "Y".[2] This latter judgment relates to the landmark ruling that, in cases of patients who are either minimally conscious or experiencing a prolonged disorder of consciousness (PDOC), where treating doctors and families (and those with a stake in the welfare of the patient) all agree that clinically assisted nutrition and hydration (CANH) should be removed, there is no longer a legal requirement for the case to be referred to the Court of Protection. However, there is still an expectation that in cases where, "the way forward is finely balanced, or there is a difference of medical opinion, or a lack of agreement to a proposed course of action from those with an interest in the patient's welfare, a court application can and should be made" (paragraph 125). In the context of CANH, the perception within the legal profession is that the authorities are placing increasing emphasis on what P would have wished. This clearly slides towards the "substituted judgement" end of the best interests' continuum and is an interesting development.

In addition to these planned changes to the legislation and to legal practice, there appear to be a number of trends in practice that merit brief discussion at this point. One such development seems to be that the courts appear to be displaying a greater tendency to find that a person has the capacity to litigate than was previously the case. This may be occurring due to the growing realisation that appointing the Official Solicitor to represent a party in proceedings could be perceived as an invasion of an individual's rights. It has also been observed by legal practitioners that the courts are focusing on doing whatever is reasonably practical to enable a person to give their best evidence. These developments in the legal context mirror those observed in the clinical context and represent a significant cultural shift towards placing the person's rights and autonomy at the centre of decision-making by them, or for them. In that regard, the MCA (2005) can be said to have achieved great things. However, not all observers share this positive perspective on developments in the implementation of the spirit of the MCA (2005).

2 [2018] UKSC 46

Skowron (2018) refers to the gap between "judicial rhetoric and behaviour" (p.1). His paper describes three different judicial approaches to capacity and autonomy in current practice. The first provides a simple distinction between those who have capacity and those who do not. Those who retain capacity retain autonomy and those that are deemed to lack capacity are also considered to lack autonomy. In this account, capacity serves as the threshold for autonomy, known as the "gatekeeper account".

The second approach is described as the, "insufficiency account" where mental capacity is considered necessary, but not enough in its own right, for autonomy to be respected. This account takes cognisance of the elements of, "voluntariness, [and] freedom from undue external influences" (p.9).

The final account of capacity and autonomy described by Skowron as evident in extant judicial practice is the, "survival account". In this model, the individual's, "personal autonomy survives the onset of incapacity".[3] Here the status of autonomy is such that it is protected by means of the best interests' evaluation. In reviewing these three models, Skowron points out that they fall down in their attempt to review complex moral concepts because they adopt a binary approach, which is, essentially, overly simplistic.

Not only are there tensions between the rights of the individual and the imperative of the state, but also between the clinical and legal perspectives in assessing an individual's capacity. There can be wide divergence between the legal test for capacity in a given instance and the clinical measure or assessment framework used to gather information to assist the courts in their particular deliberations.

A clear-cut example of this lies in an individual's capacity to consent to sex. The *legal* test, expressed simply, is that the individual needs to understand the mechanics of the sex act, the possibility of pregnancy following intercourse between a man and a woman and the health risks inherent in sex, such as contracting a sexually transmitted infection (STI). The *clinical* approach typically requires the individual to demonstrate a deeper, broader understanding of the concepts of sex, sexual anatomy, masturbation, sexual orientation, gender, contraception, periods, sexual abuse and the risks of exploiting others with less sexual power as well as understanding the abstract concepts of "private" and "public". A clinician could not reasonably assess the capacity to consent to sex unless relying on an objective measure such as the Sexual Attitude and Knowledge (SAK) assessment. This particular measure has four key domains against which it measures an individual's knowledge: sexual awareness (including anatomy), assertiveness, understanding relationships and social interaction. The reason for the breadth of the scope of the SAK is that, often, in adult populations where there are cognitive limitations due to brain injury or developmental disability, an individual may well be able to cite the correct answers to a simple measure of sexual knowledge yet lack the fundamental ability to apply that knowledge to keep themselves safe. To adopt the vernacular, they can talk the talk but not walk the walk. This represents the

3 [2011] EWCOP 2443, [2012] 1 WLR 1653 [95]

well-rehearsed dissociation between "knowing" and "doing" that is often referred to in the context of executive (frontal lobe) brain injuries (Teuber, 1964).

There are also instances where information which has come to light as part of a clinical assessment of capacity is not fully taken into account by the legal professional involved in the case. One example is that of a mature gentleman who had a series of strokes and had a clear pattern of neuropathology which underpinned his inability to manage his finances. He was provided with a financial deputy by the Court of Protection. It came to light that his adult son was "borrowing" his bank card and using his father's PIN to make regular and significant withdrawals of cash from the father's bank account with no intention of paying them back. This information was provided to the deputy who did not share the concerns of the clinical team. The practice continued until the carers, lead clinician and case manager all wrote to the deputy to raise continuing, collective concerns about the financial vulnerability of the father, who had other adult children who may also have had claims on his assets. The deputy's response was to dismiss the concerns on the basis that the father would probably have made financial gifts to the son during his lifetime and probably would not have asked for such monies to be repaid were he to have retained financial capacity. For the clinicians involved this remained a safeguarding issue.

A further example of divergence between clinical and legal perspectives is provided in the case of an adult gentleman with a severe brain injury and a 24-hour care team. He was known to be drinking excessive amounts of alcohol in his own home, leading to aggressive behaviour towards care staff, several falls (with fractured bones and broken teeth) and a disengagement from his rehabilitation team. His behaviour also risked his continued contact with his much-loved children with whom he had supervised contact weekly. It transpired that his family were visiting and bringing him alcohol to "cheer him up" despite having been asked on several occasions to desist. Urgent discussions were held between the rehabilitation team and financial deputy, who, in turn, sought legal advice from counsel. The prevailing advice was that there was little point in applying to the Court of Protection for a welfare order as a means of limiting the person's access to alcohol as any such order, even if made, would be almost impossible to enforce in a person's own home, despite the fact that failure to manage this risk severely compromised this person's quality of life and level of support.

There are many instances of individuals with acquired brain injury, typically through trauma, who retain a veneer of cognitive ability, largely in terms of preserved communication function, which gives the false impression to professionals inexperienced in brain injury that they retain capacity and can make choices. This has been seen to occur with social workers, for example, who may have had little or no training in brain injury as well as those Best Interests Assessors who do not come from a clinical background. It can also occur with Independent Mental Capacity Advocates who, again, rarely have training in brain injury and who are easily persuaded that the person being assessed is somehow being misunderstood by clinical staff and being prevented from making decisions that they feel perfectly able to make, usually due to lack of insight into their injury or lack of self-awareness in terms of their cognitive and behavioural deficits as a result of their injury. George and Gilbert (2018) attribute this divergence in opinion to the difference between the "deficit-orientated" approach of the clinician and the "empowerment" approach of local authority colleagues. However, the authors also refer to Norman (2016) who reminds the practitioner that, particularly in cases of pre-frontal lobe injuries (which are common), "empowering some patients may inadvertently increase their risk". In such cases it is critical that there are clear lines of communication between those treating the person and those assessing their mental capacity.

However, despite these and other pitfalls, the MCA (2005) has brought about many positive changes, not least of which a closer collaboration between clinical and legal professionals. Long may this continue.

> vigorous interdisciplinary collaboration between legal and clinical professionals . . . is vital to the continuing development of capacity assessment as a field, and to its success as a societal mechanism for resolving individual issues of autonomy and protection.
>
> (Moye & Marson, 2007, p.9)

References

George, M. & Gilbert, S. (2018). Mental Capacity Act (2005) assessments: Why everyone needs to know about the frontal lobe paradox. *The Neuropsychologist*, 5, 59–66.

Mental Health Foundation. (2012). Mental Capacity and the Mental Capacity Act 2005: A literature review. Retrieved from www.mentalhealth.org.uk/publications/mental-capacity-and-mental-capacity-act-2005-literature-review

Moye, J. & Marson, D. C. (2007). Assessment of decision-making capacity in older adults: An emerging area of practice and research. *Journal of Gerontology*, 62B(1), 3–11.

NICE. (2018). Decision-making and mental capacity. Retrieved from www.nice.org.uk/guidance/indevelopment/gid-ng10009

Norman, A. (2016). A preventable death? A family's perspective on adult safeguarding review regarding an adult with traumatic brain injury. *Journal of Adult Protection*, 18(6), 341–352.

Pitt, V. (2010). Professionals fail to comply with Mental Capacity Act. Retrieved from www.communitycare.co.uk/2010/06/17/professionals-fail-to-comply-with-mental-capacity-act/

Ruck Keene, A. (2018). The NICE guideline on decision-making and mental capacity: Very good try but only two thirds of a banana. Retrieved from www.mentalcapacitylawandpolicy.org.uk/the-nice-guideline-on-decision-making-and-mental-capacity-very-good-try-but-only-two-thirds-of-a-banana/

Skowron, P. (2018). The relationship between autonomy and adult mental capacity in the law of England and Wales, *Medical Law Review*, doi:10.1093/medlaw/fwy016

Teuber, H. L. (1964). The riddle of the frontal lobe function in man. In J. M. Warren & K. Akert (Eds) *The frontal granular cortex and behaviour* (pp.410–458). New York: McGraw-Hill.

Index

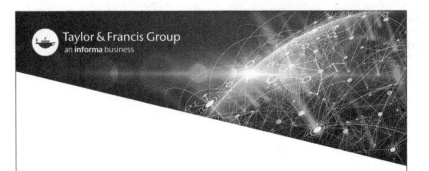